CHARLES MORGAN
THREE PLAYS

CHARLES MORGAN

THREE PLAYS

The Flashing Stream

The River Line

The Burning Glass

OBERON BOOKS
LONDON

WWW.OBERONBOOKS.COM

Contents

The publisher is grateful to the Linbury Trust for their assistance with this publication.

Foreword

Charles Morgan (1894-1958) was already a distinguished novelist with a wide international reputation before writing his first play. His involvement with the theatre as observer and critic had extended throughout his adult life until *The Flashing Stream* was produced in 1938. At Oxford he had been President of the Oxford University Dramatic Society, which, under his presidency, had produced Thomas Hardy's *Dynasts. The Times* dramatic critic, A. B. Walkley, met Morgan when reviewing this and recruited Morgan as his deputy. He succeeded Walkley as chief dramatic critic in 1924 and wrote weekly articles on the English theatre for *The New York Times.* He was, then, very much a man of the theatre before addressing himself to the art of writing a play himself.

Each of his three plays was published by Macmillan before its appearance on the stage. This collection has taken advantage of the changes that were made and recorded by Morgan in the course of production. The texts, therefore, differ from those originally printed. Each of the original editions included lengthy introductory essays on the themes with which the plays were concerned. It has not been feasible to include these in the present single volume.

R.M.
2013

In the Name of the Spirit

In reviewing Charles Morgan's first play, *The Flashing Stream* – by his own admission, speedily written in 1937 as a breather from an unfinished book manuscript – one's immediate response could be to settle back, in the stalls, attempting to draft in one's mind the icy analysis that could have found its way into a column in *The Times* the next day. But at this distance, with the benefit of Morgan's own apologia, his explicit preceding essay, *On singleness of mind* [1] – for which, he says, his play is 'a pendant'[2] – one might, in the comfort of retrospect, ask oneself whether there could have been other impulses that produced such a work: one can only surmise that there were.

The play was written three years into what would be a long term relationship with Margaret Rawlings, whom he cast as his heroine. One cannot escape the conclusion that it was Rawlings's attraction for him that defined much of Karen Selby in the play; it is her *singleness of mind* and frank sexual attractiveness – Morgan takes the opportunity to deplore that the theatre recoils from the truth that 'many women [...] have pleasure in the experience of sex'[3] – and brilliant intellectuality, that he argues in the accompanying essay. This unique part of 'a woman of passion and integrity, not a virgin, not an adulteress and not a courtesan'[4] fitted Rawlings like a glove: her performance was 'a masterpiece of sincerity, passion and warm humanity.'[5] Commander Ernest Ferrers (Godfrey Tearle) also embodies that virtue of singleness of mind which, Morgan insists, is neither selfishness nor egotism, rather 'devotion to an ideal'[6],'an absolutism.'[7] And that ideal is a noble one for it is both our essence and redemption somehow.[8]

A storyline is provided by that old post-WW1 chestnut, the super-weapon that will end all conflict. In the wardroom of a

---

1   Morgan takes great pains explaining to Louis Bonnerot that the preface was necessary so that 'the play should be *read* and not only seen in the theatre', To Louis Bonnerot, 9 December 1938

2   Foreword , xi

3   *Ibid.*, xvi

4   *Ibid.*, xviii

5   J.E. Sewell in *The Daily Telegraph*

6   Cf. To St. John Ervine, September 1938

7   Preface, p. 7

8   *Ibid*, p. 7

British Naval experimental unit somewhere in the Atlantic, under the command of Ferrers, a handful of Royal Navy boffins bring their mathematical genius to bear on the design of a guided missile that eerily anticipates the mainstay of present day international arsenals. One of the boffins, Selby, is accidentally killed in an early test. The cat is put amongst the pigeons when the Admiral and his wife arrive, bringing Selby's sister, Karen (fortuitously ranked the world's sixth best mathematician), who is recruited to replace him. Tensions run high as Karen's presence begins to stir the passions and prejudices of those with whom she must work: Ferrers and she fall in love. It is not helpful that the Admiral's classy wife, the 'horrid' Lady Helston, is also in love with Ferrers. The fetching worldliness of Karen also attracts the innocent Lt Commander Brissing, who is rewarded with an embrace and a kiss or two as the play unfolds. Analysis of a fault in the project, combined with Ferrers's adamant defence of his calculations then cause the project to be cancelled. In the final act, Lady Helston's animosity is finally revealed to Karen during an explosive exchange: 'Because you have brains, you want to submit yourself...that's why you are a slut *(FS* 234)... I wanted more and more power over him...is that being a cad?' (235). In a final twist, it is single-mindedness that suffers as Karen declares (untruthfully) that she has discovered a discrepancy in Ferrers's calculations; the decision on the experiment can be reversed; Ferrers breaks down; Karen recants and the curtain falls upon a love that is thus predictably cleansed and sealed in each other's arms.

Morgan had wished 'to write a play about a man and a woman of first-rate minds passionately in love from first to last.'[9] But exaltation of love was not all: he wanted to write about working characters, as opposed to the usual idlers of cosy drawing-room dramas. The Navy was an obvious choice given Morgan's background[10], and a naval station *ashore,* the perfect setting for the contrivance of a plot that involved a woman: the Cornelian tension between this love at first sight and duty being resolved

9   To Louis Bonnerot, 25 December 1937
10   There is an autobiographical element: educated at Osborne and Dartmouth, Morgan entered the Royal Navy and spent most of the First World War as a captured officer in the Castle of Rosendaal in the Netherlands. During the Second World War, he worked for British naval intelligence.

in the Platonic theory of an ideal world based upon mathematics as the clue to all intelligibility and truth: 'a man and a woman desperately in love, refraining from love because to them the work, the mathematics, is an absolute ideal, comparable to the ideal of the great *religieux*.'[11]

Morgan had slight misgivings about the reception of *The Flashing Stream*: he was well aware that 'the audience of what is called a "west-end" theatre is not the easiest before which to express, in the naturalistic convention, the idea implicit in the sixth beatitude'[12] – purity of heart. There was the problem of English coyness: 'a strange race' who 'assume more than their fair share of the intolerance and hysteria of the masses.'[13] However, the play was to run for six months in 1936: 'A remarkable first play'[14] which stood apart in the London theatrical season[15] as a Box Office sizzler. 'A man with a fine mind has written a fine play.'[16] Such was the success of that 'magnificent play' that the eminent James Agate himself jubilantly predicted 'a Possibility of Sensational Performance.'[17] Hugh Walpole was a great admirer and *The Manchester Evening News* prophesied that Morgan would become 'a constant star in the theatrical sky.' In post-war Paris this success was replicated.

The gripping *River Line* – first written as a novel (its title refers to an underground escape route through occupied France) – appeared later, in 1952. Prefaced by an essay 'On Transcending the Age of Violence' – how are we to act in an age of violence? – it is a poignant story of entanglement which involves an indomitable glamorous French *résistante*, Marie, brought to England by her husband-to-be, the naval officer Julian Wyburton. The shattering melodrama of the second act – a flashback that transports the characters back into a granary near Toulouse and the French Resistance in 1944, described as 'masterly as a theatrical exercise' by J.C. Trewin[18] – is disconcertingly sandwiched between the philosophising of the first and third acts (two years after the

11   To Louis Bonnerot, 25 December 1937
12   Foreword, p. xii
13   *Ibid.*, p. xviii
14   J.E. Sewell in *The Daily Telegraph*
15   Cf. A.D. in *The Manchester Guardian*
16   S.W. in *The Sunday Express*
17   James Agate in *The Sunday Times*
18   J.C. Trewin in *John London's Weekly*

war). This was very much 'the old Morgan formula': 'philosophy reaching up, up, up…to a slick happy ending.'[19] The central character is an English soldier, Heron, wrongly suspected of being a *faux Anglais* and therefore murdered by his companions and Marie, who, Morgan insists, '*had* to do what they did.'[20] A comradeship blighted by that scar upon their memory. The truth about Heron's innocence will be revealed retrospectively. With its architectonic clarity, *The River Line* is a splendid illustration of Morgan's treatment of drama as a game of draughts.[21] Though Morgan confessed that its temporal structure had been a technical challenge,[22] even the rather reluctant Kenneth Tynan, 'midst some predictable fault-finding, admitted to admiration of its qualities of 'oracular clarity' and eloquence.

The French production proved tricky; France had a special place in Morgan's heart: she was 'the heart that pumps the blood of civilization'[23], but the Resistance was still an open wound for the French; Morgan's poeticizing could have struck the wrong chord.

There is more than a formula which provides the frame of ideas upon which each play is built; there is an *idée fixe*: The Liberties of the Mind. The plots may be almost the stuff of *Boys' Own* or classic war films, but the argument is deeper and the lexicon of the mind all-pervasive. Morgan's plays are absorbing studies of human dilemma and conscience; all still very topical. He may have used the melodrama of spy thrillers (kidnapping, murder, international diplomacy etc.) but insofar as it served the ideas: his is 'the civilised melodrama, the melodrama of ideas'[24]; he was allergic to melodramatic bombast.

'New melodrama contains provocative idea' was the title of the *New York Times* review of *The Burning Glass* (1953) which was a compelling illustration of the theses put forward in his collection of essays, *The Liberties of The Mind*; 'exciting play about secret war weapon' that of *The Daily Telegraph* review. Its

19   John Barber in *The Daily Express*
20   To St. John Ervine, 20 July 1949
21   Cf. Harold Hobson in *The Sunday Times*
22   To Louis Bonnerot, 21 October 1947
23   Charles Morgan, 'France is an Idea Necessary to the Idea of Civilization',
        Reflections in a Mirror, second series, Macmillan, 1954, p. 108
24   J.C. Trewin in *The Lady*

reception was 'most cordial'[25]: indeed, it was refreshing to see a play 'which actually deals with the world in which we live.'[26] Ivor Brown praised Morgan for 'facing the greatest problem of mankind today'[27]: the use of scientific discoveries. Morgan had applied his intellectual ardour and probity to the chronicle of the technico-scientific revolution of the inter-war years – the nuclear theory of the atom - and its sinister implications during the Second World War when national survival was at stake. Prefaced with an essay 'On Power over Nature'[28], *The Burning Glass* is, in his own words, 'neither a debate nor an allegory, but a straightforward story of men and women facing a crisis in their lives'[29]; it may be described as a soul-stirring 'scientific romance' with its awareness of the sinister consequences of scientific discoveries, its indictment against that 'Force of Evil' lurking in the modern age and bewitching the spirit. With her moral instinct and idealistic acuity, Mary, Christopher Terriford's delightful wife, believes that the corruption of life – the civil uses of atomic power which, according to Morgan, would inevitably lead to 'an intolerable distortion of life on earth'[30] – is a greater evil than war (*BG* 123). And indeed, the author had anticipated such evil: 'atomic power is potentially a thousand industrial revolutions compressed into the time-space of a few months.'[31]

Geoffrey Tarran effusively branded *The Burning Glass* 'drama at its best.'[32] Morgan's main achievement had been to give credibility to genius in the theatre[33]: no mean feat! There seems to have been a consensus amongst the critics. For Alan Dent *The Burning Glass* may not have been a masterpiece but 'it is full of mind, and only the mindless can find it dull.'[34] Ivor Brown greeted 'a play which touched on the fundamentals as well as the surfaces of life, a play whose second act, if not the

25   Beverley Baxter in *The Sunday Express*
26   *Ibid.*
27   Ivor Brown in *The Observer*
28   Charles Morgan devoted an essay to *The Liberties of the Mind* in which he expressed his fears about the scientific revolution and its ever-increasing power over nature, especially atomic power. Cf. 'Mind Control' in *The Liberties of the Mind*, London, Macmillan, 1951, pp. 30-44.
29   Preface to *The Burning Glass*, p. vii
30   *Liberties of the Mind*, p. 40
31   *Ibid.*, p. 40
32   Geoffrey Tarran in *The Morning Advertiser*
33   J.C. Trewin in *The lady*
34   Alan Dent in *The News Chronicle*

other two, reminded us that first-rate story-telling can be linked with intellectual contention!'[35] Never mind the didacticism, 'it is a bracing change to have the theatre as a pulpit, even if one disagrees with its sermon.'[36]

A theme dear to Morgan's heart was the 'Liberties of the Mind', the title of a series of essays published in 1951, in which he vehemently stated his concern – a persistent one – with 'the concept of a power to dispossess men of their minds, their wills and even their individualities.'[37] Humanity, Morgan felt, was prey to a pervasive malignity, 'an alien psychology' injected into the individual: significantly, 'the power to make this injection' was 'like the power of nuclear energy in the early Nineteen Forties.'[38] Morgan would of course resort to a naval metaphor (*ad nauseam*!): man's increasing power over Nature threatens his ability to steer his ship and cuts him off from his 'spiritual origins'[39]: 'the ship was not answering her helm and there was a devil in the wind.'[40]

The Second World War left humanity 'in such a condition of drift'[41] that a spiritual ascent was necessary: the empathetic Keatsian recovery of the 'indestructible Order' of Nature 'for the terror of our world is of a reasonless chaos which is spreading, like a dreadful disease of the skin, over the whole body of experience.'[42] Another favourite metaphor, a self evident one, was, 'that disease of society which ends in the annihilation of independent thought, and of the will to independence.'[43]

In these penetratingly reflective plays, Morgan is the chronicler of the moral disturbance of an unsettled age, the mystical prophet of humanity. His scrutiny of futurity is carried out with a touching earnestness of purpose. The Brave New World may have been a well-worn subject, but there is a persuasive grandeur in Morgan's plea that is vaguely reminiscent of the very English idealistic protest of a Carlyle or Ruskin.

Bristling with oracular pronouncements, Morgan's drama is

35   *The Observer*
36   *Ibid.*
37   *Liberties of the Mind*, p. 6
38   *Ibid.*, p. 6
39   *Ibid.*, p. 17
40   *Ibid.*, p. 30
41   'This Spring', *Reflections in a Mirror*, second series, p. 19
42   *Ibid.*, 19
43   *Liberties of the Mind*, p. 40

imbued with an acute sense of man's predicament: the fear is that of 'a disintegration of himself, a breaking-up of his spiritual substance.'[44] That is why the drama is also enacted in the recesses of the soul. Morgan was always concerned with the mind, its turmoils and dilemmas, the disquietude of the modern soul; rather, with the chasm opened by the 'despiritualisation'[45] or 'soullessness' of modernity.

Despite the philosophical and poetic foundations of dramatic tension, there is no austere morality or doctrine in Morgan's *oeuvre*: his finely-shaded thought is that of the artist-moralist; it is of a delicate and scrupulous quality: it stimulates reflection, disturbs our numerous complacencies. Morgan knows how to temper his austere lessons with flashing formulae dominated by the ardour and anguish of high certitude.

Discipline was the hallmark of Morgan's career. His plays exemplify his impeccable compositional skills, those skills that made him such a brilliant reviewer. *The Flashing Stream* was, of his own admission, 'a technical exercise, a discipline, a deliberate submission to three acts, one scene, naturalistic dialogue.' Morgan subscribed to the Baudelairean merits of constraint: 'I wanted to see how much passion, how much of the relationship between love and mathematics, how much of the nature of love and genius (both these are *The Flashing Stream*) I could express within the accepted limits of the theatre. I wanted to learn to *draw* before I dared to distort in this supremely difficult medium. If this play succeeds (and its extreme intensity may prevent it from succeeding in England) I want to make experiments.'[46] Morgan was underestimating his compatriots – the play turned out to be a roaring success – but of course he was writing this to a Frenchman.

The handling of portraiture is worked out with refinement. As 'a literary gentleman'[47] with a carefully calculated persona – confessedly 'a revolutionary conservative' with a handsome profile (and flamboyant opera cloak!) – Morgan was almost bound to create well-bred characters who live in manor houses where the courtesies and formalities of the drawing-room drama

44   'Ideas at War', in *Reflections in a Mirror*, second series, p. 5
45   According to Morgan, human relationships had become 'despiritualized' ('Mind Control', in *Liberties of the Mind*, p.33)
46   To Louis Bonnerot, 25 December 1937
47   Beverley Baxter in *The Sunday Express*

are observed; even the bitter exchange between Karen and Lady Helston is not too much of a lapse of taste. The paradox of such momentous events unfolding in such half-tones of atmosphere is a tantalizing one; and, curiously, the conventions do not blur the fervent clearsightedness. Morgan's characters, it is true, play bridge and chess, discuss tragedy, Montaigne, Pascal and Flaubert, drink Musigny. The language they speak may be a trifle too meretricious or mannered – Morgan's friend Rupert Hart-Davis did warn him about a 'tendency to over-stylize [his] dialogue'[48] in *The River Line* – but these characters are all true to the law of their own being; they are all keenly alive to their fervid feelings, passions and impulses. Whether good – like Mary Terriford; evil – like Lady Helston and Gerry Hardlip; or invulnerable – like Karen Selby – they are noteworthy for the definiteness of their outline, thus seizing us with a sure conviction of their truth.

Morgan's technical mastery conveys their (as well as his own) innermost complexity. Lofty in its laconic literacy, his dramatic language has the grace of a ceremonious gesture. 'The immaculate conception of the prose'[49], so crisp, elegant and imperious, confers a sober intensity to the plays, restores to language some measure of limpidity as well as some stringency of meaning. It owes its sureness to an unfailing mental vision, and, in a way, tempers the complexities of Morgan's mind. The chess game in *The Burning Glass* may be too obvious a symbol for that singleness of mind so dear to Morgan but he himself displays those same necessary skills of concentration, foresight and circumspection.

Morgan consecrated his endeavours to a noble task: a genuine adhesion to man's moral progress, a warning against overreaching oneself, in the Faustian sense, lest one be consumed like Icarus by the terrible proximity of omnipotence. This is the blasphemy of Adam, Prometheus and Satan; it is in our demand for the absolute that the tragedy of our condition lies.

With their tragic scenario involving man, the world and the absolute, Morgan's finely wrought plays are instinct with a feverish central impulse that carries them to their lucid conclusions. With

---

48   To Rupert Hart-Davis, 25 July 1949
49   Ludovic Kennedy in *The Evening Standard*

their suspense, plot and characters, they were hugely successful in the West End, as well as abroad. Retrospectively the triad appears as a fleeting yet privileged moment of poise in the history of twentieth-century drama. Despite its anticipation of a mighty collapse, it envisaged, beyond its compelling blending of self-analysis and circumstances, the reconciliation of beauty and lucidity, a permanency of utterance. Besides, Morgan claimed to be merely 'awake' rather than 'an alarmist.'[50]

Writing in a darkening period Morgan was making a case for the poet's eminence as a moral conscience. The merit of his plays lies, ultimately, in their raising the supreme question of the ethical value of literature. A humanising force, literature cultivates human judgement and thus is a protection against endemic barbarism. Despite the doom and gloom that beset Morgan's mind (and Europe) a braced energy animates his belief in human grandeur: 'the Spirit of Man' is 'greater than all human manifestations of it'[51] – it is 'that immortal part of us.'[52]

The production of *The River Line* in October 2011 at the Jermyn Street Theatre in London may have marked the commencement of a revival of the much neglected Charles Morgan.[53] Nowadays, his antiquated stiff-upper-lip urbanity and meditative charm may not be a crowd-puller, but Libby Purves puts her finger on their compelling interest: 'this marvellous play demonstrates how seriousness, too, can thrill, particularly when teamed with a tense wartime tale.'[54] As Dominic Cavendish opines in *The Daily Telegraph*: 'some plays lie buried and forgotten for years – and are then exhumed, with their quality to astound left entirely intact'.[55]

Carole Bourne-Taylor
Brasenose College, Oxford

50   *Liberties of the Mind*, p. 7
51   'Ideas at War', *Op. Cit.*, 12
52   *Liberties of the Mind*, p. 44
53   Paul Taylor heralds a rediscovery of Morgan, in *The Independent*, 14 October 2011
54   Libby Purves, *The Times*, 10 October 2011
55   Dominic Cavendish, *The Daily Telegraph*, 10 October 2011

THE FLASHING STREAM

Characters

COMMANDER HENRY CARR, R.N.

DENHAM (Corporal of Marines)

LIEUT.-COMMANDER PETER BRISSING, R.N.

COMMANDER EDWARD FERRERS, R.N.

LIEUT.-COMMANDER RICHARD SANDFORD, R.N.

LADY HELSTON

REAR-ADMIRAL SIR GEORGE HELSTON,
Bart., C.B., R.N.

THE RT HON. WALTER HARROWBY, P.C., M.P.

KAREN SELBY

CAPTAIN WINTER, D.S.C, R.N.

The play was first performed at the Lyric Theatre, London under the direction of Mr Godfrey Tearle, on Thursday, 1 September 1938, with the following cast, here given in the order of their appearance:

COMMANDER HENRY CARR, R.N.	Mr. Leo Genn
DENHAM (Corporal of Marines)	Mr. Roger Maxwell
LIEUT.-COMMANDER PETER BRISSING, R.N.	Mr. Anthony Ireland
COMMANDER EDWARD FERRERS, R.N.	Mr. Godfrey Tearle
LIEUT.-COMMANDER RICHARD SANDFORD, R.N.	Mr. Laurier Lister
LADY HELSTON	Miss Marda Vanne
REAR-ADMIRAL SIR GEORGE HELSTON, Bart., C.B., R.N.	Mr. H.G. Stoker
THE RT HON. WALTER HARROWBY, P.C., MP	Mr. Felix Aylmer
KAREN SELBY	Miss Margaret Rawlings
CAPTAIN WINTER, D.S.C., R.N.	Mr. Desmond Roberts

Time: The Present

Scene: The living room of the officers attached to the Commander Ferrers' experimental unit in the British island of St Hilary, in the Atlantic.

Act I

Scene 1: An evening, early March

Scene 2: After dinner, the same evening

Act II

Scene 1: The morning of July 15

Scene 2: August 16. 5 p.m.

Act III

Mid-October

Producer	Mr. Peter Creswell

ACT ONE

The Block House, formerly a fortress, on high ground three miles from Kendrickstown in the British island of St. Hilary in the Atlantic.

The scene is a big plain room of stone and whitewash, furnished as a naval mess. It is the general living room of the officers attached to COMMANDER EDWARD FERRERS' experimental unit. The stage directions which follow are given from the point of view of the audience.

On the right is a door which leads to the dining room and to other rooms of the Block House. Below this are two drawing-office desks, each with a light above and a high stool before it.

On the left is a staircase which runs up a few steps, then turns at right angles and continues to ascend, along the left wall, in the direction of the audience. At the turn of the staircase is a door, like the door of a huge safe, leading to the Control Room, which is FERRERS' own workroom. The staircase then leads on towards FERRERS' bedroom.

In the crook of this staircase is a piano, so placed that a player's back is to the room. Near it, running up and down stage, is an oblong table with a cloth of Service pattern, and beyond this, downstage, is a settee. Behind the settee a small table for drinks. Other tables and chairs. The upholstery is of leather. Maps, charts, a few pictures.

Beyond this room, in the centre upstage, there is to be seen through an archway, which may be closed by sliding doors now open, a verandah with a small table and some chairs. Sky beyond and indication of flowering shrubs. The verandah is approached from within the room by a few wide shallow steps, and whoever leaves the verandah for the open air goes down steps to the garden level. The verandah is, in effect, a platform at the back of the stage.

It is a blue, glowing evening of March. Daylight fading.

DENHAM, a marine servant, is polishing glasses. COMMANDER CARR, in mess-dress, enters downstairs from FERRERS' room. He is about forty-seven, solid, kindly, able; never openly emotional; the balance and common sense of a brilliant group of men.

CARR: *(Shouting upstairs.)* Ferrers!

FERRERS: *(Off.)* What?

CARR: Where did you leave it?

FERRERS: On the piano. *(As CARR goes to piano, picks up cigarette case and hands it to DENHAM.)*

CARR: Denham. Cigarette case. Take it to Commander Ferrers. He's upstairs dressing.

DENHAM: Very good, sir.

CARR: And you might report progress. We don't want him late for his guests.

DENHAM: I'll give him a jog, sir.

CARR: Which means?

DENHAM: Tell him his watch is slow, sir.

CARR: *(Smiling.)* He's pretty close on the mark. You won't catch him that way.

DENHAM: I'm not saying he'd swallow it, sir. But it do give people a turn to say their watch is slow. May think you're a liar, but they can't be that sure. It's like winkin' the eye about a man's girl. She may be an angel with knobs on, but it makes him look slippy.

CARR: Go easy, Denham. He's on edge. He's done two men's work since Mr Selby was killed. Go easy.

DENHAM: Very good, sir.

CARR: Find out if you can how he wants people seated at tonight's dinner. I suppose he'll have the Admiral's lady on his right and Miss Selby on his left. Find out where he wants the First Lord and the Admiral. The rest of us can arrange ourselves. The Flag-Captain too. Where's he to go? Ask that if you can. But use your judgment, Denham. Don't worry him for orders. He doesn't like invasions of this place – particularly female. *(Takes papers from table and crosses to settee.)*

DENHAM: Some of us could do with a bit more of it, sir.

CARR: More what?

DENHAM: Skirt, sir.

CARR: I dare say. *(Sits.)* But that isn't Commander Ferrers' view. As long as the experiments go on, the fewer people get their noses into this Block House the better – men or women.

DENHAM: It's more than a year now, sir. It comes a bit hard on the married men.

CARR: It does. I'd have brought my own wife out if there'd been a chance of it, but there's only one house in Kendrickstown that hasn't fallen to pieces, and the Admiral's wife has that. Anyhow, Denham, what about the single men?

DENHAM: It's harder on the married, sir.

CARR: Is it?

DENHAM: What I say is: if it's not, it ought to be.

CARR: Are you a puritan, Denham?

DENHAM: No, sir, Primitive Methodist. (Then seeing that his leg has been pulled.) Well, sir, you're married yourself. It's not for me to be telling you. I only hope some of the hands'll stick it. They're weak – sailors. (CARR is reading paper; then as the significance of DENHAM's remark strikes him, he stops.)

CARR: Did you say 'stick it', Denham?

DENHAM: I did, sir.

CARR: What, exactly, did you mean by that? Is there trouble?

DENHAM: Oh, I'm not suggesting mutiny, sir. Nothing of the kind. Commander Ferrers, he only has to look in on 'em when they're in the workshops and make one of his jokes straightfaced without batting an eyelid and they'll sit here in this sweaty island till he tells 'em to quit. But it's easier for us up at Headquarters than it is for them in the workshops.

CARR: In some ways I suppose it is. But they know what we're driving at.

DENHAM: They do and they don't, sir. They know that what they're making is a kind of aerial torpedo. They call them Scorpions, same as us, but –

CARR: *(Rises and sits on arm of settee.)* If the Scorpions work, no bomber can live in the air. Isn't that something?

DENHAM: That's what I keep telling 'em, sir. But some people want to know everything – specially the engineering kind. You and the Commander and Mr. Sandford and Mr. Brissing, you send down designs for separate parts, and they make 'em blind and they make 'em accurate, but they can't piece 'em together. More than a year of that. It takes some sticking.

CARR: But they must work blind, Denham. No one outside can have the complete plan. Too much hangs on it.

DENHAM: I know, sir. But it's not knowing how long it will last. If I could write and say: 'Home by Christmas' it'd be easier. I'm not complaining, sir. If the Scorpions is going to mean no enemy can touch us by air, all right. But the last trial didn't come to much, except that Mr Selby was killed.

CARR: Wasn't meant to. It was preliminary.

DENHAM: *(A little too familiar.)* When's the next to be, sir?

CARR: When we're ready. *(This is a snub.)*

DENHAM: Very good, sir. *(Moves to exit.)*

CARR: *(Takes material for letter-writing and lays it out on the table.)* Are Mr Selby's things all packed up?

DENHAM: Yes, sir.

CARR: Everything in? Ready to be shipped home?

DENHAM: Commander Ferrers went through 'em himself, sir.

CARR: I see. *(CARR is unscrewing and testing his fountain pen.)*

DENHAM: With Mr Selby dead, sir, and the work slowed down, perhaps the Admiralty would be sending out someone to help the Commander?

CARR: Mathematicians of the Ferrers and Selby rank don't grow on raspberry bushes, Denham. There aren't twenty in the world – and they have jobs, and most of them aren't English.

DENHAM: I see that, sir, but –

CARR: There's no but about it. Here we are and here we stay until this thing succeeds – or fails.

FERRERS: *(Off.)* Carr, where the hell are those cigarettes?

CARR: All right!... Take them.

DENHAM: *(To FERRERS.)* Coming, sir. *(Exit upstairs. CARR sits down at the table and begins to write letter. Enter LIEUTENANT-COMMANDER BRISSING, R. He is in dress-shirt, trousers, patent shoes, braces – no tie. Young, handsome, a little vain, potentially a lady-killer, but that is not his profession. A 'star' Gunnery Officer, he has first-rate intellect.)*

BRISSING: *(Off.)* Denham!... Denham! *(Entering.)* Hullo sir! Where's Denham?

CARR: *(Steadily continuing his letter.)* Gone up to Ferrers.

BRISSING: He put me out lightning conductors. Why are we in mess-dress?

CARR: Because, my boy, the First Lord of the Admiralty is dining tonight.

BRISSING: Even so –

CARR: And because the Admiral's wife thought she'd like our legs to look pretty.

BRISSING: Ferrers' legs.

CARR: May be.

BRISSING: How that woman loves to give orders!... I can't find my tie.

CARR: It's in the loop of your shirt.

BRISSING: Where?

CARR: Hanging down your back.

BRISSING: Damn! *(Finds it.)* One of the disadvantages of a celibate life is that there are no mirrors. What are you doing, sir?

CARR: Writing a letter home.

BRISSING: You won't get far with it this evening.

CARR: I shall when they've gone. I write a kind of serial letter. A bit at any odd time. Then put them together when there's an outgoing mail.

BRISSING: I scribble mine at the last moment. *(Tying his tie.)*

CARR: The other way keeps you in touch. It's more like talking. Something comes into your head and down it goes. My wife does the same.

BRISSING: *(Enviously.)* You must feel *safe*!

CARR: She permits me that illusion. Is Sandford dressed?

BRISSING: Out of his bath. ... Things seem to have happened since we went away.

CARR: You and Sandford gave things time to happen. Nineteen hours over leave.

BRISSING: I know. Completely genuine breakdown.

CARR: Have you reported?

BRISSING: Couldn't until we had got into uniform. Ferrers said much?

CARR: About you? Very little. Bit awkward that neither of you was here for the First Lord's inspection this morning, but Ferrers and I took him round. Last night was the trouble.

BRISSING: why?

CARR: Someone from here had to go down into Kendrickstown and call at the Admiral's house as soon as the First Lord had landed from his liner and settled in.

BRISSING: Wasn't that up to Ferrers himself?

CARR: He wouldn't go.

BRISSING: But why?

CARR: Just wouldn't. *(Abandons letter.)* You know, Brissing, he's devilish on edge. Sounds mad, but, in some odd way, he goes on looking for Selby.

BRISSING: Did you gather they were as close friends as that, when Selby was alive?

CARR: I didn't – not fully. And it's not all personal. Mathematics means more to Ferrers than anything on earth. It's his language. It was Selby's too and it's not ours. What they cared about wasn't the Scorpion itself but the maths of the thing. That's the point. Without Selby he's alone in a foreign country.

BRISSING: Even so, I don't see why he couldn't pay a duty call at the Admiral's house.

CARR: Because Selby's sister is there.

BRISSING: And the Admiral's wife. She'll have her knife into him if he doesn't play his cards. Ask me, he's a fool to avoid her.

CARR: Yes, but I don't think you're fair to her.

BRISSING: Why should I be?

CARR: She's unhappy, you know. Most bitter people are. And I believe that in her own queer way she loves Ferrers.

BRISSING: She has an odd way of showing it. Why d'you think she patronizes Sandford? She doesn't care a damn for *him*. Trouble is, Sandford himself is badly hit, but he'll get over it. *(Sits on settee.)* Meanwhile, she's dangerous to Ferrers. She sees him here, shut up, working like hell, concentrated on his job. That fascinates some women. It's odd. They want to break up a man's work because it keeps them out, and they want to be – the inspiration of it. That's her ladyship's trouble. Any man who's running a show is fair game to Lady H. If she was in a train, she'd try to seduce the guard. If she lived in Rome, she'd pester the Pope. And when she got no change, she'd hate them. Ferrers is precisely the kind to drive her mad. If he had a bit of sense, he'd play down to that woman.

CARR: By which you mean – go to bed with her?

BRISSING: You have the simple mind of a happily married man, sir. No – on the whole – not. He'd have to get out again. Then there *would* be hell to pay. But he might at least go through the polite motions of thwarted longing. *(Enter DENHAM, downstairs.)*

CARR: All right?

DENHAM: Coming down, sir.

BRISSING: I'd better get dressed before he comes. *(Exits, R.)*

CARR: Did you get the orders? What about the seating at dinner? Where are the ladies to go?

DENHAM: I asked him, sir.

CARR: Well?

DENHAM: He said I was to give you the message in his own words, sir.

CARR: Well, go on.

DENHAM: He said: 'Tell Commander Carr that he can put the women where the – '

CARR: All right, Denham. Carry on now.

DENHAM: Here he is, sir. *(Moves towards door R. Enter FERRERS. He is dark, keen, very alive. In his walk, the buoyancy of a single-minded man with natural authority; in his abrupt manner the impatience of one who knows that the minds of others move slower than his own. To fools, he is arrogant, but not in face of his own job. His imagination can leap to other people's point of view; when it does, it endows him with rare sympathy and tenderness. CARR sits down again to his letter.)*

FERRERS: Denham! *(DENHAM stops. FERRERS crosses to him, and holds out his wrist-watch.)* Look at that watch. *(Pointing to clock.)* And look at that clock.

DENHAM: Yes, sir.

FERRERS: Well, look at it. You can't see it from here.

DENHAM: *(Turns, stands at attention.)* Yes, sir.

FERRERS: Well?

DENHAM: I'm sorry, sir. But it did the trick, sir.

FERRERS: It did. Time for a gin before they come. One pink, one orange, Denham.

DENHAM: Very good, sir.

FERRERS: Tell the sentry to report at once when he hears the Admiral's car on the lower road.

DENHAM: Very good, sir. *(Exits.)*

FERRERS: *(To CARR.)* I wish you hadn't let us in for this.

CARR: I couldn't help it. Admiral's orders.

FERRERS: He can't have ordered himself to dinner in our mess.

CARR: He made it pretty clear. It's the First Lord's idea, I think.

FERRERS: Harrowby. He's an odd cove. I like politicians when they have brains. ... But the women?

CARR: That's Harrowby's idea, too. After all, you've got to see the Selby girl some time. *(Rises.)*

FERRERS: I suppose so.

CARR: Her brother may have been a civilian, but she probably thinks of you as his commanding officer. There'll be things she'll want to ask.

FERRERS: I don't want to go over and over it. Selby's dead. All our work's held up without him. I can't say: 'That's the desk your brother worked at. That's the settee he sat on to drink gin. He died happy, talking of you.'

CARR: It happens to be true.

FERRERS: What?

CARR: That he died talking of her.

FERRERS: He died talking of calculation-groups forty-three to eight. Group 46 was on his mind. There's something new to come out of that. I can't get –

CARR: May be. But he talked of her too.

FERRERS: Apropos of Group 46. He said she'd know. He always said she was a finer mathematician than he was himself. ... My God, what a waste! Why I let him of all men go up as an observer –

CARR: *(Putting writing material into drawers.)* It wasn't your fault. He asked for the job. You have no need to blame yourself.

FERRERS: Haven't I? I let him go ... What have you been packing away in there? Not work?

CARR: Only a letter. *(DENHAM comes in with drinks and goes out again.)*

FERRERS: What's the girl's name?

CARR: What? Selby.

FERRERS: I know that. I mean the other name.

CARR: Karen.

FERRERS: I remember. Karen Selby. Well, here's to her. *(Drinks.)* She's a mathematician anyway. *(Enter BRISSING and SANDFORD, R. FERRERS gives his glass to CARR, and turns to the newcomers. CARR puts down the glass and moves away to piano. The following passage is strictly Service. SANDFORD is quieter than BRISSING, but of a steadier and even deeper intelligence. He is a romantic where BRISSING is a realist. Towards women a little too doglike.)*

FERRERS: Why didn't you report?

SANDFORD: We weren't in uniform, sir.

FERRERS: Well, this isn't the uniform to report in.

SANDFORD: There wasn't time for a double change. I'm sorry, sir.

FERRERS: What happened?

BRISSING: My mare went lame just after we had started for home, sir. I had to wait with her while Sandford went for another mount.

SANDFORD: It took me eight hours, sir. I lost my way. When I found him, my own horse was all in. Anyhow it was dark. We had to camp again and come on at sunrise.

FERRERS: All right. Carry on. *(BRISSING and SANDFORD begin to mix cocktails.)* You'd better get your drink in before the women come. After that you'll have to talk. ... Brissing, you're the poodle-faker in this mess. When the car is reported, go out and meet them. They'll like that.

BRISSING: Aye, aye, sir. I'll tell the sentry. *(Moves up steps to verandah.)*

FERRERS: That's done... *(To SANDFORD.)* Dick, your job is to keep Lady Helston in a good temper. Is that congenial?

SANDFORD: I'll try. *(BRISSING returns.)*

CARR: It may not be easy. As far as I could gather, the Selby girl isn't a joy to her.

BRISSING: Another woman wouldn't be.

SANDFORD: Well, if you had a perfectly good blue-stocking thrust on you as a guest –

BRISSING: Why 'thrust'? Anyhow where else was the girl to go?

SANDFORD: *(To BRISSING, angrily.)* I dare say there is nowhere else. That doesn't make it easier for Lady Helston. That's why I said 'thrust'.

CARR: It's more or less true, I'm afraid. She was in the same liner with the First Lord. He took her under his wing to the Admiral's house.

SANDFORD: With the result that Sybil Helston –

BRISSING: *Sybil* Helston! Damn it, you worry that woman's name as if it were a bone. *(To FERRERS.)* Mr President, sir, can we have a round of drinks off anyone who repeats a lady's name more than three times a minute? *(Enter DENHAM.)*

DENHAM: Sentry reports car approaching, sir.

FERRERS: Hell's bells! On you go, Brissing.

CARR: Bring them in by the verandah. *(Exit BRISSING.)*

SANDFORD: Why that way?

CARR: Avoid the smell of cooking.

SANDFORD: *(Laughing.)* Bless you, sir. You're the sanity of this place.

FERRERS: *(Who is walking up and down in a state of extreme nervousness.)* Why in God's name can't women leave you alone?

CARR: It's not the girl's fault. She didn't know Selby was dead when she sailed. Harrowby told her on board – from his own wireless. Be gentle with her, Ferrers. ... If you can't, be gentle with yourself.

FERRERS: You saw her last night?

CARR: Yes.

FERRERS: Speak to her?

CARR: A bit.

FERRERS: What's her line?

CARR: Didn't say much.

FERRERS: About Selby, I mean.

CARR: Asked where he was buried. I told her. She said: 'Why didn't you bury him at sea?'

FERRERS: *(Interested.)* Did she?

SANDFORD: Bit odd for a girl.

FERRERS: What?

SANDFORD: To think of that.

FERRERS: Why odd?

SANDFORD: Lady Helston has a horror of burials at sea. She says it's so lonely.

FERRERS: Burials are. What's the point of dying, if you can't be alone even then? *(Enter from verandah MR HARROWBY, First Lord of the Admiralty, dry, thin, deliberate, silky – with a twinkle; REAR-ADMIRAL SIR GEORGE HELSTON, BART., a good seaman but unimaginative, easily flattered because he is weak and full of vague good-will and likes to be liked; LADY HELSTON, much younger that her husband, at once bright and intense. She is well bred, well dressed, affected, but no fool. FERRERS, CARR and SANDFORD go forward to meet their guests. Greetings.)*

LADY HELSTON: *(To FERRERS.)* What a lovely room this is! *(To ADMIRAL.)* George, isn't it a lovely room? *(She sits on the settee.)*

ADMIRAL: Well, my dear, you're the expert on interior decoration.

LADY HELSTON: It's not that. It's the atmosphere of it!

SANDFORD: We find it a bit monastic.

LADY HELSTON: That's why it's such a perfect background for a party.

SANDFORD: *(Ingratiating.)* I have mixed you your own cocktail.

LADY HELSTON: *(Snubbing him.)* Dick, that's sweet of you, but may I have sherry? *(To FIRST LORD, who is talking to FERRERS.)* We owe it to you, Mr Harrowby, that we're asked here at all. Commander Ferrers never gives a party if he can help it. Do you, Edward?

FIRST LORD: Well, you mustn't expect the prior of a monastery to invite temptation into it.

LADY HELSTON: Not even with whitewash as a background? I always wear a dress with flame in it and trust to Edward's imagination to supply a forked tail.

FERRERS: Where are the other guests?

LADY HELSTON: *(To ADMIRAL, irritably.)* Where *is* that girl?

ADMIRAL: Winter's following with her in his car.

LADY HELSTON: I know that. But they ought to be here by now. They started just behind us.

FIRST LORD: *(Now alone with FERRERS.)* She may disturb the monastery a little.

FERRERS: Who?

FIRST LORD: Miss Selby.

FERRERS: *(Sharply.)* Why do you say that?

FIRST LORD: The more because in her case the disturbance will not be deliberate. She doesn't need flame in her dress. Are you a judge of women, Ferrers?

FERRERS: Not by profession, sir.

FIRST LORD: Good. But I hope an observant amateur? It is, I think, important.

LADY HELSTON: *(Cutting in.)* What is important?

FIRST LORD: To have a good memory, Lady Helston. I was trying to recall those lines of Pope's:

'I know a thing that's most uncommon,

Envy be silent and attend.

I know a reasonable woman,

Handsome and witty but a friend.

Not warped...'

Do you remember, Ferrers?

FERRERS: I'm afraid not, sir.

FIRST LORD: Perhaps we shall be reminded before the evening is out.

BRISSING: *(In verandah.)* This way. Shall I lead on? *(But he stands aside and KAREN SELBY appears. She is dark and not conventionally pretty. Her power is in her movement, her voice, the impact of her imagination and intelligence. She is wearing an evening dress, beautifully made and of one flat colour – or, preferably, of black, for she is in mourning for her brother, and, if the actress likes black on a white background, KAREN brought a black dress on her voyage. She pauses on the top step.)*

LADY HELSTON: Edward, you must do the introductions. You haven't met Miss Selby.

FERRERS: *(Down L.C., facing front.)* No. *(Faces KAREN.)* Look, Brissing, you've met. He's the gunnery expert.

KAREN: I'm afraid we nearly ran him down. *(She comes down the steps.)*

FERRERS: You saw Carr yesterday evening. *(CARR shakes hands with her.)* That leaves Sandford. Dick, come and be introduced. *(SANDFORD is handing sherry to LADY HELSTON. Now he comes to KAREN. The FLAG CAPTAIN enters, prim, efficient, hard, shifty. He is greeted by FERRERS.)*

SANDFORD: *(To KAREN.)* How d'you do. I have to apologize.

KAREN: For what?

SANDFORD: Five minutes ago I decided you were a perfectly good blue-stocking.

FIRST LORD: I can assure you she's neither.

KAREN: Neither?

FIRST LORD: A blue-stocking – nor perfectly good.

KAREN: *(With a shade of serious emphasis.)* That's true.

FIRST LORD: This is an officer I haven't met. You are a torepedo-man, Mr Sandford?

SANDFORD: Yes, sir. Brissing and I *(He draws BRISSING in.)* were away fishing. His mare went lame.

FIRST LORD: Any fish?

FLAG CAPTAIN: If there were, they'd have gone off in this weather. *(They drift away, talking of fish. ADMIRAL, FIRST LORD, SANDFORD, BRISSING are in one group. CARR is talking to LADY HELSTON.)*

KAREN: *(To FERRERS.)* You are Edward Ferrers.

FERRERS: I am.

KAREN: My brother always wrote of you by both names. That's why I used them. I think of you that way.

FERRERS: I see.

KAREN: He loved you. You know that?

FERRERS: *(Cold but trembling.)* We were good friends.

KAREN: I'm sorry. You hate to talk of him.

FERRERS: I'm sorry for your sake, Miss Selby. I ought to have said so. Coming out here – *(He abandons polite condolence.)* It's my work takes me back.

KAREN: Group 46?

FERRERS: *(Suspicious.)* What do you know of Group 46?

KAREN: You needn't worry. He didn't give away any secrets. All I know is part of the mathematical process – nothing of what it's leading to. It was in Robin's last letter.

FERRERS: I see. Do you make anything of it?

KAREN: Yes.

FERRERS: How great a mathematician are you?

KAREN: I –

FERRERS: No. You can answer that to me. Selby said you came before him. Is that true?

KAREN: Yes.

FERRERS: Well, thank God you can say it. Do you always tell the truth?

KAREN: About mathematics. *(There is a pause, neither can speak. KAREN goes to the top of table and sits.)*

CARR: I suppose it depends on what you really believe in.

LADY HELSTON: I've given up believing in anyone.

CARR: That may happen to all of us if the luck breaks. Still there are *things* you can believe in – if not people. Aren't there?

LADY HELSTON: *(Bored.)* There may be.

CARR: More sherry?

LADY HELSTON: Dickie mixed me my own cocktail. Can I have that? *(Three bells sound.)*

CARR: Of course. *(FERRERS returns towards KAREN. On the way, meets CARR.)*

CARR: *(To FERRERS.)* Which is her Ladyship's cocktail?

FERRERS: She's drinking sherry.

CARR: She's mixing them. *(FERRERS reaches KAREN.)*

FERRERS: You have nothing to drink.

KAREN: *(Looking into his face.)* He never sent a photograph. I've never seen one.

FERRERS: Of what?

KAREN: Of – any of you. *(She turns her head away suddenly.)* I think I *should* like a drink. *(BRISSING has come down with ADMIRAL and FIRST LORD and is within earshot.)*

BRISSING: I've got one for you. *(He goes to table.)*

FIRST LORD: Ferrers, have we a minute before dinner?

FERRERS: It's overdue, sir.

FIRST LORD: Never mind. I'd like a word. *(He draws FERRERS aside.)*

ADMIRAL: This is your first experience of a naval mess, Miss Selby.

KAREN: I went to a dance in a Yugo-Slav warship at Corfu.

ADMIRAL: They have a drink called Šljivovica. It's a kind of plum-brandy. *(The dinner bugle sounds.)* You don't recognize the dinner bugle.

(Sings.) 'Officers' wives have puddings and pies,
Sailors' wives have skilly.'

LADY HELSTON: George, in a moment you'll be teaching Miss Selby knots and splices.

ADMIRAL: I should like that.

KAREN: So should I.

CARR: *(Detaching KAREN from them.)* Are you a painter, too, Miss Selby?

KAREN: A painter? No. Why?

CARR: Only that your brother was. He and I went out sketching together. That's one of his things over there. I'll take it down for you.

KAREN: No, don't do that. *(They go over L. BRISSING hesitates but KAREN signs to him and he follows.)*

LADY HELSTON: George, I want you to do something for me.

ADMIRAL: What, again?

LADY HELSTON: Now don't be crusty. It makes you seem older than you are. This is quite simple.

ADMIRAL: As long as it's not a Service matter. I've been wanting to say for some time my dear, that on Service matters you really must leave me to myself. *(KAREN, BRISSING and CARR go on to verandah.)*

LADY HELSTON: Don't you value advice?

ADMIRAL: Of course I do. Of course I do, between ourselves. But you must be more discreet. People will begin to say –

LADY HELSTON: This isn't a Service matter. It's personal. Don't you think, after dinner, Commander Ferrers might show us his Control Room?

ADMIRAL: Show you, you mean?

LADY HELSTON: He never has. He always avoids and hedges. Perhaps he thinks you wouldn't approve. If you issued an order –

ADMIRAL: But, my dear, this is a dinner-party. An order –

LADY HELSTON: Don't be stupid. If you say you approve, that will be enough.

ADMIRAL: Better leave Ferrers alone.

LADY HELSTON: But you don't disapprove?

ADMIRAL: N-no.

LADY HELSTON: That's all I want. *(Enter DENHAM.)*

DENHAM: Dinner is served, sir.

ADMIRAL: *(Glancing round and seeing that FERRERS is occupied with FIRST LORD.)* Shall we lead on, Ferrers?

FERRERS: Please, sir *(General drift towards door R.)*

FIRST LORD: Don't think I'm trying to force your hand, Ferrers.

FERRERS: What you suggest can't be done, sir.

FIRST LORD: Possibly not. But can anything else be done? Who else is there?

FERRERS: Aren't there any men in the world?

FIRST LORD: Not here. Not with her qualifications. You see, Ferrers, I'm getting old. Women, so to speak, don't hang out flags for me – white or red – though sometimes I get a glimpse through a window in passing. The things that chiefly interest me are (a) cats, (b) the safety of Great Britain. And whether it's a man or a woman sells me the cat I want – or the peace of the world – makes no odds to me, as long as I get it. You are younger.

FERRERS: The thing won't work, sir.

FIRST LORD: Still young enough to be afraid of women – or of yourself… Mr Sandford spoke of the lady as 'a perfectly good blue-stocking'. I presume he hadn't seen her.

FERRERS: I have. However good she is at her job, she can't work in this unit.

FIRST LORD: You dislike her?

FERRERS: That's not the point, sir. I –

FIRST LORD: Never mind. Never mind, then. We must not spoil our dinner. *(The others are all in the mess-room. The FIRST LORD and FERRERS move to the door. On the way the FIRST LORD stops. His bantering tone is gone.)* Tell me, Ferrers, is it true that Miss Selby is among the first six mathematicians in the world?

FERRERS: I'm not good at team-making, sir. Can you tell me who are the first six poets in the world?

FIRST LORD: My question was, I admit, a crude one. Still, you can answer it.

FERRERS: The answer is: roughly – yes.

FIRST LORD: The first six?

FERRERS: Selby said her work in the astronomical observatory at Green Hill was beyond anything of his.

FIRST LORD: That is what I want you to consider while you eat your soup. *(They move on. He stops again.)* Imagine her in trousers, my dear Ferrers. In dealing with women, I have found it a useful exercise. God so made a woman that in trousers a part of her truth conspicuously appears.

FERRERS: Not unbecomingly.

FIRST LORD: No. … No. … But with a salutary candour.

Curtain.

SCENE 2

The same, after dinner. The stage empty and almost dark. DENHAM brings in coffee and liqueurs, puts them down and turns on the lights. The diners begin to enter from the mess-room. When they have disposed themselves, the FIRST LORD, ADMIRAL and FLAG CAPTAIN are at the piano, and remain there in conference, unheard except when, in the chance silence of the others, a sentence or two of theirs comes through. The FLAG CAPTAIN is sceptical and disapproving of what is being said to him.

LADY HELSTON and SANDFORD are on the verandah.

FERRERS takes CARR by the arm, brings him right down stage past the others and talks with him eagerly. CARR is laughing good-humouredly.

FERRERS: *(Cutting him short.)* Yes, I know. But he means it.

CARR: That she should come here?

FERRERS: In Selby's place.

CARR: Who said politicians were without ideas?

FERRERS: But seriously. You have your head screwed on – perhaps better than any of us.

CARR: At first glance, I like the girl.

FERRERS: As a girl?

CARR: As a human being, too. She runs straight – and fast. *(Their talk continues.)*

LADY HELSTON: *(From top step leading to verandah.)* Are we going to play, Captain Winter? *(She comes down into the room.)*

FLAG CAPTAIN: *(An awkward courtier. Now a little vague, for he has been interrupted.)* Charming. Charming... Bridge?... Yes, I'd like a game presently. *(KAREN and BRESSING enter from garden and separate. She comes down to desk R.)*

LADY HELSTON: *(Mimicking.)* Charming. Charming... Out on the verandah I think. *(To BRISSING.)* Or will the cards blow away?

BRISSING: There's not a breath.

LADY HELSTON: *(To SANDFORD.)* What are they up to, Dick?

SANDFORD: Who?

LADY HELSTON: Over there. A conspiracy? *(DENHAM enters with coffee and goes to KAREN and BRISSING who has now rejoined her.)*

SANDFORD: Harrowby is probably telling his best story.

LADY HELSTON: *(Going across again.)* Mr Harrowby, is it true that all the wickedest stories come from the House of Commons?

FIRST LORD: Not *from*, Lady Helston. We keep them to ourselves.

LADY HELSTON: That's selfish. Why?

FIRST LORD: Because they're so often true. *(Turns back.)*

LADY HELSTON: *(Takes coffee. To SANDFORD.)* Now you try.

SANDFORD: What?

LADY HELSTON: To break them up.

SANDFORD: Why should I?

LADY HELSTON: They're scheming something... Try. You'll see.

SANDFORD: *(Glancing.)* Better leave them.

LADY HELSTON: *(Contemptuously.)* You may be right.

BRISSING: Are we quarrelling? *(Moves to LADY HELSTON. Takes her cup.)*

LADY HELSTON: Not yet.

BRISSING: Then let's begin. *(LADY HELSTON towards verandah.)*

SANDFORD: *(Nettled.)* It has nothing to do with you – whether I do what Lady Helston wants or not.

BRISSING: *(To KAREN.)* Getting a rise out of Dick Sandford is only a game, Miss Selby. In this place you take your entertainment where you find it. Brandy? *(There is a momentary silence as he pours it out.)*

KAREN: I'll have the cigarette you offered me before dinner. *(She sits on the settee.)*

FLAG CAPTAIN: I think you have too much confidence in him.

FIRST LORD: What do you say, Admiral?

ADMIRAL: I don't like it myself, sir. But I see no other way of getting the work done. I repeat I don't like it, but if your view is set, I don't oppose it. *(LADY HELSTON and SANDFORD are occupied with each other.)*

BRISSING: *(To KAREN.)* What are they talking about?

KAREN: Who? I didn't hear.

BRISSING: The First Lord and his cronies… You're not hearing much this evening.

KAREN: I'm sorry.

BRISSING: Are you usually absent-minded?

KAREN: No.

BRISSING: I thought not.

KAREN: Was I at dinner?

BRISSING: Ferrers was on your other side at dinner.

KAREN: *(Deliberately flat.)* My brother had told me so much about him that –

BRISSING: Listen. They'll drag you into bridge.

KAREN: They can't. I don't play.

BRISSING: Good. Then let's clear out of this.

43

KAREN: Clear out?

BRISSING: Into the open. Walk down to the signal station. The moon's up. I'll tell you why before you ask. I –

KAREN: You do believe in progress!

BRISSING: *(Looking at her.)* So do you.

KAREN: I see. But do you usually rush your fences quite like –

BRISSING: No. But if I don't have you to myself now, it's ten to one I never shall. I'm drunk of course. Anyhow you think I am which comes to the same thing.

KAREN: No. I think you're in love… Not with me… Is that true?

BRISSING: *(Astonished by her intuition and grateful for it.)* Yes. Now you'll hate me.

KAREN: No. I never hate people in love. If I were in love and he – hopelessly out of reach – anyhow I'm made that way.

LADY HELSTON: *(Returning to them.)* Dick says we might make a four and leave the conspirators to conspire.

KAREN: I can't play. *(She rises.)*

LADY HELSTON: A mathematician who can't play bridge! Edward can't lose.

KAREN: I'm sorry.

SANDFORD: *(Eagerly to LADY HELSTON.)* Come down to the signal station.

LADY HELSTON: *(To disappoint him.)* If you will come too, Miss Selby?

KAREN: *(To BRISSING.)* I should like to.

BRISSING: *(As LADY HELSTON and SANDFORD move up towards the verandah, he steps in front of KAREN.)* No. Why the hell should you?

KAREN: *(Smiling.)* Fate.

BRISSING: Or drink… I'm sorry.

KAREN: *(Takes his arm.)* I like live animals.

BRISSING: *(Suddenly.)* Are *you* in love?

KAREN: *(A short, astonished laugh.)* Give me time.

BRISSING: You asked *me*!

KAREN: I *told* you! *(KAREN and BRISSING go out by verandah. LADY HELSTON and SANDFORD are near the verandah steps. The conference by the piano has broken up and the FLAG CAPTAIN intercepts her.)*

FLAG CAPTAIN: Now what about bridge?

LADY HELSTON: Is the fate of nations sealed?

FIRST LORD: Probably it is.

LADY HELSTON: Then let's play.

FIRST LORD: Not for me, I'm afraid, unless it's backgammon.

LADY HELSTON: You, Dick?

SANDFORD: *(Hating it.)* I'm bad you know.

LADY HELSTON: I know you overbid. Never mind. It passes the time. That's three. *(She turns to FERRERS.)* What about you, Edward?

FERRERS: Bridge? Carr will play.

CARR: *(Doing his duty pleasantly.)* Certainly. *(He begins to move up towards the verandah.)*

FERRERS: Well, Carr, that's your last word?

CARR: Yes. I see no other way.

FERRERS: I think you're mad.

CARR: I have a thousand less exciting defects, but unfortunately not that.

FERRERS: I thought so until tonight.

LADY HELSTON: *(To FERRERS.)* What are you two so deep in?

FERRERS: We were discussing whether men grow to resemble their dogs. *(The bridge players go off to the verandah.)*

ADMIRAL: Ferrers, the First Lord has been telling me of the proposal he made to you before dinner. I gather you are against it?

FIRST LORD: Oh come, Helston, that's a very leading question. Let us take it easy. *(The ADMIRAL and FIRST LORD sit at table L., but FERRERS remains restless.)*

FERRERS: *(Standing, centre.)* Have you spoken of it to Miss Selby?

FIRST LORD: Certainly not.

FERRERS: Mustn't that be done? What's the good of discussing whether we'll have her until we know whether she's willing to come?

FIRST LORD: Or I might say, is it not perhaps indiscreet to ask a woman to change her whole way of life until we know whether you are willing to employ her? … No, Ferrers. This is a matter of choosing your own personnel. Not only that – but the member of your staff who is to be your own closest associate. I issue no orders.

ADMIRAL: Certainly, I don't.

FIRST LORD: *(To FERRERS.)* But I should like to understand your objections.

FERRERS: Among men – aren't they plain enough?

FIRST LORD: Not if the men are doing a job that means anything. Women have worked with men before.

FERRERS: *(On arm of settee.)* This is a naval mess. Try bringing a girl to live in a wardroom at sea.

ADMIRAL: But she wouldn't *live* here.

FERRERS: In effect she would, sir. We work to all hours. … And this place is more cut off than any ship at sea. This island stays put in the Atlantic. It doesn't go into harbour and give leave.

FIRST LORD: Sandford said 'monastic'. Does young Brissing treat it so?

FERRERS: In fact he does – not without dust and heat. The local alternative isn't all it might be – and he's devoted to some girl in England. Carr is married. Sandford – *(He glances at ADMIRAL and hesitates.)* – Sandford sticks to his job. I won't have them disturbed. I won't have myself disturbed. Besides, if she came, where *would* she live?

ADMIRAL: That is a difficulty.

FIRST LORD: Is there no inn?

ADMIRAL: There's a native inn. It is a house – that also supplies what Ferrers calls the local alternative.

FIRST LORD: Most unfortunate. No other quarters?

ADMIRAL: None, except in my own house.

FIRST LORD: Would that be inconvenient?

ADMIRAL: To me not at all. I should have to consult my wife.

FERRERS: *(Interrupting.)* None of that is the point. If she comes at all, quarters shall be found. *(He rises. To FIRST LORD.)* You still don't understand, sir, what the difficulty is.

FIRST LORD: What is it, Ferrers?

FERRERS: Have you any real notion of how this place is run? We five – we four – live a very curious, specialized life.

FIRST LORD: In what sense?

FERRERS: What do you think we have in common? We're all naval officers – that may be – Selby wasn't even that – but the Navy, as such, isn't what holds us here. Carr's older; when this is through he'll take a fourth stripe and retire; but he's giving up here and now what is life to him – wife, sons growing up, a daughter he worships – the honest-to-God existence he loves – all on this gamble. Dick Sandford's the finest torpedo officer in the Service; Brissing's gunnery isn't far behind; they're young, desperately ambitious, and they're losing sea-time; they're out of touch. Here they live – no women, no leave, no company but their own, prisoners for all intents and purposes – all for an invention of mine. The Government thinks it's wildcat –

FIRST LORD: No.

FERRERS: Some do.

FIRST LORD: Not the Prime Minister.

FERRERS: Isn't it true the Admiralty is impatient for results?

ADMIRAL: *(Rises.)* That's not unreasonable. My wife's brother, Brian Wedgcroft, who's a member of the Board, feels, I know –

FIRST LORD: I think it would be better if Admiral Wedgcroft were left to speak for himself.

ADMIRAL: As you please. I wanted Ferrers to understand what the Service point of view is.

FIRST LORD: By all means. Shall I put it? The point is, Ferrers, that some extremely sound officers feel – well, not that the thing's wildcat – but that it is slow in proving itself. Meanwhile, the Prime Minister and I are behind you. But politicians come and go; the Navy goes on forever. Would that represent your brother-in-law's opinion, Helston?

ADMIRAL: Politely put. *(Sits.)*

FIRST LORD: But we politicians are sometimes firmer in the saddle than others suppose. The Prime Minister doesn't make a habit of resigning. As you grow older, resignation seems less and less productive. You can take it that the Admiralty are backing you, Ferrers.

FERRERS: I'm grateful. But I see Wedgcroft's argument. I'm expensive. Workshops. Foundry. Destroyers for patrol. A power station. Wireless. A squadron of aeroplanes. As every month passes in Whitehall 'extremely sound officers' add up the bill. I don't blame them. The question is: how long will it last?

FIRST LORD: As long as my confidence in you lasts.

FERRERS: *(After a moment's thought.)* Why do you, sir, believe in me in that way?

FIRST LORD: Why do your shipmates here believe in you? It is a power some men possess.

FERRERS: *(Returning eagerly to the point he was making.)* It's not so much me personally, as the idea. It's their belief in the thing itself that holds us together.

FIRST LORD: An act of faith.

FERRERS: What's more – a continuing act. Not the burst of enthusiasm that makes a bank-clerk enlist or a woman run off to a new faith-healer, but day after day, month after month. … There's not a man here that hasn't a touch of genius of his own – but they have to work on my lines;

cancel their work at my order; sweat for days, and then, because I want to try out another possibility, break up all they've done and start again.

ADMIRAL: Plain obedience to orders.

FERRERS: No, sir. It's less simple. It's subjecting your imagination to orders. Nothing on God's earth is harder to men of imagination. There's only one thing makes it possible – an absolute acceptance and, within the stress of the job itself, singleness of mind. That's what the girl would destroy.

FIRST LORD: Necessarily? Because she's a woman?

ADMIRAL: You mean, there would be jealousies, Ferrers?

FERRERS: No, sir. There might be. That's not the point.

FIRST LORD: Not?

FERRERS: I wish I could make you see, sir. We carry on by one saving grace – by knowing and feeling the difference between on duty and off duty. A woman can't. She can obey or she can think for herself. She can be a subordinate or an independent human being. Magnificent as each. But she can't, for months at a stretch, be *both* in relation to the same man. My officers can be and are. A woman doesn't divide up her mind as we divide ours. If I suggested to Carr that he should do something he didn't believe in, he would argue and criticize. So he should. That's what he's here for. If I gave him an order, he'd obey. That obedience would be final and absolute – nothing personal about it. The girl might obey too. I dare say she would. But it would give her a sense of – not rebellion but of – inferiority. Either she'd begin to enjoy it and become a slave, like a whipped dog, or she'd nurse her personal criticism to poison her Service obedience. A woman is a personal animal. That's her greatness. But this particular job needs –

FIRST LORD: Go on, Ferrers. What does it need?

FERRERS: *(This carries the whole emphasis of the play and is spoken very slowly, clearly, quietly.)* I think the rarest thing in the world, sir – impersonal passion.

FIRST LORD: Thank you. I am glad I interrupted my journey to Buenos Aires. You have answered your own question: why do I believe in you? *(After a pause.)* But – 'impersonal passion'? There are women who have been great saints.

ADMIRAL: Bless my soul, this girl isn't –

FIRST LORD: No, Admiral, as you shrewdly observe, probably she is not. But the great female saints have not all been, as women, cold… Really, you naval officers take an extremely odd view of the sex. You recognize no intervening territory between Belgrave Square and the shady side of Burlington Street. You put all your money on matrimony or the mantelpiece.

ADMIRAL: It seems to work.

FIRST LORD: With ladies themselves? Of course it does. You act upon the principle that some women live by falling on their feet; the rest by – assuming a different posture; naturally they like to know which attitude is expected of them. It prevents confusion and shortens procedure. But though such maritime distinctions do, no doubt, facilitate the Navy's silent progress from drawing room to alcove, they are the ruin of philosophy. You mustn't assume, Admiral, that because a girl has bright eyes the angels have lost interest in her.

ADMIRAL: Angels my foot! Why are we talking of angels? *(KAREN and BRISSING return to the verandah. They do not enter the room and those on the stage do not see them.)*

FIRST LORD: Because they are extremely relevant. Do you suggest, Ferrers, that women haven't the capacity for impersonal passion? No religieuses? No artists? No women of science? … No mathematicians? … Come.

FERRERS: They may be capable of it in relation to a God they worship.

FIRST LORD: And to a picture they paint? And to a poem they write? … Well?

FERRERS: This isn't her picture. It's mine. And I'm not God.

(Enter DENHAM.)

DENHAM: *(To FERRERS.)* Master-at-Arms reports fort cleared up for rounds, sir.

FERRERS: Brissing, take rounds for me.

BRISSING: Aye, aye, sir. *(To DENHAM.)* Waiting now?

DENHAM: Yes, sir.

BRISSING: *(To KAREN.)* Sorry, I must go the rounds. *(BRISSING follows DENHAM out by the door R. KAREN, on the top step of the verandah, makes a movement as if to descend, then, seeing that she is eavesdropping, turns and goes.)*

FIRST LORD: Women who vanish when they're not wanted are rare… Well, Ferrers?

FERRERS: If I do what you ask, sir, there's no going back.

FIRST LORD: If you don't, there's no going forward. See her, Ferrers.

ADMIRAL: *(Looking round and seeing KAREN on the verandah.)* I'll bring her in. *(He goes out.)*

FIRST LORD: See her. That's all I ask.

FERRERS: I *have* seen her.

FIRST LORD: What?

FERRERS: I said: I have *seen* her.

FIRST LORD: *(Serious.)* Ah!… *(Then on the principle that the only way to treat a serious emotion is lightly.)* Historians tell us, my dear Ferrers, that, on appropriate occasions, ladies and gentlemen of the Middle Ages shared the same bed but placed a drawn sword between them.

FERRERS: Did no one ever put the sword into its sheath? Human nature must have changed *(FIRST LORD has moved up stage, meets ADMIRAL as he enters with KAREN. Sound of chatter from bridge players. SANDFORD comes in, from verandah to fetch LADY HELSTON's fan.)*

ADMIRAL: Who's wining, Sandford?

SANDFORD: We are, sir.

ADMIRAL: You and –

SANDFORD: Lady Helston, sir.

ADMIRAL: Thank God for that. *(Exit SANDFORD.)*

FIRST LORD: *(To KAREN.)* Is there a good view from the signal station?

KAREN: You can hear the water sucking into the coves under the cliff. It makes you want to throw yourself in.

FIRST LORD: Come, Helston. If I were drowned, that would be most unfortunate. You shall go with me and prevent a bye-election in the East Riding. My majority is only seventy-two. *(ADMIRAL and FIRST LORD go out. FERRERS has seated himself at the big table. KAREN comes forward, but he does not look at her and she is left stranded in mid-stage. She would go out, but suddenly he says:)*

FERRERS: Come here, please. *(She obeys and stands beside him, but at a little distance, waiting. Then he looks at her – a long gaze – and jerks his head away. From now onward he is forcing himself to speak to her strictly on Service, as he would to a junior officer – and he leaves her standing.)*

You work in the Green Hill Observatory?

KAREN: Yes.

FERRERS: For how long?

KAREN: Three years now.

FERRERS: You like it?

KAREN: Yes. It's the nearest thing to pure mathematics anyone has ever been paid for.

FERRERS: Who's your chief?

KAREN: Sir Henry Savernake.

FERRERS: How old is he?

KAREN: Seventy-four.

FERRERS: And you?

KAREN: Thirty.

FERRERS: Not twenty-nine?

KAREN: Thirty. *(A smile.)* I always tell the truth about mathematics.

FERRERS: So I see. *(Pause.)*

KAREN: Are there more questions?

FERRERS: I'm afraid so.

KAREN: May I sit down?

FERRERS: Of course. I'm sorry. *(He rises, and she seats herself at once on the arm of the settee.)*

KAREN: *(A smile.)* You can assume that I am standing – for drill purposes.

FERRERS: What do you know of 'drill purposes'?

KAREN: It's a phrase Mr Brissing has just taught me. *(Pause.)*

FERRERS: *(Sits.)* Miss Selby, it has been suggested that you should take your brother's place.

KAREN: *(It is not a question.)* Here.

FERRERS: For many reasons I'm against it; I dare say you are. But we're in a hole. There's no one else to do the job, and the job must be done. The First Lord pressed me. I promised to talk it over with you. You would receive your brother's pay and allowances. You know what they were?

KAREN: Yes.

FERRERS: Enough?

KAREN: More than I get.

FERRERS: I take it you'd lodge with Lady Helston.

KAREN: Does she know?

FERRERS: Not yet.

KAREN: What will she say when she does?

FERRERS: Does that matter?

KAREN: Not to me... All right. Go on.

FERRERS: You would lodge with her but live in this mess, as a member of it, and work under my orders.

KAREN: I understand.

FERRERS: If the thing's impossible, say so. We'll leave it at that.

KAREN: It is not impossible... What will my work be?

FERRERS: *(Surprised.)* What *would* it be?

KAREN: That door leads to the Control Room? My brother worked in there. *(She looks round the door.)*

FERRERS: He and I worked together… *(KAREN touches the leather of the settee.)* What are you looking at?

KAREN: It's all new tonight. Soon I shall know every scar on the leather of this sofa. And the ink-stain on that desk. *(To desk R.)* Whose desk is it?

FERRERS: Brissing's.

KAREN: *(Moving towards the other desk.)* And Mr Sandford there? *(She points to the Control Room.)* Is that a special lock?

FERRERS: The door of the Control Room needs two keys, used together. I carried one; your brother the second; Carr has it now… There's no reason you shouldn't smoke. Will you?

KAREN: I'd rather not – yet. *(Moves across top of table L.)*

FERRERS: Is there – anything else you'd like? I forget this is a party.

KAREN: *(Sits in chair at end of table.)* Nothing. I want you to forget.

FERRERS: *(Relieved.)* Thank you. Then we can get on. You know what kind of work we do here?

KAREN: Roughly. Anti-aircraft.

FERRERS: You have heard people speak of Scorpions?

KAREN: Since I came here.

FERRERS: Your brother didn't write of them?

KAREN: Never.

FERRERS: Good; but he might have without real harm. The word's a nickname – a cover – no more. Scorpions are a form of aerial torpedo. The object is to destroy enemy aircraft – but not by direct hits. You grasp that?

KAREN: Not yet.

FERRERS: To hit an aeroplane with a shell is the devil. His speed's too great; he turns too fast. Scorpions work on a different principle. They're not shells fired from a gun to hit or miss. They move under their own power, as a torpedo does in the water. Roughly speaking, what they are is very small high-speed aeroplanes without a pilot. They carry a high explosive charge. *And they follow the enemy in the air –*

KAREN: How – follow?

FERRERS: First, by wireless steering from the ground, you get the Scorpion within reach of the enemy. Then the whole point of the thing is this. The Scorpion is fitted with sensitive receivers – two sets of them. The vibration of the enemy affects one set and moves the Scorpion's rudders. The enemy may twist and turn like a hare, but a Scorpion has the legs of the fastest machine designed and moves continually towards the centre of vibration – follows it in the air. When near enough, it explodes.

KAREN: *(She rises and moves behind the table until level with FERRERS.)* As though the enemy were a magnet, drawing the torpedo on to itself?

FERRERS: In effect, yes.

KAREN: I see. What makes the charge explode when you want it to?

FERRERS: Again, the enemy vibrations acting on the second set of receivers. They detonate the charge.

KAREN: If the enemy cuts out his engine, what then?

FERRERS: He loses speed. He can't manoeuvre. If he does it often, the fighters get him.

KAREN: What about interference from other machines in the air and your own vibrations?

FERRERS: One and a half seconds!

KAREN: How? – one and a half seconds?

FERRERS: To see that snag. You're quick. Do you see the way out – how to eliminate?

KAREN: Not yet.

FERRERS: It took us three months.

KAREN: It's done, then.

FERRERS: Your brother found that. Yes, it's done.

KAREN: Even then, doesn't the effect of vibration vary with the type of engine?

FERRERS: How much do you know of the mathematics of vibration? *(Enter LADY HELSTON.)*

LADY HELSTON: *(Echoing.)* How much *do* you know, Miss Selby, of the mathematics of vibration? Really, Edward, are you bullying her already?

FERRERS: *(Rising reluctantly.)* Your bridge isn't over yet?

LADY HELSTON: Dickie's gone to fetch a wrap I left in the car. *(Sits on settee.)* Give me a cigarette. *(To KAREN.)* It sounded as if you were being given a lesson. But I'd forgotten – you are quite a mathematician yourself! I was rather good at it at school, but of course one can't keep up everything. Edward said once that mathematics were a form of poetry. *(To FERRERS.)* Didn't you?

FERRERS: I was very foolish if I said that to you. But you can't have invented it. *(He lights her cigarette.)*

LADY HELSTON: Thank you. You do know how to light a cigarette, Edward. I give you marks for that. Did you learn that in your monastery?

FERRERS: I learnt it from a woman, who, if you give her a chance, always pokes her nose into a flame.

LADY HELSTON: *(To KAREN.)* You see? I told you he was like that. I don't know what it means, but didn't it sound fierce? I expect that was because I interrupted the lesson. Couldn't it go on?

KAREN: I'm afraid you'd find it dull.

LADY HELSTON: Not as dull as you think. I know him better than you do. He has all the virtues – except that he won't learn.

FERRERS: What ought I to learn?

LADY HELSTON: *(Counting on her fingers.)* Well, first, which side your bread is buttered. Brian said in his last letter – but, perhaps that's a naval secret.

FERRERS: Then don't pass it on. Sir Brian Wedgcroft is Lady Helston's half-brother, Miss Selby. He happens also to be Second Sea Lord. Admirals to right of us. Admirals to left of us. Ours but to do and die.

LADY HELSTON: No need to die, Edward.

FERRERS: Only to do what you tell me.

LADY HELSTON: *(Unperturbed.)* I should adore that. Like having a tame tiger. Or would you eat me? I should adore that too. *(Yawns.)* I've always thought the lady of Riga had it both ways.

FERRERS: Granted a Freudian tiger.

LADY HELSTON: It must have been. Everything is. Specially limericks and nursery rhymes. Are mathematics Freudian, Miss Selby? Until this evening, I thought they were completely sexless.

KAREN: But I thought you said you were good at them at school.

LADY HELSTON: I expect those were what Edward calls pure mathematics.

FERRERS: Didn't they produce results? Poor Sybil, you must have had a tedious girlhood. Not an admiral in the dormitory. Or were you captain of the hockey eleven and the glory of the Guides?

LADY HELSTON: In fact I was. Edward is always right except when he thinks he is. Tell Miss Selby about her girlhood, Edward. It would interest her enormously. And then you shall take us round.

FERRERS: Round what?

LADY HELSTON: All the mysteries. *(To KAREN.)* You know, on board a warship, they take you everywhere. Conning-tower, turrets, plotting-house, engine-rooms – everywhere. That's the difference between a ship and a house. Civilians take pretty women higher and higher; naval officers take them lower and lower. Dull women are left on the upper deck; moderately attractive ones are shown the boiler rooms; I expect you would be mathematical for hours in the double-bottoms or the bilge. But Edward won't show anyone anything. The workshops yes – lathes and oil and soapy water and the foundry and the Power House and this place, but there's a little holy of holies in there – *(Moves towards Control Room.)* – that no one has ever gone into until tonight.

FERRERS: Why do you want to?

LADY HELSTON: Bluebeard.

FERRERS: No, but why *do* you want to? It interests me to know.

LADY HELSTON: Shall I tell you? Because you're so stubborn about it. It's such a silly mystery. Can you tell me why you don't want me to?

FERRERS: I can, but it wouldn't seem a reason to you.

LADY HELSTON: Do you think I'm going to steal a secret formula?

FERRERS: You wouldn't know which to steal.

LADY HELSTON: Well?

FERRERS: It's where I work. It's where I think and imagine. It's where everything else is shut out.

LADY HELSTON: But Carr and Brissing and Dickie – they come in.

FERRERS: Sometimes – on duty. Nothing personal comes there. I don't want to refuse things to you – but don't ask this. There is such a thing as an absolute rule. Think I'm a fool if you like, but try to see what kind of a fool I am.

LADY HELSTON: I don't think you a fool. I'm very fond of you, Edward. But I think you are stubborn and proud. I've never heard of such a thing! The Admiral's wife asks – *asks* – to be shown into your Control Room and you blankly refuse. Well, my dear Edward, this time you can't refuse. It happens to be the Admiral's order.

FERRERS: Do you mean that?

LADY HELSTON: I asked him before dinner. He said I could go in. Now what do you say?

FERRERS: That was not an effective order. It isn't one he could possibly give.

LADY HELSTON: And why not?

FERRERS: Sybil, don't go on with this. Let's forget it.

LADY HELSTON: Answer my question, Why isn't it an order he could possibly give?

FERRERS: Because he can't give as a reason for my resignation that he ordered me to admit his wife into my Control Room. If you were in your senses –

LADY HELSTON: Do you mean you'd resign rather than let me in?

FERRERS: It would never come to that. I have told you – the order is one he couldn't possibly give. Now, please, forget it.

LADY HELSTON: *(Very quietly.)* I have a good memory. You had better go on with your mathematics while you have time. *(SANDFORD appears in verandah with her cloak.)*

SANDFORD: Here it is. Will you put it on now?

LADY HELSTON: I will. *(She sweeps out. SANDFORD follows.)*

KAREN: Can't you do anything? That is really dangerous.

FERRERS: As much to you as to me.

KAREN: I wondered whether you knew that. *(FERRERS sits at the table. KAREN behind it, level with him.)*

FERRERS: How much do you know of the mathematics of vibration?

KAREN: As it happens, a lot.

FERRERS: But not as a specialist?

KAREN: As a specialist.

FERRERS: How? How did you come to it?

KAREN: By way of music. I spent a year once on the vibration of strings.

FERRERS: My God, is that true?

KAREN: Does it seem foolish?

FERRERS: Go on. Go on. I want to hear this.

KAREN: Mathematics is a cold thing to most people. It's not to me… *(She breaks off.)* Probably, if I go on, you will – not want to use me… You see – *(She crosses above the table to the centre.)*

FERRERS: Get on. Get on.

KAREN: People think it mad – anyhow in a woman – to be a mathematician. Even mathematicians themselves think that – some of them. They look at me. I know what they're thinking. 'You!' – because I'm not ugly – and not cold. As if they'd found me selling matches or scrubbing floors. And others think I'm not doing my job in the world. They want me to use my brains their way – converting someone, compelling someone – politics, economics, anti-war. For me to shut myself up in the Green Hill Observatory seems to them just funk – an escape from life. *(Sits on the arm of the settee.)* If you won't march in one of their regiments you are always accused of escaping from life. Mathematics isn't that to me. It's one of the ways of listening. It's one of the ways of being and loving. One of the ways. They don't want to listen. They want to shout and compel. But the world is growing tired of the regiments. They fail everywhere. The misery they want to cure by force is the misery they have created by force – and will create again. Suddenly men and women will grow tired of marching in step and shouting choruses. We shall listen again, when we are still. The world is beginning to listen again. It is beginning to watch again. *(Moves down L above table.)* In poetry, the thing comes through words. Music says it direct. Saints and lovers know it. And mathematics… I want to listen; I must communicate but not through words. And mathematics, to me – oh, the agony of trying to say in words what can only be said – *(She is laughing and almost crying.)* But I needn't say it to you. You *know* it.

FERRERS: You must never say it to me – if we are to work here together.

KAREN: *(Sits at foot of table.)* I never shall again. But you had to know whether I am – the kind of – mathematician you can work with.

FERRERS: The only kind. *(Long pause.)* Do you understand what it would mean – your living here?

KAREN: I think so.

FERRERS: An absolute discipline – you, me, all of us.

KAREN: I accept that. Why are you afraid?

FERRERS: You are a woman men desire. That's the danger.

KAREN: I desire men. Isn't that the safety?

FERRERS: Safety? You could drive them mad.

KAREN: Cold women drive them mad. It's they who dangle and bait and hang out for a price. They can despise men's desire because they don't share it. It's their vanity; they can't cut it out. They tease an agony to keep themselves alive. Hasn't the Navy a word for them?

FERRERS: It has.

KAREN: Now are you beginning to know me?

FERRERS: *(He moves to her.)* Tell me one thing more. When we met – before dinner – you said your brother had never sent home photographs. Why did you say that?

KAREN: It just – came out.

FERRERS: You saw a physical likeness between me and – what you had expected?

KAREN: Not so much physical… I don't know… Yes, that too I suppose. It was queer – wasn't it?

FERRERS: Our meeting?

KAREN: Our recognizing each other.

FERRERS: I knew without looking at you. I knew the feel of the air about you.

KAREN: I knew before I came in. *(FLAG CAPTAIN, LADY HELSTON, ADMIRAL, FIRST LORD and SANDFORD have come in from verandah. FERRERS crosses below settee to desk R, taking as he passes a cigarette from the table behind the settee. The party is about to break up. General buzz of conversation.)*

ADMIRAL: Well, my dear, ready to start? *(SANDFORD follows LADY HELSTON with her cloak, holding it out.)* You had a pretty good evening. What did you win?

LADY HELSTON: I left it on the table. I thought you would pick it up.

ADMIRAL: *(Opening his fist.)* And so I did. Here you are. *(Counts money into LADY HELSTON's palm.)* Fourteen and sixpence.

LADY HELSTON: What do you expect me to do with that?

ADMIRAL: Well –

LADY HELSTON: I haven't my bag.

ADMIRAL: Your bag –

FERRERS: Bag!

LADY HELSTON: On the table. Didn't you see it? *(But CARR, ever watchful, has brought it and hands it to her.)*

CARR: Is this it?

LADY HELSTON: Thank you. Could someone give me a note for all this silver? *(They begin to search for a note in their pockets. SANDFORD is still holding out the cloak. It is CARR who finds a note.)*

CARR: I have a note, I think. *(LADY HELSTON begins to counts out money on the table.)*

FERRERS: Sandford.

SANDFORD: Sir?

FERRERS: Down masts and sails.

SANDFORD: Aye, aye, aye, sir! *(He throws cloak over his arm and sits.)*

ADMIRAL: Now. We really must be getting on. Ferrers, your decision in the morning?

FERRERS: I have made it, sir.

ADMIRAL: Yes, yes, but it will keep. *(To FIRST LORD.)* I hope we haven't tired you, sir. It's getting late.

FIRST LORD: Not at all. I think it has been a most successful evening. I hope you agree, Ferrers?

FERRERS: It's stopping too soon.

ADMIRAL: *(To BRISSING.)* The car's there?

BRISSING: Yes, sir. *(Comes down from verandah.)*

FLAG CAPTAIN: I'll go on ahead. I want to look at my tail lamp. Good night, Ferrers.

FERRERS: Good night, sir.

FLAG CAPTAIN: You'll be my passenger again, Miss Selby?

KAREN: Please. I'll follow you out. *(Exit FLAG CAPTAIN, R. BRISSING goes with him.)*

FERRERS: *(Stopping KAREN.)* Must you?

KAREN: What?

FERRERS: Go. I want to show you the Control Room. *(LADY HELSTON hears and rises. KAREN stops FERRERS talking and turns her back.)*

CARR: I'm very sorry. No one seems to have a ten-shilling note. *(Reluctantly.)* There's a pound.

LADY HELSTON: That will do. Thank you. *(Gives him the silver.)* Now I owe you – what? Four and six? Is that right, Miss Selby?

KAREN: Five and six.

LADY HELSTON: Oh, thank you. I'm not a mathematician.

ADMIRAL: Now are we all set?

LADY HELSTON: If I might have my cloak, *(FIRST LORD takes it from SANDFORD.)*

FIRST LORD: *(Politely impatient.)* Let me. *(She puts it on.)*

FERRERS: *(To KAREN.)* Well, tomorrow. Can you start work then?

KAREN: I will.

FERRERS: She won't head you off?

KAREN: No.

FERRERS: She will if she can.

KAREN: No. I promise. Good night. *(Moves upstage to L of steps.)*

FERRERS: Good night.

LADY HELSTON: Who will do what if she can?

FIRST LORD: *(Quickly.)* Good night, Ferrers.

FERRERS: Good night, sir. And thank you.

FIRST LORD: Ah, well. It's pleasant to be thanked for getting one's own way.

FERRERS: I have mine too – as far as I can see it.

LADY HELSTON: *(To FERRERS.)* Good night. I think it has been a charming conspiracy. *(To ADMIRAL.)* It will give us something to talk about on the way home. *(General good nights from which, as they drift towards the door, the following emerge.)*

SANDFORD: *(To LADY HELSTON.)* I'll see you out.

LADY HELSTON: You overbid that last time, Dickie.

SANDFORD: Did I? I thought my diamonds –

LADY HELSTON: Well, never mind. I don't mind losing.

SANDFORD: But you won… You've left your fan. *(Retrieves it and follows her out.)*

CARR: *(To KAREN.)* I owe a shilling to you.

KAREN: Me?... Oh, I see.

CARR: I'd have let her get away with it.

KAREN: I was afraid you would.

CARR: And may I say I'm glad – about the other thing?

KAREN: I hoped you might feel that… I didn't even hope you'd say it. Until tomorrow then. *(She shakes hands and moves up steps.)*

CARR: Tomorrow.

FIRST LORD: *(To KAREN.)* I wish I were coming with you.

KAREN: You mean there'll be questions. *(BRISSING enters on verandah. KAREN greets him. They go out together.)*

FIRST LORD: Well, she has to be told some time. Good night, Carr… Ferrers. *(FIRST LORD goes out. CARR goes at once to the drawer in which he put away his letter. Takes it out, sits at table, unscrews his fountain pen, begins to write. Meanwhile –)*

FERRERS: Now the damned party's over, I wish it wasn't. *(Pause. CARR writes.)* I'll get things ready for the morning. Give me your key. *(CARR hands him the key and goes on writing. Sound of cars starting. FERRERS jangles two keys in his hand. Restless, irresolute. Goes to SELBY's watercolour and peers at it.)* She doesn't paint, does she? *(Enter BRISSING on the silence.)*

BRISSING: She doesn't need to. *(Silence. He mixes two whiskies and sodas from a hissing siphon. Outside the sentry sounds six bells.)* That girl has a flank like a racehorse. *(FERRERS turns. BRISSING holds out a whisky and soda to him, offering it. FERRERS shakes his head and points to CARR. BRISSING puts the drink at CARR's elbow. CARR looks up, nods, returns to writing.)* 'Night. I'll turn in. *(BRISSING goes out R carrying his whisky.)*

FERRERS: Still writing home?... Keep dogs there?

CARR: Pair of retrievers. *(FERRERS sits down on arm of chair. CARR takes a gulp of drink, and continues to write as the Curtain falls.)*

ACT TWO

SCENE 1

The same. Nearly four months later; 15 July. Just before eleven in the morning. Hotter weather. Loose covers of Service pattern – white with blue piping at edges. SANDFORD and BRISSING, at their desks, working at plans. Since the party, the furniture has been moved. The settee is L. The long table is down stage R. Plans lie on it to which both SANDFORD and BRISSING from time to time refer. The dress of the day is full whites, but the officers, while working, wear, within limits, what they please. Silence when the Curtain rises. BRISSING turns off light over his desk and moves to table. Continues to work, then breaks off.

BRISSING: *(Hot and exhausted.)* Phew!

SANDFORD: *(Tired, driving himself, on edge.)* The thing won't fit. If he wants the fulcrum of spindle 84 at point six-two of its length, any conceivable gadget will foul the compensating mechanism.

BRISSING: *(Without turning from his own work.)* You'd better conceive a gadget that won't.

SANDFORD: *(Goes over to BRISSING, paper in hand.)* But look at this –

BRISSING: For God's sake, go to hell.

SANDFORD returns to his desk. Silence. After a time BRISSING lays down his own pen.

BRISSING: Now what's the trouble?

SANDFORD: This. *(At table.)* Fulcrum at point six-two. As far as I can see the spindle action depends on that. If we shift it a hair's breadth, the whole of his new calculation series loses its effect.

BRISSING: It's not Ferrers'; it's hers.

SANDFORD: She works so damned fine – like painting a miniature. It may not be necessary to carry precision so far. *(To verandah steps.)* Where the hell is that woman?

66

BRISSING: She's not back. Ferrers kept her at it all night or nearly. She didn't push off until five this morning.

SANDFORD: The man's insane.

BRISSING: He works himself harder.

SANDFORD: *(Down centre.)* That isn't the point. Karen turns up at Helston's house at all hours. Sybil hates it.

BRISSING: Does she enter the times in a register?

SANDFORD: She's often awake.

BRISSING: She would be – and she would tell you.

SANDFORD: It's not because –

BRISSING: Dry up. I'm not going to quarrel with you about Lady H. Let's get back to this spindle of yours.

SANDFORD: No. You say things and then run away from them. What have you against her? In a way, as Karen's hostess, she is responsible.

BRISSING: *(Mocking.)* In a way, as Karen's hostess, she *is* responsible.

SANDFORD: If there's a scandal in this place –

BRISSING: Who's going to make scandal if she doesn't? Ferrers carries his damned austerity too far. So does Karen. They never touch, even when they're working side by side at the same table. He puts down a T-square; she picks it up from the desk; it's not even handed between them.

SANDFORD: They daren't touch. If they did –

BRISSING: What if they did?

SANDFORD: You'd go mad for one.

BRISSING: I?

SANDFORD: You want her.

BRISSING: I'm not a monk, if that's what you mean.

SANDFORD: *(Moves to BRISSING.)* You want *her*. I'm not blind. Oh, the love of your life may be in London. Meanwhile Karen –

BRISSING: She belongs to Ferrers. *(He rises.)*

SANDFORD: If she did – if you knew it – here, now – if you watched it going on – could you work in this place? *(No answer.)*

BRISSING: *(At last.)* Anyhow, Karen does her job.

SANDFORD: Oh, she does her job. *(He follows BRISSING with his eyes. The chair to L of table is now between them.)*

BRISSING: Do you know any other woman who would do it as she does – and not play men up?

SANDFORD: You have it your own way.

BRISSING: Isn't it true?

SANDFORD: No, it's not. She may think it is. But she's in love. If Ferrers lifted a finger, she's go to him tonight. Sybil says –

BRISSING: My god, can't you keep off that woman? If she could, she'd break this place because Ferrers won't let her run it. She may yet. She has the Admiral in her pocket. She treats you like a dog and all you do is lick her boots. Ever since Karen has been here – four months now – that woman has used you. You come back here yapping her opinions as if they were your own. You've forgotten they're not your own. 'If there's a scandal in this place, she's responsible.' Aren't those her words? And who said Karen was willing to be Ferrers' mistress? Lady H again. She's a candidate herself and you know it.

SANDFORD: *(Trembling with anger.)* Now you can take all that back.

BRISSING: Not a word… She has no use for you except as a poodle on a string.

SANDFORD: Take it back.

BRISSING: I've been wanting to say it for weeks.

SANDFORD: Take it back!

BRISSING: Are you going to fling yourself at me in defence of your lady-love?

(SANDFORD throws chair upstage and springs at BRISSING's throat. BRISSING throws him off, his back to the table. SANDFORD collects himself to attack again; then collapses centre. BRISSING picks him

up, props him on table, and shakes him, saying: 'Dick! Dick!'. SANDFORD recovers.)

SANDFORD: I could have killed you then. Do you know, while I was standing there, I couldn't see your face.

BRISSING: One of the rewards of attempted murder.

SANDFORD: Now, what are you going to do?

BRISSING: Withdraw, apologize, get on with the job. Come on, Dick. It's the only sanity in this place. *(SANDFORD tries to rise but can't move.)*

SANDFORD: I'm weak as a kitten… I believe I was mad then.

BRISSING: I'll get you a drink. *(He goes to mix it. FERRERS comes in.)*

FERRERS: Why drink now?

BRISSING: Dick threw a faint, sir.

FERRERS: Nonsense. *(To SANDFORD.)* Stand up. *(SANDFORD stands and sways. FERRERS grasps him by both arms.)*

FERRERS: To hell. What *is* this? You look as if you'd been drugged.

SANDFORD: I'm all right, sir. I can go on.

FERRERS: I dare say… Have you two been scrapping?

BRISSING: Let it go, sir.

FERRERS: Why?

BRISSING: Because it went very far and –

FERRERS: How far?

BRISSING: *(Quickly and steadily.)* It went very far and came back again. Please let it go, sir. *(Pause. Six bells are struck.)*

FERRERS: Yes. All right… Why aren't you both in the workshops? I thought you had a bench test this morning.

BRISSING: We have,

FERRERS: At what time?

BRISSING: Eleven.

FERRERS: It's struck. *(Enter KAREN.)*

FERRERS: Why are you back? I told you not to come till the afternoon. You haven't had five hours sleep.

KAREN: *(Takes smock from hook.)* I thought you wanted me. *(To SANDFORD.)* Have you been working on that spindle, Dick?

SANDFORD: I began on it.

KAREN: *(Puts on smock.)* There's a point I want to show you. I remembered it after I'd gone last night. *(She goes to table.)* Look.

FERRERS: Not now. They are due in the workshops. *(To BRISSING and SANDFORD.)* Better go on... Dick! *(BRISSING goes out.)*

SANDFORD: Yes, sir.

FERRERS: Are you all right?

SANDFORD: I am now, sir.

FERRERS: Cancel the bench test if necessary. Turn in and sleep.

SANDFORD: I can carry on.

FERRERS: No one's worth swinging for, you know. *(He turns away abruptly and SANDFORD goes out.)*

KAREN: What's wrong?

FERRERS: Nothing. *(Picks up chair.)*

KAREN: Shall we work in the Control Room or here?

FERRERS: *(Sits at table.)* Here. The papers are in my cabin.

KAREN: Have you been up all night?

FERRERS: I worked upstairs a bit after we'd shut the Control Room.

KAREN: Why not sleep now?

FERRERS: I'll take it sudden, when I need it. Get the papers. Ring the bell as you go. *(She goes up to his bedroom, ringing the bell. Enter DENHAM.)*

FERRERS: I want some water.

DENHAM: Aye, aye, sir.

FERRERS: Wait. I thought you were a marine.

DENHAM: I am a marine, sir.

FERRERS: Then don't say: 'Aye, aye, sir.' Everything's 'very good' to a marine.

DENHAM: Very good, sir.

FERRERS: Lucky to be a marine. Have you a kettle boiling?

DENHAM: Yes, sir.

FERRERS: Bring some tea for Miss Selby. *(Exit DENHAM. KAREN returns. Spreads out papers.)*

KAREN: Was that my fault? *(Sits at table.)*

FERRERS: What?

KAREN: Those two. Something had happened. Had they been quarrelling?

FERRERS: Not about you. At least – why should they quarrel about you?

KAREN: I wanted to make no difference to this place – except my work.

FERRERS: Then, for God's sake, let's assume you have made none. *(He rises suddenly and takes his cap.)*

KAREN: Where are you going?

FERRERS: Carr's in the Power House. I promised to go over. *(BRISSING appears on verandah.)*

KAREN: *(To FERRERS.)* I thought we were to work together.

FERRERS: I'll go to Carr first.

KAREN: You can't go now.

FERRERS: Indeed I can.

KAREN: I have something to tell you. *(Rises.)*

FERRERS: It can wait.

KAREN: No. It's urgent. *(Moves to FERRERS.)* Last night Lady Helston –

FERRERS: Get on with your work and leave me to mine!

KAREN: Very well. *(She sits down, her back to him. He moves towards her, almost touches her, turns abruptly away, sees BRISSING.)*

FERRERS: *(To BRISSING.)* What about your bench test?

BRISSING: Dick's adjustments aren't ready, sir. They'll be a quarter of an hour *(FERRERS goes out R.)*

BRISSING: *(In front of table.)* Why do you stand for it?

KAREN: Because –

BRISSING: Service?

KAREN: Yes.

BRISSING: Liar.

KAREN: I said I'd go through with this.

BRISSING: *(Sits on table facing front.)* That's no reason he should refuse to listen when you have something to tell him.

KAREN: He and I understand each other.

BRISSING: Or is it that a woman will stand anything from a man she loves? They say so in books.

KAREN: Do they? It's not true.

BRISSING: *(Quick on his cue.)* No, but it is true she'll stand anything if he loves her. Isn't it? Isn't it?

KAREN: Ferrers can run this place in his own way.

BRISSING: Not *if* he loves you.

KAREN: What?

BRISSING: I said: Not if he loves you – as you think he does. Does he?

KAREN: Love me?

BRISSING: That's what I'm asking. That's what you're beginning to ask yourself. Isn't it? I've asked it too. I know what it feels like.

KAREN: You?

BRISSING: About my own girl. She's not faithful to me, you know.

KAREN: How much does that matter? Did you expect her to be?

BRISSING: I hoped like a fool.

KAREN: Two years?

BRISSING: It's two years for me – too.

KAREN: Faithful?

BRISSING: Women are different.

KAREN: Not all.

BRISSING: I know. Sorry. It's hell for you... Karen, why should it be hell for either of us – if you feel as men feel. Why should it? I know I'm not the man you want. You're not the girl I want – not *the* girl I want. Still, when sane people are hungry they have dinner together. *(She looks at him but doesn't answer.)* All right. I've said it. Now you can tell me off.

KAREN: You are an odd human being. Why did you say all that to me?

BRISSING: One of us had to.

KAREN: You don't love me.

BRISSING: Did I say I did?

KAREN: *(Holds out her hand.)* No... Kiss me.

BRISSING: *(Rises.)* Stand up to be kissed. *(She obeys. They kiss.)*

BRISSING: Well?

KAREN: Five minutes ago that was impossible. It still is. ... Just abject starvation. Both of us. No, my God, why should I cry?

BRISSING: Kiss me again. *(Takes her.)*

KAREN: *(A bleak surrender.)* As much as you like...

BRISSING: And you?

KAREN: Very well. As much as *I* like. *(They kiss.)*

BRISSING: Enough Karen?

KAREN: *(Perhaps consenting.)* I suppose so.

BRISSING: Tonight? Don't turn your face away. Look at me. Answer me. *(She quietly releases herself.)*

KAREN: What *are* we?

BRISSING: *(Striding away and turning to speak.)* Oddly enough, we are the people for whom the estate of matrimony was ordained. 'That have not the gift of continency.'

KAREN: The *gift*? Does the Prayer Book say that?

BRISSING: It does – though the modern priests tried to cut it out. *(Enter DENHAM with tea.)*

KAREN: What's this, Denham? I didn't order tea.

DENHAM: Commander did, Miss. Water for himself. Tea for you.

KAREN: I see… Thank you, Denham; I need it. *(Exit DENHAM.)*

KAREN: *(Passing her hand across her forehead.)* That's coming up to breathe!

BRISSING: And think?

KAREN: Yes.

BRISSING: Do you want to think? *(Pause.)*

KAREN: Do something for me.

BRISSING: You have a habit of not answering questions.

KAREN: If there isn't an answer.

BRISSING: Will there be an answer tonight? … Will there, Karen?

KAREN: Do something for me… When's your bench test?

BRISSING: *(Looking at watch.)* Five minutes.

KAREN: Go to the Power House. Find Ferrers. Make him listen. He thought what I had to say about Lady Helston was something – personal to us. It's not. Last night – early this morning, rather – when I got back, she was waiting for me. She has made the Admiral choose the earlier date – for the trial.

BRISSING: But he –

KAREN: It gives us short of a month.

BRISSING: But Ferrers postponed it.

KAREN: He wanted to, but the Admiral won't forward the postponement. His message to the Admiralty will go tonight.

BRISSING: But it's mad! Sandford and I can't be ready.

KAREN: You'll have to be unless the Admiral can be made to change his mind. He's coming here this morning.

BRISSING: *He* – here! Why? Couldn't he send for Ferrers?

KAREN: Not when he feels guilty. It salves his conscience this way. He likes to be liked… But Ferrers must know.

BRISSING: He must indeed. I'll tell him. *(Exit BRISSING. KAREN pours herself out tea and is settling down to her papers when SANDFORD comes in, wearing overalls.)*

SANDFORD: *(To the absent BRISSING.)* We're all set. *(To KAREN.)* Where's Brissing?

KAREN: The Power House.

SANDFORD: But he ought to be in the workshops. We're held up.

KAREN: You'll have to hold up a bit longer. *(Looking straight at him.)* Did you know we were to run the trial in one month?

SANDFORD: Two.

KAREN: One. Lady Helston told me early this morning… How long have you known?

SANDFORD: I knew that Sybil wanted –

KAREN: Did you tell her you needed an extra month on your detonator receivers?

SANDFORD: I told her the whole damned thing. I don't suppose she listened but I made it as clear as I could for babes and sucklings. I said: The receivers, because we've got them placed wrong, are subject to screening and interference.

KAREN: Did that amuse her? It doesn't sound like an amorous conversation.

SANDFORD: She said: 'Well, can't you place them right?' She just can't grasp what it means. But when I told her that my job was to shift things about inside the Scorpion so that the detonating receivers could be repositioned, she saw that. 'Like repacking a trunk,' she said.

KAREN: Poor Dick. Did you tell her you needed more than a month to repack your trunk?

SANDFORD: Yes, I did.

KAREN: It made no odds?

SANDFORD: On the contrary.

KAREN: And you still love her?

SANDFORD: That seems mad to you?

KAREN: No. Men can love women they despise. There aren't any rules. *(Enter FERRERS, CARR, BRISSING.)*

SANDFORD: *(To BRISSING.)* You promised to be back ten minutes ago. They're all standing by.

FERRERS: For what?

SANDFORD: The bench test.

FERRERS: Wash it out. I want you here. *(Goes to bell and rings.)* Is that my water? *(Drinks.)* Brissing, get the Admiral's house. Find out where he is. If he's there, ask if I can come down to see him at once. *(BRISSING makes telephone call. Enter DENHAM.)*

FERRERS: Send down to the workshops. Tell them Mr Sandford and Mr Brissing's bench test must wait.

DENHAM: Is that all, sir?

FERRERS: Yes.

DENHAM: Very good, sir. *(Exit DENHAM.)*

FERRERS: Now. Sit down, please.

BRISSING: *(On telephone.)* Do you know where he is?... All right, thank you. *(To FERRERS.)* He's on his way here, sir.

FERRERS: Very well. We must think quickly. You all know what the position is. *(To KAREN.)* Does Sandford know?

KAREN: I have just told him.

FERRERS: I want you opinions. Carr?

CARR: *(Slowly and deliberately.)* For the full trial we need six completed Scorpions – more if possible. The bodies are complete, the engines are fitted; what remains –

FERRERS: No, Carr, I'm sorry. Usually I bless your leisurely methods; they keep us sane. But there's not time. The point is: I have asked for a postponement to September 12. The Admiral is tying me to the date we originally fixed, four weeks from now, August 9. Can it be done – or not?

CARR: If you mean, can my wireless be ready – the answer is: yes.

FERRERS: Good… Brissing?

BRISSING: Well, sir, from this point onwards, Sandford and I more or less work together I think we can get the vibrational steering to work on the reduced power. That's OK if you come in on it.

FERRERS: I?

BRISSING: And Karen.

FERRERS: I see. Aren't you giving too much credit to what she and I can do? Remember, there's less than four weeks. I don't like the look of it. Anyhow we've left Sandford's department out of account.

SANDFORD: That's a real snag – the detonator mechanism. The Lord knows how long that will take. We're on it now, sir *(Bending over his plan.)* That spindle takes up space. It seemed all right before, but if I shift it –

FERRERS: Is it coming?

SANDFORD: I shall probably have the new drawing out tomorrow or the next day. Then we have to manufacture. Then test. If it's not a go, we have to start again.

FERRERS: In which case, a month won't be enough?

SANDFORD: No, sir.

FERRERS: Two months?

SANDFORD: With reasonable luck. There's nothing wrong in principle. It's a question of trial and error to get the positions right.

FERRERS: Very well. Do I accept the earlier date or not?

BRISSING: No, sir! If you stand up to him, he'll give in. He's not doing this off his own bat.

FERRERS: Dick?

SANDFORD: I don't know. You decide, sir. I'll get it through somehow. I'll *make* the damned thing work.

CARR: My deliberate view is – I wouldn't be rushed, Ferrers. We've been on this job nearly two years. It's madness, for the sake of an extra month.

FERRERS: May be. But this isn't an easy bluff, Carr. If I refuse to run the trial on August 9 and the Admiral sticks his heels in –

SANDFORD: *(Unexpectedly.)* I warn you. He will. *(They all look at him.)* He won't budge. He's been holding out against this. He's been holding out like hell. And now he has given in – he won't go back. Sybil will see he doesn't. *(He stops. They all gaze at him.)* And the wind at the Admiralty blows her way.

FERRERS: There you are, then, Carr. That's the choice. Either I accept August 9 or – we must be prepared to pack up this place.

CARR: *(With steady determination.)* As I see it, it's a matter of principle. Pack and be damned.

BRISSING: I'm with you.

FERRERS: You haven't spoken, Karen.

KAREN: I take your orders, sir.

FERRERS: Then we are decided.

CARR: Are you? *(Enter DENHAM.)*

FERRERS: Well?

DENHAM: The Admiral, sir. And his lady. *(Exit.)*

BRISSING: And his lady?

FERRERS: Brissing, bring him in. Don't encourage her. Perhaps he'll have the grace to leave her in the car. *(Exit BRISSING, R.)*

CARR: But if we know she's there –

FERRERS: For once we can forget it. *(BRISSING enters R, hurriedly points to verandah.)* Damn it, she can't do us more harm than she's done. *(Silence while they wait. Enter ADMIRAL. They all rise.)*

ADMIRAL: *(Nervous and affable.)* Good morning, gentlemen. Good morning, Miss Selby.

FERRERS: Good morning, sir.

ADMIRAL: I wanted a word with you, Ferrers.

FERRERS: Alone, sir?

ADMIRAL: N-no. Better with all of you, since you're here.

FERRERS: I've been on the telephone to you house, sir. You had already left. I was suggesting that I should come to you.

ADMIRAL: To me? About what?

FERRERS: The same subject, sir.

ADMIRAL: But this is a matter –

FERRERS: Not new to us, sir.

ADMIRAL: I don't understand you, Ferrers.

FERRERS: Miss Selby had orders at five o'clock this morning from Lady Helston.

ADMIRAL: Eh? Oh, that may be. That may be. I believe I did mention it to her. *(Silence.)* Well, gentlemen, I knew this wouldn't come easy to you. That's why I preferred to come up here and have it out with you myself. As you know, for some time past the Admiralty has been pressing me very hard. They feel that these experiments have – Anyhow, Ferrers, August 9 was originally your own date. Then you ask for postponement to September 12. How do I know you won't ask for a further postponement to October or November?

FERRERS: That's always possible.

ADMIRAL: You see how difficult – Is there any reason we shouldn't sit down and talk this out man to man? *(All sit.)* I want you, gentlemen, to accept this as I accept it. We all have to adjust our plans from time to time. I want there to be no sense of injustice. If there's a difference between us –

FERRERS: There's nothing to discuss, sir. As I see it. *(Enter LADY HELSTON. They rise, except KAREN. Silence, resenting her presence. Even LADY HELSTON is a little embarrassed.)*

LADY HELSTON: Good morning, everyone. George –

ADMIRAL: No, no, my dear! You can't come in here.

LADY HELSTON: But, George – it's like an oven in the car –

ADMIRAL: I'm very sorry, my dear, but –

LADY HELSTON: I simply wanted somewhere cool to sit.

ADMIRAL: But not in here, my dear. We're discussing a Service matter.

LADY HELSTON: I suppose there is no objection to my sitting on the verandah?

ADMIRAL: *(Ushering her out.)* No, none whatever, as long as –

LADY HELSTON: *(Going.)* I'll go right to the other end – you needn't think –

ADMIRAL: That's not the point. *(He leads her off.)* I'm sorry, gentlemen. *(He returns and goes down to the table.)* You, Ferrers – you were saying –

FERRERS: In my view, sir, there's nothing to discuss. I understand your decision is that we are to run the trial on August 9. Very well, that leaves me with one course open.

ADMIRAL: Now, Ferrers, don't be hasty. Don't say what we shall all regret, I admit you have been – Still, the interests of the Service come first. There must be no question of resignation. We are naval officers, not politicians.

FERRERS: I have no intention of resigning. Or of begging for time. Either you trust me or you don't. Meanwhile, I accept your order.

ADMIRAL: *(Surprised: looking from face to face.)* And these gentlemen – are they agreed?

FERRERS: They will take my orders.

ADMIRAL: You make it easy, Ferrers.

FERRERS: That's as you see it, sir.

ADMIRAL: I haven't the least doubt in my own mind that by August 9 – I'm delighted that's settled – and much quicker than I could reasonably have expected. *(Endeavouring to be hearty.)* I really needn't have turned my wife out at all. *(Goes and calls.)* Sybil, dear… It's all right, you can come back now.

LADY HELSTON: *(Reappearing.)* Thank you, George. You didn't keep me waiting very long after all. I wish all your Service meetings were as abrupt.

ADMIRAL: Ferrers has smoothed everything out, by accepting the earlier date.

FERRERS: I have accepted an order.

LADY HELSTON: *(At foot of steps.)* Can you carry it out?

FERRERS: There's one thing you can do for us, sir, if you would.

ADMIRAL: I'll do anything on earth.

FERRERS: We shall be working here, pretty well night and day. All leave will be stopped for men and officers. And we want to be left alone.

ADMIRAL: Quite – quite.

FERRERS: Will you issue an order, sir, that no one is to come here except strictly on duty by your written order or mine?

ADMIRAL: Certainly – I can quite understand the necessity –

LADY HELSTON: I understand too. It is deliberately aimed at me! *(To FERRERS.)* Do you deny that?

FERRERS: *(Makes no reply.)*

LADY HELSTON: You ask my husband for an order to shut me out, and you ask for it in my presence.

FERRERS: You are here by your own choice.

LADY HELSTON: Do you think I want to come here? *(She is now so angry and so unhappy that she cannot finish her sentences.)* Naturally I have taken an interest in the place. The rugs you are standing on are mine. The piano is mine. And when you found a girl coarse enough for your taste –

(KAREN rises.) Do you think I wanted her in my house? She was quartered on me. I accepted even that.

ADMIRAL: Sybil, Miss Selby is our guest.

LADY HELSTON: She's not. Make no mistake about that. She *was.* She came slinking back to our house at all hours of the night and morning. You think I don't know what was going on?

FERRERS: That's not true. Miss Selby –

LADY HELSTON: I don't want to hear about her. I'll have no more of it. She can sleep where she likes and how she likes, but not in my house. You think that because you are an indispensible expert, you can do as you like. You will soon find out you can't. You've had your bluff called and you know it. Ask Mr Sandford if he can be ready. *(To SANDFORD.)* Can your detonator be ready? Can you re-pack your ridiculous trunk? *(To FERRERS.)* Don't imagine you can treat me like this and get away with it. *(To ADMIRAL.)* Do you mean to issue that order?

ADMIRAL: You had better go to the car.

LADY HELSTON: I asked you a question.

ADMIRAL: Mr Brissing, open the door. *(Exit BRISSING, R.)*

LADY HELSTON: You mean that? Then give your own orders for Miss Selby's luggage to be moved where you please. *(Exit LADY HELSTON, R.)*

ADMIRAL: Miss Selby –

KAREN: Don't trouble about me, sir.

ADMIRAL: What shall you do?

KAREN: If I have permission, move here.

ADMIRAL: There are no other women here. You would be – afterwards, I mean – in the eyes of the world –

KAREN: I came here to work.

ADMIRAL: Look here, Miss Selby. That house is my house –

KAREN: Let me come here, sir.

ADMIRAL: So be it. *(At the door.)* Get the job done, gentlemen. Then women don't matter. *(Exit ADMIRAL.)*

FERRERS: This evening we'll get out a new work schedule. You'd better go back to the Power House, Carr. *(To BRISSING, who has entered R.)* Can you get your bench test through before the hands pack up for dinner?

BRISSING: The first part we can. The rest later. *(BRISSING and SANDFORD move towards door.)*

CARR: Ferrers, why did you do that?

FERRERS: What?

CARR: Accept the early date.

FERRERS: We won't crawl to her. That's what she wants. Poor old boy, he's in a worse fix than we are.

CARR: But if we're not ready – that's what she wants more. *(CARR and BRISSING go out R.)*

FERRERS: We shall be – if you don't stand in doorways arguing… Dick, before you go, show me the spindle that's worrying you. If we don't get that detonator right, we're done. The charge won't go off. These people are like children. If they don't see their puff of smoke, they'll think the whole invention has failed. Show it to me. I may get a line on it.

SANDFORD: *(Showing his drawing.)* It's this. Karen's idea is that if we shift the fulcrum of 84 to point six-two from *that* end we get –

KAREN: *(Over their shoulders.)* You see, if the Scorpion inclines from the vertical while the spindle is lifting, it's all right up to 38 degrees. After that – not. Where we've had detonator failures, the inclination has in fact been more than 38. There may be other causes too. Dick's trying to eliminate this one.

SANDFORD: But if you shift the fulcrum, you foul the compensating mechanism – and the compensating mechanism can't be shifted.

KAREN: That may be so unless –

FERRERS: That's enough. Dividers. *(Holds out his hand for them. Works with dividers on drawing.)* Slide rule. *(Works it.)* The odd thing is – we've tackled this problem before. You did, Karen.

KAREN: Never.

FERRERS: You did. I remember it now. Like a face. Every calculation has a face, You remember the expression of it even when you've forgotten the detail. You said we should have to fit a gyro – *here*. You began the gyro calculations.

KAREN: I didn't.

FERRERS: Not on this?

KAREN: Never.

FERRERS: *(Remembering.)* It was your brother. Now I've got it. Go on, Dick, get down to your bench test. Karen and I will work on this. I don't know how far Selby took it but the beginning's there. Go on. Go on. *(He gets SANDFORD out of the room.)* This may be the answer to the whole damned thing. If it is, and if we can get it through in time, Dick's spindle mechanism can be cut out. That will cook her ladyship's goose. *(Rises.)*

KAREN: 'If it is.'

FERRERS: Well, find out. Your brother's stuff is still there.

KAREN: Any idea of its number?

FERRERS: None. It's an early series. Probably B or C. We'll have to search the pigeonholes. *(KAREN rises. He is moving towards the Control Room but stops.)* Drink your tea first. You're tired. *(She hesitates – but she is tired, and sits down.)*

KAREN: You're tired, too. *(Puts out her hand to touch him. At once he moves away.)*

FERRERS: When this job's done –

KAREN: What shall you do then?

FERRERS: Do? Make my soul. It's about time. There's a devilish arrogance in doing things – if you do them well. Don't you feel it yourself? For instance, standing at that desk with Dick Sandford. He's as keen as a knife. He has one of the clearest and quickest mechanical minds I've ever known. He could construct anything from a torpedo to a lady's wristwatch. *And* he gets a move on. But he keeps to the road. After the first mile, the second; after the second, the third; quick but always on the road. He never jumps, he never flies; he doesn't – just *see*. I do. And you do. Don't you feel sometimes like an eagle taking a chicken for a walk?

KAREN: *(Laughs.)*

FERRERS: And we call that genius. Anyhow we let other people call it genius for us. It's not, you know. Not the genius that matters, anyway. In itself, the genius of action and intellect isn't much more than a trick. It's a damnable false pride. I have no illusions about the job we're doing here. If it comes off, we shall be told we have saved the world. I shall be invited to dine by the warlords one evening and by the pacifists the next. But all we shall have done is to make the air unsafe for bombers. Large numbers of people will live a few years longer. I doubt if that's a service to the world if they don't know how to live at all.

KAREN: You haven't talked to me of anything – except the job – for months. Why do you now?

FERRERS: Because I'm tired and you are – and we have to go on one month longer, the hardest of all. And because, in the end, this thing may seem to have failed.

KAREN: But why today, suddenly? You were on your way to the Control Room. Then you stopped and changed – as if you were a human being. Why now?

FERRERS: Was I wrong?

KAREN: So desperately right... Did you know?

FERRERS: I knew I was losing you.

KAREN: I was losing myself.

FERRERS: Karen, how unhappy are you?

KAREN: If I could put a circle round any instant of time and keep it always, I'd choose this... It's strange. We've struggled so long not to talk in this way – and now we do – and it's – safe and – oh, it's not! It's not! *(He has taken both her hands.)*

FERRERS: Let it be unsafe, Karen. Once. It may never come again. Put a circle round this moment too. *(FERRERS is drawing her to him, but she does not yield.)*

FERRERS: Why do you say no?

KAREN: Not now. Not yet. It would blind us. *(He lets her go. Beneath this impact, they talk as much to themselves as to each other.)*

FERRERS: Then –

KAREN: *(Her hand across her eyes.)* It's true. I can scarcely see you.

FERRERS: *(Holding out his empty hands.)* I still have the weight of your hands… How cool they are.

KAREN: What time is it?

FERRERS: *(He is by the table.)* Here's the slide-rule where I put it down.

KAREN: What made you order this tea for me?

FERRERS: I think I did.

KAREN: Ages ago. *(Silence.)*

FERRERS: Now I can work.

KAREN: Yes.

FERRERS: *(Taking out his key.)* Come and unlock. *(She rises and puts her hand inside her dress for the key she carries on a chain round her neck.)*

KAREN: I haven't got it.

FERRERS: *(On steps L.)* What?

KAREN: I haven't the key.

FERRERS: *(Returning towards her.)* Where is it? You were never to let that key out of your possession.

KAREN: I don't. I carry it always – on a chain – round my neck.

FERRERS: Well?

KAREN: I'm sorry… Why are you so angry?

FERRERS: It's no good being sorry. Where is it?

KAREN: It's at the house. I'd been working all night. I was half-asleep when I dressed this morning. I forgot to put it on – that's all. Why are you so angry? You frighten me.

FERRERS: Do you remember taking it off? Why do you take it off at all?

KAREN: I put it on again before I sleep – always.

FERRERS: Did you, this time?

KAREN: I don't remember.

FERRERS: Do you remember anything?

KAREN: I was deadbeat. Don't you understand? Why does it matter so much? You have only to send for it.

FERRERS: Now we can do nothing. I'm shut out of my own Control Room. We can do nothing, nothing all day until your damnable carelessness is made good.

KAREN: If you sent a messenger in the car –

FERRERS: *(Takes hold of her.)* Will you stop talking? Stop. Stop.

KAREN: Your hands! You are hurting!

FERRERS: *(Letting her go violently.)* I wish to God you weren't a woman. Because you are I can do nothing. You can do this and you can stand there and say you're sorry. I can do nothing to you. It's like being bound with cords. It's like being divided from you by a wall of glass. Get out of the room. Out of my reach. Out of my reach.

KAREN: You can do what you like.

FERRERS: Come here. Let me look at you. Inside you, what are you thinking?

KAREN: Of your suffering.

FERRERS: You are not thinking at all about the key.

KAREN: It's of no importance. Nor what you do to me. Nor what I have done.

FERRERS: *(Coming out of a dream.)* None… *(He sits on settee.)* This is one of the episodes in our lives we shall both forget. We shall seem to remember it.

KAREN: *(Kneels at his feet.)* I shall say: 'Do you remember the day when you could have beaten me because I had forgotten the key?' And you will say: 'I remember.'

FERRERS: But we shan't recognize ourselves in the remembrance.

KAREN: I think that must be true of murderers – they don't recognize themselves in the remembrance.

FERRERS: If I had struck you then – to the world the blow would have been everything – and to you?

KAREN: Whatever it was to you – not more or less. *(Enter BRISSING.)*

BRISSING: Karen, the Admiral's coxswain brought up this key. Found on your dressing table.

KAREN: Thank you… *(He puts the key on the table and she moves towards him.)*

BRISSING: What?

KAREN: Peter, there isn't any answer.

BRISSING: No answer?

KAREN: To the question you asked. There can be no answer. There could never have been. Do you understand?

BRISSING: Yes… I see… I'll be getting back. *(Exit BRISSING.)*

FERRERS: What question was that?

KAREN: Something he and I got muddled about. It doesn't arise now.

FERRERS: For God's sake put that key round your neck and keep it there.

KAREN: When this is over, will you give it me?

FERRERS: That depends.

KAREN: On what?

FERRERS: Listen. Let's get this straight. We love each other. Is that true?

KAREN: I love you.

FERRERS: But if this job goes wrong, we shall never marry. *(He waits for her answer but gets none.)* Do you understand that?

88

KAREN: No.

FERRERS: Then you don't understand me… And, my God, you don't understand yourself. How long are you going to want a man you despise?

KAREN: Despise.

FERRERS: Pity, then. Have you ever been maternal towards anyone you loved? You'd soon tire of me if that was what I needed. Anyway, I don't want pity – not from you. I'm a god to you or nothing. I know that. If this job crashes, I'll pay someone else to wheel my bath chair.

KAREN: I thought *I* was arrogant – but you frighten me.

FERRERS: That's why you love me.

KAREN: *(Looking at him for a long moment.)* Is that why?

FERRERS: Isn't it? Anyhow, it's one of six reasons why I love you. Does that make the arrogance worse?

KAREN: What are the other five?

FERRERS: My dear, if the trial succeeds, I will prove the other five. Then you shall have your key, if you'll take it.

KAREN: *(Steadily, deliberately.)* And if we fail.

FERRERS: No, my Karen, if this thing fails, that's an end for us. Let's believe it won't fail. Come and unlock me. *(He moves to the Control Room, leaving KAREN C.)*

Curtain.

SCENE 2

Five weeks later. 5 o'clock, 16 August. The big table is on the right littered with the papers of an interrupted conference. Chairs are set near it. The room looks untidy, used and stale, for the conference has been going on all the afternoon. BRISSING alone on sofa, bored and kicking his heels. Rises, empties ashtrays into waste paper basket, and piles them on piano. Picks up papers from floor.

BRISSING: *(Singing.)* 'As far as I know

It's the end of the show

And now we go home to bed – to bed

And now we go home to – '

89

(Telephone rings. Goes to it.) Yes. Block House. Brissing speaking. Hullo, Flags. Oh, yes. You bet he's still here – and the Admiral. The inquiry's still going on. Having a tea interval. Well, it's damned irregular. Do you usually distribute signals by wardroom telephone?... Don't be a fool, Flags. Of course I'll take it. Hold on. I haven't a pad. *(Fetches signal pad and pencil. Sits to write.)* Carry on. Dictate… P.M.O. Hospital, Kendrickstown to Flag. Regret report Flight-Lieutenant A.J. Murphy died 4.23. I'll read back. *(Repeats casually at high speed.)* OK?... What? Oh, they've been going over the same ground all the afternoon. The Admiral's trying to be judicial. I don't believe he'll close down on us. But the Flag-Captain's dead against us. He's a clever swine. He baits Ferrers. That makes it worse. One thing about it, if they pack us up, it means a spot of leave… All right. *(Rings off. Goes towards mess-room door, signal pad in hand. KAREN enters, walks past him in silence.)* What are the chances, Karen?

KAREN: They go for facts. The trial failed – anyhow they think it did. I said what I could.

BRISSING: *(Admiring.)* You did your bit – like hell! The Admiral lapped it up! *(Sits on table.)*

KAREN: He wanted to, I think. But it needs courage if the Admiralty expects him to report against us.

BRISSING: Are you sure they do?

KAREN: Wedgcroft will be against us. How much ice does he cut?

BRISSING: He's not all the Admiralty, though he is Lady Helston's brother.

KAREN: Edward says the Treasury is through. They want results. All they get is eight Scorpions that didn't explode their blank charge *and* a crashed aeroplane *and* the observer dead.

BRISSING: *(Holding out pad.)* The pilot too. Murphy died in hospital half an hour ago.

KAREN: *(Having looked at it.)* That doesn't make it easier.

BRISSING: The Flag Captain will make the most of it.

KAREN: Oh, Peter, if they do close us down, it will kill *him.*

BRISSING: Ferrers.

KAREN: *(To herself.)* The principle isn't affected by the detonator failures. Why can't they see? I think the Admiral does see – in his heart.

BRISSING: But if he sees that, he *can't* close us down.

KAREN: Can't he? I believe I know him better than you. He's not a coward and he's not dishonest and he's not really convinced. It needs guts to be convinced of anything – and stick to it. In the past, men on the spot had full powers. They were expected to use their imagination. Whitehall let them be. Now, speed of communications has made every kind of mess of the world. It has taken the heart out of all but the greatest men. You have to be a lion not to be led on a string. The Admiral's not a lion. He's an affable dog who knows his master's voice. He'll begin to say to himself: 'Well, I dunno. P'raps I'm wrong.' That's what he'd like Edward to say: 'Well, I dunno. P'raps I *am* wrong.' It's a polite habit. Modest. Charming. … Damnable. *(Down to settee, and sits.)*

BRISSING: *(He crosses to KAREN, leaving signal pad on table, Shy, consoling.)* I hate this – for you. If things go wrong, for me it's different. First I get leave – London. I shall see her. Then Guns in a Home Fleet cruiser.

KAREN: *(Coming out of her own trouble.)* You heard from her last mail? Didn't you?

BRISSING: How did you know?

KAREN: Because you didn't tell me.

BRISSING: I see… I'm sorry. I'm afraid I have poured out my heart a bit. I suppose I'm damned young still. *(Portentously.)* She's older then I am, you know.

KAREN: *(Smiling.)* You didn't confess that. Much?

BRISSING: Two years.

KAREN: Grey?

BRISSING: *(Laughs. Takes her hand affectionately. Kisses it.)* Bless you. You'd be good with puppies.

KAREN: *(Vehement.)* What did you say?

BRISSING: *(Taken aback.)* I only said – you'd be good with puppies. Why?... I'm sorry if – I only meant you'd be good to me.

KAREN: You've repaid it.

BRISSING: How?

KAREN: By saying that... You'll go to London –

BRISSING: We'll meet.

KAREN: *(Keyed up.)* Of course. You'll ask me to lunch and tell me about her. After a bit we shall meet again. You'll tell me about your children.

BRISSING: Karen, what's wrong?

KAREN: Don't forget to ask me, because I shan't forget ever. The man who said – today of all days – I should be good with puppies.

BRISSING: My dear –

KAREN: It's all right. *(She goes up to him and kisses him.)* What about that signal?

BRISSING: They're coming out. *(Enter ADMIRAL, FLAG CAPTIAN, FERRERS, SANDFORD and CARR. KAREN to piano. BRISSING to table to pick up signal pad.)*

KAREN: I'm sorry, sir.

BRISSING: *(To FLAG CAPTAIN, presenting signal.)* Signal for you, sir. Relayed from Flag, sir.

ADMIRAL: The tea wasn't as good after you'd gone, Miss Selby.

FLAG CAPTAIN: *(To ADMIRAL.)* Young Murphy's dead, sir. Died 4.23... Relayed from Flag. *(Presents signal.)*

ADMIRAL: I see. Do we know anything about him? People and so on? Not a married man?

FLAG CAPTAIN: No, single.

ADMIRAL: Good… Well, we'd better get on. Are you ready, Ferrers? *(Sits at table. FLAG CAPTAIN also. SANDFORD and BRISSING on settee.)*

FERRERS: Yes, sir. But there's no need to take up more of your time, sir. Miss Selby has put my case very clearly. Clear to me, anyhow. I have nothing fresh to add. *(Sits below desk R facing upstage.)*

ADMIRAL: But I have more to ask. I want no regrets.

FERRERS: I understand that, sir.

FLAG CAPTAIN: Sarcasm does no good, Ferrers.

ADMIRAL: *(Smoothing over.)* Was that sarcasm?

FLAG CAPTAIN: Ferrers said, sir, that –

ADMIRAL: Never mind. I didn't hear it. Now, let's get on. Men get tired, you know. *(But he is on edge himself and shouts at CARR who is wandering about the room.)* Sit, Carr. Don't wander about like a dog that's lost its tail. *(CARR sits on stool before upstage desk.)*

FLAG CAPTAIN: *(To BRISSING.)* Ashtrays.

BRISSING: What, sir?

FLAG CAPTAIN: What the devil have you done with the ashtrays?

BRISSING: Emptied them.

FLAG CAPTAIN: Well, where are they? *(BRISSING collects the pile from piano, and distributes them. Meanwhile –)*

ADMIRAL: Now then. *(CARR rises and moves L.)*

FLAG CAPTAIN: Before we begin I should like to say one or two words, sir, entirely in Ferrers' own interest. I feel that his attitude throughout the afternoon has been most unhelpful. I hope –

ADMIRAL: I expect a dish of tea has done all our tempers good. Admirable tea, Miss Selby. Nothing like making it oneself.

FERRERS: *(Angry.)* In any case, what is this? A court martial?

FLAG CAPTAIN: Certainly not, but it remains true –

FERRERS: Then I don't want a prisoner's friend.

FLAG CAPTAIN: You will please not interrupt me when I am speaking.

FERRERS: *(Unrepentantly.)* I apologize, sir.

ADMIRAL: *(Affably amused to BRISSING, who is still slowly distributing ashtrays.)* Well, have you finished?

BRISSING: Yes, sir.

ADMIRAL: Quite finished? Every ashtray in its place?

BRISSING: Yes, sir. *(Sits again on settee.)*

FLAG CAPTAIN: *(Irritable.)* Well, sit down and keep quiet, young man. Now, Ferrers. *(Seeing CARR standing up at back of room.)* Well, what is it?

CARR: I...er... Nothing, sir. *(Sits down again.)*

ADMIRAL: Yes, Carr. I should like to hear you.

CARR: It's this, sir. Ferrers is up against it in a very special way. I speak a bit of his language – enough to see the difficulties – but the truth is that none of us understands it. Except Miss Selby.

FLAG CAPTAIN: Then he might take the trouble to learn ours.

KAREN: You wouldn't ask a musician to learn ours.

FLAG CAPTAIN: And why not? Don't they talk like ordinary people when they're not playing their music? Except that most of them seem to be Poles – or mad.

KAREN: Yes, sir, but that's different. What they say in words isn't what they say in music. If it were, there'd be no need of the music.

FERRERS: The Flag Captain isn't interested in music, Karen.

ADMIRAL: *(To CARR.)* You were saying – 'in *his* language', Carr?

CARR: The language of mathematics, sir.

ADMIRAL: I see. Still, we must do the best we can to meet each other halfway. Eh, Miss Selby?

KAREN: I know, sir. But sometimes there isn't any halfway. Just as there isn't really any halfway between a music-hall song and Beethoven's Fifth. *(Pause.)*

ADMIRAL: Now, gentleman, I must write my report this evening. Since the trial we have spent a week – your own officers, Ferrers, and independent officers from the Fleet – investigating the causes of failure. We have had their reports. Today we have heard their evidence. *(KAREN moves behind settee and sits in chair by piano.)*

FERRERS: I don't admit failure, sir.

ADMIRAL: That's one of the difficulties. It would be simpler if you did.

FERRERS: I admit that the detonators –

ADMIRAL: One minute, please. You will have your chance. First, I don't want to misrepresent you. I will go over the facts as I shall report them. You can check as I go. Now, Ferrers. Follow my notes. If I'm wrong, stop me. Murphy and Gaisford took up their aeroplane. As soon as you located them, you launched your first Scorpion. It followed them in the air. *(FLAG CAPTAIN yawns and fidgets.)*

FERRERS: Will you make that point, sir? It *did* follow them. It followed them close.

CARR: It passed very close, sir. They nose-dived to avoid it.

ADMIRAL: I accept that. But when close, the vibrations of the plane ought to have fired the charge. Isn't that so? In war, high explosive that would bring the plane down. In this case a blank charge that should have given off a puff of smoke. Is that right, Ferrers?

FERRERS: Yes, sir.

ADMIRAL: But there was no puff of smoke. That means you failed to fire the charge at the appropriate moment. The Scorpion lost power and fell.

FERRERS: The facts are right, Not your conclusions from them.

ADMIRAL: But there are seven more facts. Murphy and Gaisford began a second run. You launched a second

Scorpion. Again it followed them. This time it hit them, brought them down – with what results we know.

FERRERS: It proves at any rate that the Scorpion followed them.

FLAG CAPTAIN: That's brutal and callous.

FERRERS: It proves the vibration-steering worked.

FLAG CAPTAIN: It proves –

ADMIRAL: Steady! The Scorpion ought to have exploded. It didn't explode. Isn't that a second failure?

FERRERS: You can put it so.

FLAG CAPTAIN: And there's this point. You saw Murphy and Gaisford crash into the sea. Even then you didn't break off your mad series of failures.

FERRERS: The destroyers were under them. There was nothing I could do.

FLAG CAPTAIN: You don't seem to care how many you kill. But Whitehall will care. You must be stopped.

FERRERS: If I had stopped then, you would have said I had failed. I ordered another plane up.

FLAG CAPTAIN: Do they matter so little, these poor men? You can count Miss Selby's brother among them.

FERRERS: *(Rises, furious.)* I know that. I was his friend. What does he or any of us matter if the thing is right?

FLAG CAPTAIN: You must be mad, Ferrers. You couldn't speak in that way. *(FERRERS sits again.)*

ADMIRAL: *(To FERRERS.)* You do make it hard. Still – there's little more. Are these the remaining facts? You sent up another aeroplane. This time we have the observers' reports. They did six more runs. You launched six Scorpions –

FERRERS: And each time followed them in the air.

ADMIRAL: But you didn't explode.

FERRERS: I followed them in the air. The observer reports that.

ADMIRAL: But failed to explode.

FERRERS: Yes.

ADMIRAL: Six times.

FERRERS: Yes.

ADMIRAL: Eight in all.

FERRERS: Eight in all.

ADMIRAL: Is there any answer to that?

KAREN: Mr Sandford and I gave the answer in great detail this morning, sir. The detonators didn't work.

FLAG CAPTAIN: Eight times?

SANDFORD: *(Rises.)* They are all positioned the same, sir. If one is wrong, they all are. *(Sits.)*

FLAG CAPTAIN: You say the detonators. And yet you say the invention is not affected in principle. *(Rises.)* Now, listen to me, Ferrers. What causes, or should cause, your detonator to fire the charge?

FERRERS: Air vibration on sensitive receivers.

FLAG CAPTAIN: Exactly! And vibration is the root if your theory, isn't it?

SANDFORD: *(Rises.)* I should like to say, sir –

FLAG CAPTAIN: Be quiet, Mr Sandford. *(SANDFORD sits. To FERRERS.)* Isn't vibration the root of your theory?

FERRERS: Yes.

FLAG CAPTAIN: Vibration should explode your detonators?

FERRERS: Yes.

FLAG CAPTAIN: And the detonators failed to explode?

FERRERS: Yes.

FLAG CAPTAIN: Then your whole theory breaks down! *(Sits.)*

FERRERS: No. The receivers are not yet rightly placed. Would it have proved that Watt was a fool if the lid of the kettle had stuck?

ADMIRAL: There's no proof that the fault was in the detonator receivers. There can be none. Such Scorpions as we recovered were too much damaged. The independent officers simply say they don't know. Sandford says –

SANDFORD: Damn it, sir, I made the thing. It's my child.

ADMIRAL: A mother isn't always the best judge of her own child.

KAREN: That wasn't Solomon's opinion, sir. *(This is a relief.)*

ADMIRAL: Thank you, Miss Selby, we needed that. You say there was a detonator fault, Sandford. What was it? *(SANDFORD hesitates.)* Come, that, surely, is a fair question.

SANDFORD: *(Rises.)* Sounds like it, I know, sir. I'll never be able to convince you that it isn't. Our trouble at the end was simply how to place the detonator mechanism. When the difficulty arose, I had to repack the whole inside of the torpedo. Meanwhile, Ferrers was working on a new gyro-gear which would save space. I knew we were taking a chance. It's a thousand to one that the fault is still the effect of screening on the detonator receivers. Our time was cut down from two months to one. The tests were rushed through.

ADMIRAL: That's too vague, Sandford. Can't you go further?

SANDFORD: Not now, sir, I can't.

ADMIRAL: It may be vital.

SANDFORD: *(Desperate.)* I can't, sir. I – *(But there is nothing more he can say. Sits on arm of settee.)*

ADMIRAL: That's the end then.

KAREN: Give us time, sir. It's *so* near. We can re-position the existing detonator mechanism. Or we can work out the alternative. Then the thing will prove itself.

ADMIRAL: We can't go on indefinitely without results. Listen, Ferrers, you may be right. *(All rise except FERRERS.)* I may be looking now at the man who has it in his power to make Great Britain an island again. If I report against you, this station will be closed down. This isn't work you can do without government backing. I may be breaking the one man who might save civilization. To avoid that, I will take great risks. I came here prepared, against the evidence, to advise further experiment, if you frankly admitted an error in your own calculations and were prepared to correct it. *(Waits.)* Well, Ferrers? *(Silence.)*

FLAG CAPTAIN: There's no more to say, sir.

ADMIRAL: I want the Commander's answer. Are you willing to reconsider your formula from first principles?

FERRERS: No, sir. If I do, calculation simply stops. It's like denying that twice two make four. You can deny it in words, but, if you do, you can't go on. It's not modesty and sweet reason to deny it. It's barren folly.

ADMIRAL: Then you won't go back?

FERRERS: I can't, sir.

FLAG CAPTAIN: If we did give you more time – more money, more lives to throw away – who would be responsible next time you failed? *(With venom.)* I can tell you. One of your staff, Ferrers. Sandford again, or Carr or Brissing. Perhaps even Miss Selby by that time. Anyone but you.

FERRERS: You can think that if you like. I can't lie about my own work.

ADMIRAL: Doesn't it occur to you – even as a possibility – that you may *be* wrong?

FERRERS: *(Quietly.)* I'm as sure of this as I am of the existence of God. *(ADMIRAL turns, facing upstage.)*

FLAG CAPTAIN: I believe you're mad, Ferrers.

FERRERS: That's a feather in my cap.

FLAG CAPTAIN: And if it were proved that your calculation was wrong – what then?

FERRERS: When it is proved to me that my truth is my lie, then for me all truth is lying and I am mad.

KAREN: I know that he is right. *(ADMIRAL to foot of steps C.)*

FLAG CAPTAIN: Well, sir?

ADMIRAL: *(Turns to front. A long pause.)* I wash my hands of it.

KAREN: I know deep down. I do know.

ADMIRAL: Other men have believed in themselves, Miss Selby. Other women have believed in them. I don't blame you. Goodbye, Ferrers. *(ADMIRAL and FLAG CAPTAIN go out all standing as they go, even FERRERS on his feet. When they have gone, he slumps on chair.)*

CARR: Sybil Helston will have a good evening. Play piquet, Dick. That table's a shambles. Come to the mess-room. *(CARR and SANDFORD go out.)*

BRISSING: Karen, make it four and bridge. Oh, you don't play. Five and poker. *(No answer.)* Hell, I'll play Miss Milligan. *(Exit BRISSING.)*

FERRERS: What's the time?

KAREN: Six-eight.

FERRERS: Still accurate. *(Rises.)* As if there were work to do.

KAREN: There still is.

FERRERS: Not for me.

KAREN: This particular invention isn't everything.

FERRERS: What do you mean? Pluck up courage and make something else in the service of mankind? What – an electrical bicycle? *(Sits on corner of table.)*

KAREN: If you never invent anything that people manufacture and use, it doesn't matter to you – any more than it matters to a poet whether the world decides he's morally helpful. Mathematics is a thing of its own. Absolute.

FERRERS: But one must exercise it on something. There must be a theme.

KAREN: Before I came here, much of my work was useful – anyhow to astronomers – to navigators, too, remotely. But much of it was quite useless. What it came down to was discovering the natural laws of an imaginary universe. I was happy – using myself. Dead single-minded.

FERRERS: I've been happy here. You're good to work with.

KAREN: Oh –

FERRERS: What?

KAREN: I was thinking of something Brissing said while you were at tea.

FERRERS: What did he say?

KAREN: Something about – dogs.

FERRERS: Dogs?

KAREN: Well, about – oh, never mind that. I'm good to work with. I meant to be.

FERRERS: You'll go home.

KAREN: Let me wait and clear up. If I were a man I should.

FERRERS: You're not.

KAREN: You said, long ago, you would treat me as a man. Now I claim it.

FERRERS: They'll cut down the salary list. You're supernumerary.

KAREN: I know.

FERRERS: *(Rises.)* Why, in God's name, are we talking like this?

KAREN: *(Rises.)* Because we're still afraid of each other.

FERRERS: We were right to be afraid.

KAREN: While there was work to spoil. Not now. There's only one real misery in life – to be entangled.

FERRERS: *(An outburst.)* You don't know what I've had from women!

KAREN: I can guess.

FERRERS: Open a door – and be damned if they'll walk in. Shut it, bolt it and they'll *break* in. And once in, it's for ever and ever, unless *they* want to go out again. Then it's 'Goodbye, my lady. I am honoured to have served your turn. Please allow me to be eternally your friend and pay the damage for the next lock you break…'

KAREN: I see.

FERRERS: You have been honest, Karen. Always, with me. From the beginning of your life, I think. If you were a tart, you'd be an honest tart. There was a girl kept a bar once.

In fact she wasn't a tart – men fell in love with her. They proposed marriage and meant it. Half the young bloods in the Service – peerage, money, brains – she could have put a dozen careers in her pocket. But she wouldn't. Even when she herself loved one of them – she still wouldn't. My God, I admire that woman. She may have had fifty lovers. I don't think she did. She may have. It makes no odds. What she said, you believed. Honest – like you.

KAREN: Honest. Good to work with. Good with puppies. Respectable virtues.

FERRERS: Puppies?

KAREN: That's what Brissing said.

FERRERS: Karen! I see everything ahead like a blank wall. *(To settee.)* There's something I want to say to you. Just for the satisfaction of having once said it, I suppose. That first day, in this room, do you remember we were by the table? I sat down and left you standing? Do you know what I saw?

KAREN: A junior officer being interviewed. *(Crosses to him.)*

FERRERS: No. A woman – naked. I want you to know. That and – *(A long pause.)* Oh, it *is* true that one thinks and feels and wants two things at the same time. People who write arrange the emotions in order – first a man doesn't desire a woman, then he does, then desire grows, as they say, to 'something more' – it's all beautifully ordered, everything in its sequence. It's all a lie. The emotions aren't a reasonable sequence. At the same time, I saw you as – oh, something to eat, and behind that, like a fate, as something to worship. At one and the same time! And I said: 'She'll break up this work; she's hell; she'll play her own game.' And at the same time I knew: 'She's the Holy Grail.' … Well, that's said.

KAREN: That was honest, too.

FERRERS: If today hadn't gone as it did… I'll tell you that, too. If it hadn't, I mean if we had been going on working here, I should have taken you if I could.

KAREN: My dear, I am all yours. *(Kneels, sitting back on her heels.)*

FERRERS: Not now.

KAREN: Always, without terms. From the beginning, to the end, without terms, yours absolutely.

FERRERS: I'm broke, my Karen.

KAREN: *(Sharply – angry.)* Broke?

FERRERS: I don't mean money. I'm a broke man.

KAREN: All the more –

FERRERS: *(Resenting pity.)* All the more!

KAREN: *(Trying to recover.)* Not 'all the more' – the same, absolutely.

FERRERS: Too late, Karen.

KAREN: You think I'm pitying you! I – you! Why are you so afraid of hurting, I wonder.

FERRERS: Because I know myself. I hurt too much.

KAREN: Afraid of believing, too.

FERRERS: I have believed too much.

KAREN: Believe now. *(Her arms about him.)* Believe now.

FERRERS: *(Takes her passionately. Then, in bitter reaction, but still holding her.)* You know what would happen?

KAREN: What would happen?

FERRERS: The man you love was proud as Lucifer. Possessed by your own devil of genius. That's the kind goes phut. Not if I was twenty-five. But as things are, we should drift about Swiss Cottage in gallant poverty. You'd work in your Observatory and keep me. Or you'd get me a job there and we'd promote ourselves to Kensington. People would say 'Wasn't your husband a mathematical genius?' Someone would give me a teaching job – I'd fly out and lose it – and, my God, you'd endure that, again – and again – and again. As I grew older, I should get the smug pride of the genius who's missed it – the little man whose poetry the world is always too stupid to read or whose music is too exalted for anyone to listen to.

KAREN: *(Trying to break free.)* Oh, stop! You're cruel.

FERRERS: No. Stay in my arms while you hear it. Then you'll know. You'd be in my arms then. Month after month, year after year. Night after night.

KAREN: Happy – happy – happy with each other.

FERRERS: Not if I hated myself. Then I should hate you. And I should hate myself all right. We shouldn't dare speak of Kendrickstown. Happy – with you! – you're the one woman above all others who would drive me mad.

KAREN: Because I love you?

FERRERS: Because you had my own faith in me. You thought – didn't you? – I was going to save the world? You'd see the world-shaker come home every evening with his latch-key. 'Well, my dear, did you have a good day at the office?' Oh no. If any woman's going to wake on my pillow, it must be one who doesn't know. I could say to her: 'Yes. For about three years I tried some experiments under the Admiralty. They were extraordinarily interesting at the time.' She'd believe me, She'd be proud of my bridge. 'That's what comes,' she'd say, when we added up the score, 'that's what comes of having been a mathematical genius.' She –

KAREN: Let me go, then.

FERRERS: Kiss me. *(Violently.)*

KAREN: Oh my God!

FERRERS: *(Kisses her again.)* Now I'll remember.

KAREN: What?

FERRERS: This too. And when she says – oh whatever she says – I'll feel that ribbon, across your shoulder, under your dress – now. *(Drops her.)* Shall I ever feel it? Or just forget.

KAREN: Do something for me. Be still. Quite still. I want you here. Be still and remember. *(Draws him down.)* I love you, always, without terms, as I wish I could believe you love me. I shall try to remember too. But it's the chance things one remembers. My father tying a balloon for me. It was a piece of red wool. I suppose I shall forget this – I shall try to remember. *(Trying to plant them in her memory.)* I shall say:

'The lamp. His fingers on my flesh. His wrist on mine.' But I shan't *feel* your wrist on mine. O my beloved, can you believe in only one absolute thing? There is an absolute love. They are the same, I think. *(He moves.)* A little longer. Be still and remember. I love you always – through all follies, all unfaithfulness – through every failure and denial – *all parting* – always – to the end.

FERRERS: Karen, that's the hope of madmen.

KAREN: So is the love of God.

Curtain.

ACT THREE

Two months later. October. 3 p.m.. Very hot, Dress: full whites. Signs of dismantling. Packing cases. Some of the pictures gone from the walls. CARR is on piano-stool, idly strumming. BRISSING, on his knees, is hammering a packing case. They are all ill-tempered and on edge – the spirit gone out of them. Except CARR, they have drunk enough. The tune CARR plays is 'Farewell and Adieu' – see beginning of this book for words. He uses it throughout the opening of this scene, quietly or loudly, as a counter to the nerves of others – as a nurse uses a song to lull fractious children, at last tempting them to join in. SANDFORD enters downstairs L, carrying a pile of books.

BRISSING: *(Stops hammering.)* You can say what you like The First Lord wouldn't have come from England again without a reason.

SANDFORD: It wasn't to save this place. *(Putting down books.)*

BRISSING: I'm not so sure. This morning he was out to listen. So was the Admiral at the inquiry two months ago. Twice Ferrers' damned obstinacy has chucked the game away. *(KAREN drifts in from verandah and lies on sofa down stage, turning over illustrated papers. They take no notice of her.)*

SANDFORD: *(To BRISSING.)* Not so loyal now!

BRISSING: It was you let him down over the detonator. *(Echoing ADMIRAL.)* 'What was the defect? Surely that's a fair question, Mr Sandford?' You hadn't a damned thing to say. *(Begins to hammer again.)*

CARR: Dry up, Brissing.

BRISSING: Why should I? We've go to pack. *(Hammers.)*

CARR: *(A calm man now at breaking-point. Almost a cry of agony.)* No, no! Stop! What's the hurry? We've got a fortnight.

BRISSING: Go to hell!

CARR: All right! You play your tune. I'll play mine.

BRISSING: You only know one. *(As BRISSING continues to hammer, CARR turns again to the piano. He plays and sings his loudest. One by one, the others join in – a jangled, unprofessional chorus. One by one, they stop, but the piano continues, and one of them – KAREN perhaps – takes the last lines alone. Silence. CARR transposes a few bars into G minor. They are appeased and surprised by their appeasement.)*

BRISSING: *(To CARR.)* Sorry sir, I'm a fool… Cut for drinks.

SANDFORD: I will.

BRISSING: Karen, you coming in?

KAREN: If you bring the dice over to me. *(They bring dice.)* Lady Helston's coming here. *(CARR stops playing and turns. KAREN throws dice, using for this purpose the floor beside the settee.)*

SANDFORD: What for?

KAREN: *(Having thrown twice more.)* She telephoned a message asking if she could. She's going to England in the First Lord's ship tomorrow. *(SANDFORD throws three times quickly during what follows.)*

BRISSING: Do you mean, a farewell call on the Mess? It's not possible.

KAREN: The message was that she wanted to see me.

BRISSING: You're going to?

KAREN: Yes.

BRISSING: *(Having thrown dice only once.)* Ha! Four straight aces. Good enough? You're lurked, Sandford. *(SANDFORD rings bell.)*

CARR: Does Ferrers know she's coming?

KAREN: I asked his permission.

SANDFORD: Women beat me. Why didn't you refuse to see her?

KAREN: I don't believe in refusing to see people. You wonder afterwards what they were going to say. *(Enter DENHAM.)*

SANDFORD: Two whiskies. What for you, Karen?

KAREN: I don't want one.

SANDFORD: But you came in.

KAREN: Still, I don't.

SANDFORD: *(To DENHAM.)* All right, two then.

DENHAM: Very good, sir.

KAREN: Denham, Lady Helston is coming to see me, Show her straight in when she comes.

DENHAM: Very good, Miss. *(Exits.)*

KAREN: Can I have this room?

CARR: Why not the mess-room? This is like a carpenter's shop.

KAREN: I think this would be good for her.

BRISSING: We'll clear out the packing-case. *(To SANDFORD.)* Give me a hand. *(They carry it out.)*

KAREN: *(To CARR.)* Don't go for a minute.

CARR: I don't see what good it can do – her coming here.

KAREN: It's not that I want to talk to you about. *(BRISSING returns to pick up hammer, etc. KAREN is turning over illustrated papers again.)*

BRISSING: That's hopelessly stale. Lord Coverdale has been dining at the Savoy with the charming wife of Mr Lionel P Soot of Boston, Mass., for the last six weeks. *(Enter DENHAM with drinks.)* Take the other through to Mr Sandford. *(Exit DENHAM. BRISSING offers another paper to KAREN and sits on back of settee.)* Try this one. There's a whole page of the people who found the photographer on Mr Cochran's first night. The civilization we have failed to save… Sorry, I must still be sober. I'll remedy that defect, *(Exit BRISSING with drink.)*

KAREN: Sit for a moment. *(CARR perches himself on the arm of her sofa.)*

KAREN: This is very like hell.

CARR: My dear – as bad as that?

KAREN: Those two are drinking a lot of drink.

CARR: Naval officers can drink a lot of drink.

KAREN: You are the only one who isn't rattled.

CARR: You *will* go on hoping. I write things off.

KAREN: Like Antony? 'Things that are past are done with me.' They are done with him too.

CARR: Ferrers.

KAREN: He's not fighting any more. When I heard the First Lord was coming out from England, I thought there was still hope.

CARR: Politicians aren't gods from the machine.

KAREN: If he means to do nothing but back the Admiral, why come?

CARR: To square his own yard arm. A lot of money has been spent in this place. Three lives too, and the Admiralty has nothing to show for it. There'll be questions. Harrowby will have to tell discreet lies in the House of Commons or square the Opposition. He can do it better if he can say he's been here.

KAREN: I see. Just that.

CARR: I think so.

KAREN: *(After a pause.)* Do you believe in him?

CARR: The First Lord?

KAREN: In Edward. The others have begun to shake.

CARR: Brissing and Dick Sandford? You know why?

KAREN: That's what I want to know.

CARR: I see their point of view. If Ferrers had eaten a bit of humble pie and admitted he was wrong, the Admiral would have given him more time.

KAREN: *Would* have? Not now?

CARR: Now? It's too late. We're for home in a fortnight. Didn't you hear Brissing nailing down the coffin?... What they say is: If Ferrers really knows that he's right, why the hell didn't he go through the motions of putting his pride in his pocket? We aren't Christian martyrs refusing a pinch of incense to the altar of Caesar.

KAREN: So they think he ought to lie about his own work?

CARR: They say: If the job is everything to him, wouldn't he lie to save it – unless he really *is* wrong and doesn't believe in the thing any more?

KAREN: They think he's afraid to go on? And you?

CARR: Do you understand him yourself?

KAREN: Yes. But I love the queer being. I know how his mind works and his bitterness – *and* his infernal humility.

CARR: Humility! Isn't it pride?

KAREN: It's not his prestige he's thinking about. And not the job. That's where you're on the wrong track. You expect him to care about being the famous man who saved the world. Anyhow, you think he ought to want to save the world. Well, he doesn't. He doesn't give a farthing for the world's comfort – or his own. They can use his Scorpions or not – that's their affair. What he does care about – as an artist cares about his art – is mathematical truth. That is absolute. That's a religion. He won't go back on it. *(A pause.)* But it's going back on him. *(She says this in such acute personal distress that CARR moves across and puts a fatherly hand on her.)*

CARR: What is it that's on your mind?

KAREN: He might lose faith in himself.

CARR: That's not your fault.

KAREN: Isn't it? He thinks I doubt him. Brissing, Sandford – now me. He found me the other day going through old calculations and he said: 'Well, Karen, have you found the howler?' He thought I was looking for it.

CARR: Were you?

KAREN: I was going through *his* calculations – and my brother's – the ones I hadn't a share in.

CARR: But what for?

KAREN: The joy of it – like a gallery of masterpieces. He didn't believe that. And if now – *(She shakes her head violently and rises.)* – I daren't – I daren't do anything that would make him believe I doubted him.

CARR: Why should you?

KAREN: There's one chance to save this place.

CARR: There was. He didn't take it. He won't now.

KAREN: There's still one chance. *(Enter DENHAM quickly.)*

DENHAM: The car's here, Miss. *(Exit.)*

CARR: I'll escape by the verandah. Give us a word when she's gone. I don't want to blunder in on her. *(Exit CARR by verandah. DENHAM shows in LADY HELSTON.)*

DENHAM: Lady Helston, Miss. *(Exit DENHAM.)*

LADY HELSTON: I wasn't sure you'd want to see me.

KAREN: The message was: you wanted to see me. I wondered why.

LADY HELSTON: I am leaving for England tomorrow morning.

KAREN: So I heard… Won't you sit down?

LADY HELSTON: For a moment. Why in this room?

KAREN: If you came to triumph, I thought you'd like it. If you came to apologize, it's suitable too.

LADY HELSTON: I haven't come for either. *(Sits on settee.)*

KAREN: I know. You came because you had to. Isn't that true?

LADY HELSTON: As a matter of fact, I had made up a perfectly good conventional excuse for coming, but I suppose I needn't trouble you with it.

KAREN: That must be the straightest thing you've ever said. I like you for that.

LADY HELSTON: I only thought that as we aren't likely to meet again –

KAREN: *(Steadily and without rhetoric.)* And as you will never be in this room again, and as you did something here that twists and torments you, and as you don't know whether you're glad or sorry or a misunderstood woman or a cad – because you are in a hopeless tangle and curious and on edge – you had to come here, and see me, and see this room once more, and find out what your sensations were.

LADY HELSTON: *(Puzzled and a little frightened by a mood and method she does not understand.)* Are you pitying me?

KAREN: I am talking about what happens to interest me at the moment. I wondered why you'd come. Now I know. You wanted a scene to wipe out the memory of the last. Do you lie awake at nights wishing you could get back to the bridge table and play a hand again?

LADY HELSTON: *(Not alive to her irony.)* Why, do you?

KAREN: I don't play bridge.

LADY HELSTON: You are an extraordinary woman!

KAREN: Why? Because I don't play bridge?

LADY HELSTON: You don't like anything I like.

KAREN: Yes I do. Men.

LADY HELSTON: But you can't *say* that!

KAREN: I can to a woman I shall never see again. Doesn't it even interest you? Doesn't anything *real* interest you? Here I am. I took the man you wanted, and you have ruined what I care for more than anything on earth. I think you are a cad and you think I'm a slut, and somehow we both think we're right. No one's the villainess in her own story. Two utterly different human beings – neither with imagination enough to see the other's point of view. And in about three minutes by the clock, when you go out of that door, we shall be dead to each other – as if we really were dead. We might as well tell the truth meanwhile. *(She crosses L below the settee.)*

LADY HELSTON: I don't know what you're talking about. If I'd had any idea you would behave like this, I wouldn't have come.

KAREN: How did you expect me to behave? *(L of settee.)*

LADY HELSTON: I thought you might be angry.

KAREN: You'd have liked that.

LADY HELSTON: Or we might –

KAREN: A reconciliation scene? Did you really think that?

LADY HELSTON: No. *(She means 'yes'.)* But we might have talked.

KAREN: Aren't we talking? And you would have sat there purring over your little drama. Somehow you'd have found out what you're longing to know. All right, I'll tell you. I'm not his mistress and never have been.

LADY HELSTON: I don't think I care.

KAREN: What *do* you care about – really care? *(Sits.)*

LADY HELSTON: I loved him.

KAREN: *(Just a denial.)* No.

LADY HELSTON: I loved him – horribly.

KAREN: *(Dead hard.)* You believe that's true!

LADY HELSTON: It is true. *(With sudden spirit, rising.)* My God, you are arrogant! Do you think no one can love but yourself?

KAREN: *(In astonishment.)* Then it is true. You did love him. We don't speak the same language, that's all. We are two women, but not the same animal. Love means power to you. *Power* – over him.

LADY HELSTON: Why is that wrong? It's natural. It's you who are unnatural. Because you have brains, you want to submit yourself. That's love to you. You want to be ordered – under his discipline. If he hit you, you'd take that. Wouldn't you?

KAREN: Yes, I would.

LADY HELSTON: *(Without venom – a statement of fact as she sees it.)* That's why you're a slut. And why you didn't save him.

KAREN: I want power *from* him. I want to be more and more myself because I love him more and more. Is that being a slut?

LADY HELSTON: I wanted more and more power over him because I loved him more and more. Is that being a cad?

KAREN: Perhaps the little words don't mean much in the end.

LADY HELSTON: I'll go. *(She reaches entrance to verandah.)*

KAREN: *(Rises.)* Why didn't I save him?

LADY HELSTON: Because you submit. Because you didn't dare. *(Exit LADY HELSTON. After a moment KAREN goes to door R. and opens it to call in the others. As she does so FERRERS comes in C and she turns back to meet him.)*

FERRERS: Disposed of? I saw her go from my window. Strangely calm. Did she come to enjoy another scene? Who played the lead in this one?

KAREN: I think it played itself.

FERRERS: Where are the others?

KAREN: In the mess-room. They'll come back.

FERRERS: I'll go then. *(He moves. She stops him.)*

KAREN: Why?

FERRERS: They go over things, Karen.

KAREN: Or are you afraid?

FERRERS: Of them?

KAREN: Of me.

FERRERS: You!

KAREN: Do you know I love you?

FERRERS: My dear –

KAREN: I wonder if you do. Do you know I believe in you?

FERRERS: Perhaps you love me too much.

KAREN: No. I believe in you – in your work.

FERRERS: *(Non-committal.)* Thank you. *(He moves again. She stops him.)*

KAREN: But remember. I said: 'I believe in you'. Remember that.

FERRERS: I will. *(He moves again. She stops him.)*

KAREN: Whatever comes, remember. *(CARR and SANDFORD come in R. FERRERS at once goes out upstairs L. SANDFORD pulls forward table from upstage R, and armchair from downstage R to RC.)*

CARR: Ferrers!... Get him back.

KAREN: No. Leave him.

CARR: We have sighted the First Lord.

KAREN: Alone? *(SANDFORD continues to put the room straight.)*

CARR: And on foot.

KAREN: Coming here?

CARR: He is here – with Brissing. We must have Ferrers.

KAREN: No, please. Not yet.

CARR: But –

KAREN: No. Take it from me. *(BRISSING shows in FIRST LORD from the verandah. DENHAM enters R. He stands and waits for orders.)*

FIRST LORD: I hope I don't intrude. I've come to pay a call on the Mess. *(Top of steps C.)*

CARR: Come in, sir.

KAREN: We are very glad to see you again, sir. *(Shakes hands.)*

FIRST LORD: Thank you. I walked up. Air and exercise. The Admiral and the Flag Captain are following in the car. We timed it to meet here as nearly as we could.

SANDFORD: What will you have, sir?

FIRST LORD: Thank you. It was rather a long walk. A gin and tonic.

SANDFORD: *(To DENHAM.)* And three whiskeys.

DENHAM: Yes, sir. *(Exits.)*

KAREN: Won't you sit down, sir?

FIRST LORD: Thank you. *(He sits in armchair. KAREN on settee.)* There's talk of a signal station on Flag Point. The Admiral thought we might have a look at it. Is it a pretty place?

BRISSING: A cigarette, sir.

FIRST LORD: A pipe if I may. It persuades the newspapers that, though uninspiring, one is English at heart. For the same reason, if statesmen must go to France, it's advisable for them to cut out Paris and go straight to Aix-les-Bains. *(There is an awkward pause and the FIRST LORD continues to make conversation.)* You have some remarkable bougainvilleas in your garden. Your cultivation, Miss Selby?

KAREN: No, sir. This – *(BRISSING.)* is the gardener.

FIRST LORD: Indeed. I congratulate you. Gunnery and gardens. And what do you do in your spare time?

BRISSING: If we get long leave after this, I mean to spend a bit of it in France.

FIRST LORD: At Aix-les-Bains, I hope.

BRISSING: No. With a car, very slowly through Burgundy.

FIRST LORD: I shouldn't inform the Admiralty if I were you. It's dangerous in England to give an impression that you like the French for their own sake. It throws suspicion on your morals. *(DENHAM comes in, hands drinks and goes.)*

SANDFORD: We shall get leave after this, shan't we, sir?

FIRST LORD: I'll take your orders. Lieutenant-Commander Brissing – Burgundy. And what after that?

BRISSING: Whale Island. Then a big ship.

FIRST LORD: *(To SANDFORD.)* And you?

SANDFORD: I'd like China.

FIRST LORD: They may have less oriental ideas at the Admiralty, but I'll see it through. *(To CARR.)* Have you any instructions?

CARR: I shall retire.

FIRST LORD: Why, may I ask?

CARR: Oh, not because of this. Family reasons.

FIRST LORD: I'm glad. No one must take a personal view of this – or of anything arising from the public service. I want there to be no bitterness if I can avoid it. You are probably asking yourselves questions. *(He lights his pipe.)*

CARR: There's one I'm always asking myself. Isn't there a kind of paradox in it all? If Ferrers had admitted an error in his calculations, you'd have let the show go forward. The Admiral said as much. So did you, sir, this morning. But because he knows he's right and says so, you close down on us. Sounds mad to me.

FIRST LORD: Gilbertian, Carr, not mad. We live in a democracy and democracy is always charitable to fools, but not to arrogant genius. It's quite simple. You can back a man who has made a mistake, but not a man who won't admit it. In one case – granted you believe in the man – there's the hope of remedy; in the other, not.

CARR: But Ferrers has admitted a detonator defect.

FIRST LORD: That might go on forever. First one minor defect, then another, and all the time his basic calculations may be wrong.

KAREN: But if he *is* right?

FIRST LORD: The Admiralty would say it's a big 'if'.

KAREN: And you, sir?

FIRST LORD: I am the Admiralty for the time being... But I should like your answer to that question, Carr. Do you believe Ferrers is right?

CARR: Absolutely.

FIRST LORD: You are a family man. You have children. One daughter in particular?

CARR: *(Astonished.)* Yes, sir.

FIRST LORD: Would you stake her future on your answer to that question? The Admiralty, you know, has more at stake than that. Would you?

CARR: *(Having considered.)* I would. *(He turns away and finishes drink. BRISSING moves upstage to verandah.)*

FIRST LORD: And you, Sandford?

SANDFORD: I haven't a daughter, sir. *(Rises.)*

FIRST LORD: Few men can be sure of that; and they perhaps are not to be envied. The question stands.

SANDFORD: Well. *(Looks uneasily at KAREN.)* I'm not a mathematician, sir.

FIRST LORD: Nor am I. I have my advisers. So have you – Ferrers and Miss Selby. The question still stands, for me and for you.

SANDFORD: Well, sir, the point is –

FIRST LORD: Thank you. The question is answered... *(To CARR.)* You see, Carr, Whitehall is not the only place. Mr Brissing has gone to consult the weather. If only I could sometimes do that during question time in the House!

BRISSING: *(Turns round – with the aggressiveness of a man who has ceased to be sure of himself.)* I'm not trying to shirk. I've believed in Ferrers through thick and think. You can't help it if you work with him. If he said 'Work on with me until we *do* get this thing right', I'd be with him –

FIRST LORD: 'Until we do', Brissing! '*Until* we do?' Then it's not right.

BRISSING: You're too quick, sir. You catch up my words. I didn't say it was wrong.

FIRST LORD: *(Doubtfully.)* No. But you did say that if Ferrers asked you to work on while he corrected his present error, you would stand by him. That is the Admiralty's point of view. *(Almost in anguish.)* But he will admit no error in himself – no possibility of error in his own work. *(Stands up.)* Miss Selby will admit none. *(Enter FERRERS, L. He is nervous and suspicious.)*

FERRERS: You, sir? I didn't know you were here. *(Angry.)* Why wasn't I told? Am I still in command here or a fool to be humoured?

FIRST LORD: I asked them not to disturb you.

FERRERS: I see. I'm sorry. Afraid I'm on edge. *(Trying to be ordinary.)* What is it Miss Selby won't admit?

FIRST LORD: That there's any mistake in your calculations.

FERRERS: Incredible. Did you ask her?

FIRST LORD: I was on the point of asking her when you came in.

FERRERS: Pity you didn't. The others think I'm a fool. Not Carr, but the others. I know that. But my bridge is still first-rate! That's a proof of mathematical genius all the world can understand! I'm lucky, really. A poet can't recommend himself to the mob unless he dies or writes cracker mottoes. *(He looks round wildly at the grave faces regarding this cheap petulance. Then with a quiet despair, no longer bitter, he adds, to the FIRST LORD.)* Heigh-ho! That's how they all talk, isn't it, sir?

FIRST LORD: Who?

FERRERS: The poor devils who were ALMOST – and just hadn't got it in 'em.

KAREN: Don't say that! Don't!

FERRERS: That's what it comes to, doesn't it? *(To foot of stairs L.)*

KAREN: Oh my God! I wish they *had* asked me that question. Why did you come in? I'm such a coward for you. *(ADMIRAL and FLAG CAPTAIN appear in verandah arch. All rise.)*

ADMIRAL: We had trouble with the self-starter. Ferrers, I wish you'd invent one that worked. *(To FIRST LORD.)* We haven't kept you?

FIRST LORD: I've had a most interesting talk. Sandford is going to China. Brissing, I'm afraid, is going to France.

FLAG CAPTAIN: *(Heavily affable.)* I wish all First Lords took as much interest in personnel.

ADMIRAL: We'd better go while the going's good... Pretty well packed up, Carr?

CARR: Most of the important things, sir.

ADMIRAL: Good. *(To FIRST LORD.)* Well, are you all set, sir? *(ADMIRAL and FLAG CAPTAIN to verandah.)*

FIRST LORD: Goodbye then, gentlemen. *(They say goodbye to him.)* Goodbye, Ferrers.

FERRERS: It's a queer business. You're right; so am I. I should do what you are doing; you'd do what I am. And we both know it.

FIRST LORD: Thank you, Ferrers. Goodbye, Miss Selby. Do you remember what Pompey said to Menas in the galley? No?... That's a pity. *(Hesitates.)* Goodbye. *(He moves to his hat and stick on table R.)*

KAREN: *(Loud, forced unnatural.)* There's something I must say. *(They all look at her; the ADMIRAL at his watch.)*

ADMIRAL: We ought to get on.

KAREN: I ought to have said this before.

ADMIRAL: I'm sure, Miss Selby, you don't wish to delay the First Lord.

KAREN: *(To FIRST LORD.)* Shall you be here again?

FIRST LORD: Never.

KAREN: Then I must say it now.

FLAG CAPTAIN: Really, is it of such importance?

FIRST LORD: I think, perhaps, it is.

KAREN: I'd rather say it to you alone.

FIRST LORD: No, Miss Selby. Whatever it is, the Admiral and the Flag Captain must hear it.

KAREN: I mean – not Commander Ferrers.

FERRERS: Not me!

FIRST LORD: *(Gently.)* Will it not have to be said to him some time.

KAREN: *(Struggling.)* I suppose so. So be it. *(She goes to FERRERS, takes his hand and faces FIRST LORD.)* I have found a defect in the basic formula.

FERRERS: *(Wrenching himself away.)* What in God's name do you mean?

KAREN: *(Louder.)* I have found a defect in your basic formula.

FLAG CAPTAIN: You can't say that now!

KAREN: I do.

FIRST LORD: A moment please. I think we should like to sit down again. *(FIRST LORD to settee. ADMIRAL to armchair. FERRERS and KAREN remain standing.)* Now.

FLAG CAPTAIN: Why didn't you say this before?

KAREN: *(To ADMIRAL.)* Since your report was sent in, I have gone over Ferrers' calculations again.

FERRERS: That's what you were spying for.

KAREN: *(Disregarding him.)* Two months. Line by line.

FLAG CAPTAIN: And you found this error, when? Since lunch? Why couldn't you tell us at the inquiry this morning?

FERRERS: What's wrong with the formula? Where is it wrong? You see, she can't answer that.

FIRST LORD: *(Giving her time.)* It is of course a question she will have to answer when the time comes. There are many highly complex matters which –

KAREN: I can answer it.

FIRST LORD: *(Gratefully abandoning his improvised oration.)* Can you? I'm delighted to hear that.

KAREN: *(Very fast.)* I found the error by examining afresh the whole of the vibration experiments on which the formula was based. From these he deduced a vibration-constant which he called K. K itself *is* constant, but in calculating vibration-effect, you have to apply a correction that varies with the density of the atmosphere. The fault is there. It is –

FIRST LORD: Greek to us, Miss Selby. The question is: Can it be put right?

KAREN: Not by me.

FIRST LORD: Not?

KAREN: He could.

FIRST LORD: I see.

ADMIRAL: Ferrers, is this new to you?

FERRERS: New! *(To KAREN.)* We have tested those experimental results again and again – together.

KAREN: I tested some. You tested some. It wasn't always a double check.

FERRERS: If mine were wrong, how could they have locked with yours? They fitted group by group like the dogs of a clutch. *(Now with entreaty close to her; his own confidence shaken.)* Tell me. Forget all these people. They lie. We all do. Mathematics doesn't. You have worked with me. I trust you. You *do* know. Tell me. Am I all wrong? *(He takes her hands and pulls her to him.)*

KAREN: You are wrong.

FERRERS: How deep does it go?

KAREN: *(Lying desperately.)* Very deep.

FERRERS: *(Turns from her.)* Then everything goes. If what it true is proved a lie, nothing is left.

KAREN: Remember. Remember. Remember.

FERRERS: Remember what? I've often wondered – what it would feel like to think you're sane, to know you are, and then to have it proved that you're mad.

KAREN: But this can be put right.

FERRERS: Unless I'm mad, there's nothing to put right. If there is, I'm mad. *(He comes away from them all, right down stage.)* Madness and sanity are two intersecting circles. Suddenly they close on the same centre. Poor Charles Lamb knew that. So the world spins. *(Fiercely, at her.)* Did you never learn that in your astronomy? *(He remains apart from them, thinking so intensely that he thinks aloud.)* The formula's right!

FIRST LORD: *(Seizing KAREN's arm.)* No, girl, leave him. Leave him a little while. He'll come back.

FERRERS: It's right! It's right!

FLAG CAPTAIN: We're no forrader.

ADMIRAL: How – no forrader?

FERRERS: It's right!

FLAG CAPTAIN: *(Contemptuously.)* Ferrers is no good. Use your eyes. Gibbering like a lunatic. He's thrown his hand in.

FERRERS: *(Passionately.)* Not to you!

FIRST LORD: *(Rises.)* One moment, please. Allow me. Commander Ferrers: As long as we, who are not good at sums, were saying 'It's you who are wrong', you told us to go to hell. That I can understand – the natural instinct of an expert. In my own case, in so far as I have expert knowledge of anything, it is of cats.

ADMIRAL: Did you say 'cats', sir?

FIRST LORD: I did undoubtedly say 'cats', sir. A pacific taste, you may think, in a First Lord of the Admiralty; *(FERRERS sits.)* but you must understand that I have not always been First Lord of the Admiralty, nor shall I always be. The Captains and the Kings depart, but the cat is, philosophically speaking, always on the mat. *(To FERRERS.)* I have an unsurpassed knowledge of them, and if a group of old women told me I was wrong and that I must re-examine all my data and rewrite all my monographs on the subject, I should tell them – I should neglect their advice. But there is one lady with whom I conduct what may be called a feline correspondence and whose opinion I respect. If she were to tell me I was wrong in some particular, I should not rest until I had, so to speak, re-examined and perhaps reconstructed my whole feline theory. You get my drift, Ferrers?

FERRERS: I'll consent to anything. If only you'll leave me alone. What is it you want, sir?

FIRST LORD: Nothing but this: your undertaking to go into Miss Selby's case with an open mind. *(Shrewdly.)* You might, meanwhile, reposition the detonator mechanism.

FLAG CAPTAIN: What does this mean? You don't intend to go on!

FIRST LORD: Certainly.

FLAG CAPTAIN: With Ferrers in this state?

FIRST LORD: I had a friend once. He was a great artist. His canvas was burned. That night he was mad – like a child with fever. Next morning, he began to paint again.

FLAG CAPTAIN: But this needs a decision of the Board of the Admiralty as a whole.

FIRST LORD: It does.

FLAG CAPTAIN: Wedgcroft won't stand for it.

FIRST LORD: *(Stern.)* No? I must ask him to breakfast. *(Silky again.)* If Admiral Helston sees fit to write amendments to his report, I will countersign them. There should be no great difficulty. You are with me, Admiral?

ADMIRAL: I am responsible on the spot, sir. We are working in the dark. If a new series of experiments were to fail, what answer could I give?

FLAG CAPTAIN: It's we who should be blamed. The naval members of the Board won't put up with it.

ADMIRAL: I agree, Winter. We've gone too far. *(To FIRST LORD.)* I can't go back, sir.

FIRST LORD: Admiral Helston –

ADMIRAL: I can't go back, sir. It's no longer a technical question with me. It's a question of character.

FLAG CAPTAIN: Character, after all, is more important than brains.

FIRST LORD: How many battles have been lost under that motto!

ADMIRAL: I'm a plain seaman, sir. I have made my report. I stand by it.

FIRST LORD: Very well. Then, Admiral, I accept your report. It shall be pigeonholed with honour. Your brother-in-law will respect you for it. And I shall overrule it… Now, we shall be late at Flag Point. *(ADMIRAL and FLAG CAPTAIN go out C. To CARR.)* You have a car? Why don't you three officers come with us? *(SANDFORD and CARR go out C.)* Mr Brissing will show me his bougainvilleas as we go… Miss Selby?

KAREN: I'd rather stay.

FIRST LORD: Goodbye, then *(They shake hands.)* You have deserved your privilege. *(FERRERS, who is wishing only to be alone, has turned away. FIRST LORD approaches him as if to say goodbye, but decides to leave him.)* Well, we shall meet again. *(BRISSING picks up FIRST LORD's hat and stick. FIRST LORD moves to table and leaves his pipe on it; then takes BRISSING with him through door. As he goes:)* Burgundy will have to wait, but good wine matures in bottle.

FERRERS: Why didn't you tell me? You must have known long, long ago. You spoke of it to them as if it were a slip in the arithmetic. The correction to K! *(She tries to speak.)* You knew well enough. 'Very deep', you said. Very deep! I should think so! If that's wrong, everything that depends on it is utterly wrong. It can't be put right. That old fool goes off saying he'll give me time. He can give me eternity. The whole thing falls down. *(Rises and crosses to C.)*

KAREN: Listen to me.

FERRERS: The calculations locked! Madness and sanity are intersecting circles. Now they run together. The corrections to K belong to the early groups, and after that everything locked!

KAREN: Stop. For one minute stop and listen to me.

FERRERS: *(To end of settee.)* Proofs are not proofs. Certainty isn't certainty. Mathematics do lie. They lie and deceive like human beings.

KAREN: *(Kneels, her arms round FERRERS.)* I was lying then.

FERRERS: Nothing is absolute. *(Looking at her.)* Nothing is true. *(Thrusting her away from him. Very quietly.)* Who are you? Why are you kneeling there? Sometimes, when you are awake in bed, thinking, between waking and sleeping, your thought runs quieter and quieter, like a flashing stream, like truth itself without reason, and you glide down that stream knowing that at the end of it – then suddenly there's a click of your mind, the shutter of a camera, and it's all gone – all gone – all gone – and the little rat Reason is gnawing inside your head again.

KAREN: Come back. Come back!

FERRERS: Who are you? Why are you kneeling there? There was a madman once who wrote – do you remember? –

'If ever in my solitary room
I in an ecstasy should lie
And God's own touch have put my Fool to sleep,

Out of his sleep, my aching Fool would cry
"Ask: where is truth?" and I should ask and creep
Out of my vision into Reason's gloom.'

(A triumphant cry.) He was happy, the man who wrote that!
He knew how the world spins! *(Enter FIRST LORD.) (In
a changed voice – a man waking.)* What is it? Who is that?
(Seizing her hands.) Karen, speak to me.

FIRST LORD: *(Appearing C.)* I came back for my pipe. I think I
left it. *(Moves towards table.)*

FERRERS: *(Recognizing him.)* I thought you had gone to
England.

FIRST LORD: To England! *(Perceiving that something desperate is
wrong. To KAREN.)* What is it?

KAREN: I don't know yet.

FERRERS: *(Almost back again from the place to which he has been.)*
The old cove has lost his pipe. Where is it?

FIRST LORD: I presume you were lying, Miss Selby?

KAREN: When did you know?

FIRST LORD: A little before you began.

KAREN: What was it Pompey said to Menas in the galley?

FIRST LORD: 'In me, 'tis villainy; in thee, it *has* been good
service.'

FERRERS: Lying? About what?

FIRST LORD: There was no mistake in your calculations,
Ferrers.

FERRERS: I know that… Oh, I remember, I remember, I
remember. *(To KAREN.)* You said there was. Why did you
say that? If I had believed you, it would have driven me
mad. *(Enter BRISSING.)*

BRISSING: The Admiral suggests, sir, that if you have found
your pipe, as Flag Point is some distance away –

FIRST LORD: Did he suggest it as courteously as that? *(To
KAREN.)* Statesmen and women, my dear Miss Selby,
must do what they can to save men of genius from men of
character. *(He kisses her hand. Goes out, preceded by BRISSING.)*

FERRERS: Now the old boy has said his piece, we can get on.

KAREN: My dear, rest a little.

FERRERS: Rest? Why?

KAREN: Because, very nearly, you have been –

FERRERS: What? Mad? Odd you should say that, there was a click in my mind, like the shutter of a camera. And a stream flashing. *(A sharp order.)* Get Sandford back. *(She does not move. He takes her hand.)* Thank you, my dear. I know. *(As she makes no answer, he looks up and finds her gazing at him.)* What is it?

KAREN: You said 'Thank you'. You said 'I know'. What did you know? *(He hesitates.)* Say it. Please say it.

FERRERS: When I shook, you held steady. When I failed, you did not despise me. That's a new world for me.

KAREN: At last!

FERRERS: Not a god.

KAREN: Like a boy with sunstroke.

FERRERS: Not your master.

KAREN: Always; but then – sleep.

FERRERS: *(Slowly, looking into her with profound curiosity.)* I have never seen you asleep. The battle goes out of people then. *(Suddenly, like a pistol.)* I love you, Karen. I love *you.*

KAREN: I love you with all my heart. *(He takes her in his arms, never moving his eyes from her face, but does not kiss her. She shows him her key.)* Tell me something. Is this mine now?

FERRERS: Will you have it?

KAREN: Yes, please… Please God. To have and to hold.

FERRERS: And don't leave it sculling about. *(Her hands and all her strength close over it.)* Karen, who was it who said: 'My head, My head.' I've heard it somewhere.

KAREN: It was the Shunnamite's boy in the Bible. He had sunstroke.

FERRERS: *(Without personal application.)* He was raised from the dead… Get Sandford back.

KAREN: What for?

FERRERS: Detonator design. It's all we need. The rest is safe, but we need that. We must drop that spindle, Karen. Back to your brother's gyro and work up from there.

Curtain.

THE RIVER LINE

'We must act like men who have the enemy at their gates, and at the same time like men who are working for eternity.'

MAZZINI, *during the Defence of Rome, 1849*

Introduction

For many years I kept press cutting books – reviews of plays and films I was in, (some good, some bad!) I never look at them. But, when I had a letter from James Hogan at Oberon Books telling me they were going to publish Charles Morgan's plays, I went to the shelf and got down two ancient blue books of 1952, and leafed through the faded cuttings with a huge wave of nostalgia. There it was, *The River Line*.

How could I have been so lucky? To be in a play by the renowned Charles Morgan, and be on stage with some of England's finest actors, Paul Scofield, Pamela Brown, Marjorie Fielding, Michael Goodliffe, Robert Hardy, John Westbrook and the American actor Phil Burgess.

Our director was the brilliant Michael Macowan. Looking back, in as detached a way as I can, I think it was a play that needed a director of his calibre. It is a play on several levels, with many layers of subtext, many moments left hanging for the audience to complete. It is literary, but charged with emotion. Complex but intensely direct. Piercing you sometimes with what is not said.

For my own part, the role of Valerie was quite a challenge for someone so inexperienced. Her character is a binding thread that connects a world she has not been physically a part of, 'The River Line' in occupied France, and the post-war world set in an English country house, where some of the characters re-live and struggle to lay to rest memories that have continued to torment them. In a way she is 'the still small voice of calm'.

We opened at the Edinburgh Festival, transferred to The Lyric, Hammersmith and then to the Strand Theatre. Most critics admired it and praised it. Some – a few – felt it was 'unplayable'. But play it we did, and the theatre was always full.

So long ago and memories fade, but I have the copy of the play personally signed to me by Charles Morgan, and his kind and generous words still warm my heart.

Thanks to Oberon Books his works will, I hope, be lifted from the library shelves and be brought to life on stage, to fascinate and intrigue us, and set us thinking and questioning once more.

Virginia McKenna, 2013

If I but had the eyes and ears
To read within what now appears,
Then should I see in every face
An innocent, interior grace,
And, as the clouds of thought unfurled,
Be native of the golden world.

For not by thought shall I acquire
Re-entrance to my heart's desire,
Nor as a ticket-tourist come
Out of exile to my own home.

All things that are of Earth or Hell
We gain or lose and buy or sell,
But Heaven's deep-enclosed delight
Is an hereditary right
Which this man's lust nor that man's hate
Nor my cold sin can alienate,
But lives my own, when all else dies,
Within my blood, within my eyes:
So true it is that my dis-Grace
Is absence from my Native Place.

Characters

Scenes

Act I

Scene 1: The garden of the Wyburtons' house in Gloucestershire. A Friday in July 1947. Before dinner.

Scene 2: The same. After dinner

Act II

Scene 1: The granary of the Chassaignes' house at Blaise in the neighbourhood of Toulouse. July 1943. 11.50 p.m.

Scene 2: The same. Twelve days later. Nearly 9.30 p.m.

Scene 3: The same. Three minutes to midnight.

Act III

Scene 1: As in Act I. July 1947. The next morning, Saturday.

Scene 2: The same. That evening.

STRAND THEATRE

LONDON

| Proprietors | - | - | - | SEND MANOR TRUST LTD. |
| Licensee and Director - | | - | - | - LIONEL L. FALCK |

EVENINGS AT 7.30
MATINEES: THURSDAY AND SATURDAY at 2.30

By arrangement with LIONEL FALCK
and STEPHEN MITCHELL

TENNENT PRODUCTIONS Ltd.

present

| **PAMELA** | **PHIL** |
| **BROWN** | **BROWN** |

in

THE RIVER LINE 6ᴰ

by CHARLES MORGAN

❧

Directed by MICHAEL MACOWAN

First Performance at the Strand Theatre on Tuesday, October 28th, 1952

PROGRAMME

From the programme of *The River Line* 28 October 1952

By arrangement with LIONEL FALCK
and STEPHEN MITCHELL
TENNENT PRODUCTIONS Ltd.

present

THE RIVER LINE

by CHARLES MORGAN

Characters in order of appearance:

Philip Sturgess (*an American*)   ...   **PHIL BROWN**

Commander Julian Wyburton (*R.N., Retd.*)
                            MICHAEL GOODLIFFE

Marie Chassaigne (*Mrs. Wyburton*)
                            PAMELA BROWN

Mrs. Muriven (*Valerie's Godmother*)
                        MARJORIE FIELDING

Valerie Barton   ...   ...   **VIRGINIA McKENNA**

Major John Lang (*called " Heron "*)
                        JOHN WESTBROOK

Dick Frewer   ...   .   **ROBERT HARDY**

Pierre Chassaigne   ...   ... **MARCEL PONCIN**

Directed by MICHAEL MACOWAN

Settings by ALAN TAGG
Costumes by MOTLEY

From the programme of *The River Line* 28 October 1952

ACT I

Scene 1. The garden of the Wyburtons' house in Gloucestershire.
July, 1947. Before dinner.

Scene 2. The same. After dinner.

ACT II

Scene 1 The granary of the Chassaignes' house at Blaise in the
neighbourhood of Toulouse. July, 1943. 11.50 p.m.

Scene 2. The same. Twelve days later. 9.30 p.m.

Scene 3. The same. Three minutes to midnight.

ACT III

Scene 1. As Act I. July, 1947. The next morning.

Scene 2. The same. That evening.

There will be two intervals of 10 minutes each

Scenery built by Stage Decor Ltd. Painted by Hubert. Ladies'
dresses designed by Motley and executed by Elizabeth Curzon
Ltd. Miss McKenna's dress in Act I by Frederick Starke Ltd.
Miss McKenna's shoes by Dolcis. Men's costumes by M. Berman
Ltd. Wardrobe care by Lux. Garden furniture by G. W. Scott.
Electrical equipment by the Strand Electric & Engineering
Co. Ltd. Properties by Robinson Bros. (Jewellers) Ltd.
Nylon stockings by Kayser-Bondor. Lighters by Ronson.
Cigarettes by Du Maurier.

General Manager	... BERNARD GORDON
Manager and Stage Director	... RUPERT MARSH
Stage Manager	... ... GWEN HILL
Assistant Stage Manager	ROSEMARY WEBSTER
Productions Manager	... ... IAN DOW
Chief Engineer	... JOE DAVIS
Chief Wardrobe Supervisor	... LILY TAYLOR
Press Representative	VIVIENNE BYERLEY
	(Gerrard 3681)

(For Tennent Productions Ltd.)

Manager for Strand Theatre.. .. .. JOHN HOLLINGSHEAD

Box Office (W. Hammond) .. .. Temple Bar 2660 and 4143

**OPERA GLASSES. Please do not forget to replace hired opera
glasses, or hand them to the attendants.**

In the interest of Public Health this theatre is disinfected exclusively with **Jeyes' Fluid**

The River Line by Charles Morgan was revived on 4 October 2011 at Jermyn Street Theatre with the following cast:

PHILIP STURGRESS	Edmund Kingsley
COMMANDER JULIAN WYBURTON, R.N.	Christopher Fulford
MARIE CHASSAIGNE	Lyne Renée
MRS. MURIVEN	Eileen Page
VALERIE BARTON	Lydia Rose Bewley
MAJOR JOHN LANG (HERON)	Charlie Bewley
DICK FREWER	Alex Felton
PIERRE CHASSAIGNE	Dave Hill

Directed by Anthony Biggs
Designed by Rhiannon Newman Brown
Lighting design by David W Kidd
Sound design by Phil Hewitt

ACT ONE

A quiet summer's evening, July 1947. Friday. A little before dinner. Full sunlight. A part of the lawn outside the drawing room of the Wyburtons' house, called Stanning Farm, in Gloucestershire. It was formerly a Dower House. Period: early eighteenth century.

The lawn is part of a plateau or ledge, looking out over two converging valleys. We are looking South by East; a few small tree-tops appearing above our upstage horizon and a tranquil, open sky, which the sun will paint gradually, give an impression of falling ground. To the South-West (up-Right) is the beginning of a wood through the branches of which, if the electrician has adequate resources, the sun may appear gleamingly, and in the recesses of which, as time goes on, owls may, perhaps, profitably hoot.

On our Left is a part of the west end of the house, the main façade of which is invisible round our up-Left corner, for the house's 'aspect' is S.S.E. What we see is the end of the drawing room. There are pleasant twelve-paned windows, through which, when necessary, light will shine out on to the lawn, and a door, now open on to the garden, with perhaps a pair of steps. This wall must be set far enough across to give us a glimpse of pictures and furniture and an active sense of there being a domestic interior.

The lawn can be as simple as the designer pleases. The essentials are: Near the house, to Left of Centre and two-thirds upstage, a table with garden chairs, a stool, and perhaps a lilo. These must appear to be 'inhabited'; books, papers, a sun-hat, a rug, are lying about. Farther downstage and to Right of Centre is an immovable seat, large enough for three, comfortable for two, preferably an eighteenth-century stone seat with a curving back. Its position is important. It is far enough from the table-group to separate (at any rate by convention) two conversations, but not so far as to give the impression that those who choose the stone seat are deliberately isolating themselves. It is easy to talk across the gap. Therefore the seat faces not straight downstage but N.N.E. Those who sit in it look out, clear of the line of the drawing– room wall, over a

rolling countryside into the backward stage-box on the audience's Left,
but if they glance over their right shoulders they take in the table-group.

When the Curtain rises, PHILIP STURGESS, an American about thirty
years old, an alive, cultivated, intelligent New Englander, who will
sometimes use a Middle West accent to amuse his hosts, is wearing a
dinner-jacket. Looks at the view, upstage with his back to us, over U/L
wall.

JULIAN WYBURTON, a hard-bitten naval commander also in a dinner-
jacket, comes in from the drawing room with a silver cigarette box in
his hand.

JULIAN: *(Looking at PHILIP and in a mocking, affectionate tone.)*
Silent upon a peak in Darien!

PHILIP: *(Rousing himself.)* I prefer Gloucestershire. These
valleys take some beating, though we have some in Maine.

JULIAN: You're down early. I shall have to desert you. Tucker
has a natural genius for ruining wine if you let him touch
it. I have left the sherry in the drawing room. Ladies may
want it there. Help yourself when you feel like it.

PHILIP: *(Grinning, and stretching himself luxuriously like a happy
schoolboy.)* I always have been early for exciting parties. I
like to sit and feel them coming.

JULIAN: *(Pleased and kindly.)* Is this to be such an exciting
party?

PHILIP: For me it is – as you know. I can't be grateful
enough to you and Marie. I owed you plenty before this,
God knows. Now if things go well – *(This seriousness is
embarrassing to JULIAN and he turns it.)*

JULIAN: My dear Philip, Marie and I didn't create the young
woman.

PHILIP: You invited her here the night I came.

JULIAN: Not for your sweet sake. We had never seen her in
our lives before. She just happened to be staying with Mrs.
Muriven.

PHILIP: I like the old lady too.

JULIAN: The Iron Duke? I wonder whether, as a hopeful
idealist, you ought to like her. She doesn't mince her

thoughts… Take a drink when you want it. I'll go and carry
up the rest… Cigarettes in the box. Yours in fact. We live
on what you brought from America. *(And he makes off.)*

PHILIP: *(Checking his exit.)* Julian!

JULIAN: What?

PHILIP: About what you call 'the young woman'. About
Valerie Barton. Tell me. Do you think I'm a fool?

JULIAN: Why should I?

PHILIP: Maybe I am. Eight days isn't long. Still, I have to go
back home. Valerie is going to South Africa, I gather. You
see, Julian –

JULIAN: Now don't start reasoning it out. Your countrymen, I
grant you, sometimes take a bit long in starting across the
Atlantic, but, when you do come, you don't waste time – in
love or war. Eight days, eight hours, eight seconds – quite
long enough to fall in love. Hence the word 'fall'.

PHILIP: Maybe she doesn't see it that way… But certainly we
have talked a lot.

JULIAN: No doubt you have. *(He is moving off into the drawing
room again, when he turns suddenly and asks in a hard, changed
voice.)* What about? *(PHILIP looks up, startled by the question,
and JULIAN repeats – an insistent staccato, separating his words.)*
What have you talked about?

PHILIP: What on earth do you mean? What should we talk
about? Ourselves mostly. Her childhood in the North
somewhere. She had a brother she likes to talk of. My
childhood, too. *(Apologetically.)* One does, you know. My
home in Maine. My job as a teacher. The chance of a
professorship at Harvard – a good outside chance anyway
– which might mean –

JULIAN: Not about the River Line?

PHILIP: She knows of course that you and Marie and I met in
occupied France. Not much more, surprisingly enough.

JULIAN: Why 'surprisingly'?

PHILIP: *(With easy good-humour.)* Well, I know I talk. I dare say
you and Marie have found me a bit of an old soldier with

my tales of battles long ago. But to Valerie, not much about war. Maybe she's had enough of it. It was two years longer for you British.

JULIAN: I shouldn't let that deter you. Othello used to charm Desdemona with talk of battles. Recognized technique.

PHILIP: Why so bitter, Julian?

JULIAN: I'm not. Just interested. It beats me why you *want* to talk of the River Line at all. Why do you?

PHILIP: That's a fair question. I'm not sure I know the answer... Partly that I was responsible for what happened... Or shall we say: One adventure in a calm scholastic life? The only time I've ever put my neck out. I'm sorry, I can't help it. For you and Marie it's different. You are professionals; I'm an amateur. You, as a naval officer first of all, and –

JULIAN: A much safer job than a schoolmaster's, I promise you. At least the Navy is not co-educational.

PHILIP: And a secret agent's? Are you going to pretend that's peaceful too?

JULIAN: Tediously celibate.

PHILIP: You laugh everything away... Tell me, how many men – and women – have you seen killed, Julian? I mean, killed...privately, apart from battle? *(This is the kind of question JULIAN hates.)*

JULIAN: Good God, what a question! I've always been taught that it's rude to count.

PHILIP: Well, I have seen one.

JULIAN: And that makes you want to talk about it.

PHILIP: Does that surprise you?

JULIAN: Only that I can't imagine it in myself. I couldn't tell that story if I wanted to. *(He is speaking now with a steely restraint which is very like contempt, half-angry, half-mocking.)* When you tell 'the River Line Story' in America what on earth *do* you say?

PHILIP: Come, Julian, you're on edge. *(Rising.)* Let me come down and help you carry up the wine.

JULIAN: There's time enough for that. I want to know how you begin.

PHILIP: *(Humouring him.)* You want me to do penance. Very well. What I say is this. Maybe, folks, you heard about the River Line? *(He is caricaturing himself now and using an exaggerated American accent.)* It was a set-up for helpin' our fliers get home when they'd been shot down. I was one of 'em. We were handed on from post to post, through Belgium, through France, into Spain – home that way. We were rafts towed down the River Line, you might say; or – *(No accent.)* Isn't that harmless enough?

JULIAN: As far as it goes. I didn't know you could speak Chicago.

PHILIP: It isn't Chicago. It's pure tall corn out of Iowa. Do I continue the performance?

JULIAN: Yes, please. It's the end that matters.

PHILIP: *(The exaggerated accent again.)* Well, boys, as I was tellin' you, on the way south – it was the last lap before the Spanish frontier –

JULIAN: Do you give the names of the places?

PHILIP: *(No accent.)* I have said Blaise.

JULIAN: Blaise is no matter. Marie was captured. She's hopelessly compromised. She could never go back anyhow.

PHILIP: Go back! Do you…the war's over, Julian.

JULIAN: Wars crop up, you know… Well, go on. You were saying: 'It was the last lap before the Spanish frontier'. What do you say then?

PHILIP: Julian, what *is* this?

JULIAN: I want to know what *you* say.

PHILIP: *(Sharply, for he is being sorely tried. No accent now. Very fast.)* Alright – I say: Marie was in charge of us. We lay up in her father's house. Three of us at first – a boy called

Dick; a fellow with long thin legs we nicknamed Heron, and myself. One night, Marie brought in another Britisher, Julian –

JULIAN: Or Wyburton?

PHILIP: Julian.

JULIAN: Are you sure of that?

PHILIP: I think of you that way. I've always called you that way. Dead sure.

JULIAN: Good. Not that it really matters. My cat is out of the bag.

PHILIP: Now can I come out of the corner. *(JULIAN, for a moment, grasps his arm, then lets it go.)* You know, Julian, if I do tell that story – or try to... *(Then he begins again.)* The facts, yes, but they don't mean anything apart from the extraordinary peace of that damned comfortless granary. And Heron, right up to the end, was the heart of it. I still have the feel of that – our group of five, bound together then and bound together still. Not only we three survivors but all five, the dead and the living, still bound together in spite of what happened –

JULIAN: Or because of it.

PHILIP: But you hate to speak of it.

JULIAN: Of the River Line? I don't hate to speak of it with you. But it's hard to speak of it without speaking of Heron, and in this house –

PHILIP: Isn't it best to speak of him quite simply and openly? What was done had to be done. *(JULIAN looks into his face and says nothing. Then:)*

JULIAN: I never speak of him to Marie or she to me... No doubt you'll tell me that is wrong psychologically. But I tell you it is necessary.

PHILIP: Because – I can say this to you, Julian – because at that time she loved Heron? *(This is true and JULIAN knows it, but it is so far from being his reason for not speaking of HERON to his wife that he is, for a moment, taken aback. Then he accepts it.)*

JULIAN: That reason will do as well as another.

PHILIP: But it is true.

JULIAN: Oh yes, it's true enough. *(They are side by side, looking out over the valley, in the open door of the drawing room MARIE now appears. She is in a simple evening dress, carrying a tray with decanter and glasses.)*

MARIE: You are very silent.

JULIAN: *(Turning.)* You dressed? What time is it?

MARIE: They may be here in a few minutes. The Iron Duke is dangerously punctual.

JULIAN: I still have the wine to do.

MARIE: Good heavens, but it will be ruined! At this hour – Musigny!

JULIAN: It was decanted long ago. It only needs carrying up.

MARIE: Well, my darling… *(Meaning: 'Well, for heaven's sake, fetch it!')*

JULIAN: Take warning, Philip. Never marry a Frenchwoman. They have a taste in wine. Even your cellar isn't your own. *(Exit D/R.)*

MARIE: *(Pouring out sherry.)* No cocktails. Better keep to the grape when it's good. Is that all right?

PHILIP: Perfect.

MARIE: Happy?

PHILIP: Very.

MARIE: On a summer's evening, looking down that valley – this must be a good place to be happy in.

PHILIP: Must be? Aren't you happy too?

MARIE: In some ways I am. Did you doubt it?

PHILIP: I confess I did before I came.

MARIE: *(With a candid non-egotism that is part of her character.)* It surprises me a little that in America you should have troubled your head about me.

PHILIP: But, Marie, it stands to reason I'm grateful –

MARIE: No, Philip, don't say what you were going to say. Blaise was…a Service incident like another.

PHILIP: Ah, you and Julian, the French and the English of your kind, you take a professional and Service view of everything.

MARIE: Is that wrong?

PHILIP: Well, I believe it's limiting. The world has to think in terms of peace or it won't have peace. Sometimes I feel with you and Julian as if you felt that the war was still going on. And so you won't talk about it. You behave as if heroism were not heroism, as if feeling were not felt. *(She flinches in protest.)* Oh, I know you *do* feel, all right. But you won't ever acknowledge it. You clip yourselves into your professional reticences as if they were a suit of armour that won't let you breathe –

MARIE: *(With emphasis.)* Or go limp.

PHILIP: But why can't you relax? Isn't it an affectation not to?

MARIE: *(With a shrug.)* A habit. A valuable one, perhaps, never, as Julian says, 'to spill over'. Aren't there enough people spilling enthusiasm and grievances in this world?… No, Philip, I see your point. But don't forget that at Blaise I was the postman and you were the parcels. You will agree that it is desirable for a postman to train himself to think impersonally of his parcels… As you know, I didn't always succeed.

PHILIP: You mean Heron?… Tell me, Marie, straight out now; you would rather I didn't speak of him?

MARIE: *(With difficulty.)* I would rather you didn't when Julian is here… But now you and I are alone, and Julian needn't be…wounded – yes, it would be a relief, from silence, to hear you speak of him to me. Don't think, dear Philip, that there is…anything wrong with my marriage – except certain silences. Julian and I love each other with all our hearts – across the silence. Heron is long dead. Is it four years?… And when one whom we have loved, however silently, is dead, all account of him from those who were with him when we were not is precious, seeming – oh, how would you say that in English? I say it so stiffly…seeming to extend his life in our memory which cannot now be extended in our experience.

PHILIP: I dream of Heron often, particularly since I've been your guest in this house.

MARIE: This house is full of him.

PHILIP: Dream and memory get mixed up. In the morning I'm never sure which is which. Last night in my dream I was back in a little dark room in Brussels where Heron and Frewer and I were first brought together – where, so to speak, the River Line began. The little grey man in charge there was cross-examining us and explaining and explaining how careful he had to be. He was terrified that a German agent might introduce himself into the line and be forwarded down it from stage to stage and then mop up the *whole* Line. In fact, he explained this to us quite calmly, but in my dream he was wild with terror. He kept on saying 'un faux Anglais, a sham Englishman, a sham Englishman – that is what we have most to fear', and in my dream, as he said this, he kept on looking at Heron –

MARIE: *(In agony, stopping him.)* Ah, Philip, Philip – no.

PHILIP: But I must tell you this, because whenever I dream of Heron it's always the same. I looked across the table at Heron and what I saw wasn't just his appearance but the essential character of him: not just his tallness and erectness and his way of carrying himself that made us call him Heron, but a kind of *movement* upward so that, in some extraordinary way, you felt that he was, physically…light?

MARIE: *(Primly because she is deeply moved.)* That is exact. Light. Not burdened. Not tethered. Light. That is…exact.

PHILIP: I believe it was that more than anything which made Dick Frewer and me…love him the way we did. Certainly it was that which prevented me from putting two and two together about him. I ought to have known. All along the line there were indications. He took French stamps out of a desk, and once he bought French stamps. What could a genuine Englishman want with French stamps? There was the incident with the German corporal. There were lots and lots of little things. Above all that he spoke the German of a German, and, for Frewer's benefit and mine, made a kind of comedy out of the way he led them up the garden path.

MARIE: Was it the fact of his being so proud of his German that first made you suspect him? Wasn't his German the very thing that, as an enemy agent, he would have soft-pedalled?

PHILIP: Not necessarily. Not on the principle of a double-bluff… But, Marie, I didn't suspect him until the last moment. You must understand that. I dare say I ought to have. The indications were all there. I dare say I was hopelessly guileless or 'unprofessional' if you like, but it's true: all the way from Brussels to Blaise, and for all the time we spent in your granary, I didn't suspect him. If I had, I should have found a way to tell you and Julian sooner…

MARIE: But why are you defending yourself? I'm not blaming you, God knows.

PHILIP: But you think I was unprofessional. *(MARIE makes a little helpless gesture at this misunderstanding.)* You must understand. In spite of all the indications I didn't *consciously* suspect. To me it simply wasn't credible that Heron was false. I loved talking to him. I loved being with him. I was thinking all the time of the personal relationship. I let all the indications go – there they were, but I let them go, until, at the very end, they rushed together and… became…certainty. You see, Marie –

MARIE: Philip, please, please get it out of your head that I am blaming you. It's all over. I'm not even accusing you of professional neglect.

PHILIP: What then, Marie? Something – not Heron's death only, but something else is troubling you. *(JULIAN appears from D/R.)* What is it?

MARIE: *(Seeing JULIAN.)* Is everything set? The wine, I mean?

JULIAN: You speak as if a dinner-party were a military operation. I suppose it is to the French. The ammunition is beside the gun. *(He looks out upstage.)* There are our guests.

MARIE: On foot?

JULIAN: Half way across the field. *(PHILIP too looks out eagerly.)* You'd better go and meet them, Philip.

PHILIP: I doubt that.

JULIAN: *(His arm on MARIE's shoulder.)* Why are you on edge? You've been talking too much or listening too much.

MARIE: I shall be all right… I get tired, quite suddenly, but it goes. *(She sits.)* Oh I wish that part of my pleasure in every pleasant thing – in just sitting here and being peaceful – weren't the negative joy of its not being hell. *(She reaches for JULIAN's hand.)* You and I shall have that all our lives. To live with the feeling that happiness is exceptional – something momentarily allowed. That's the difference between you and us, Philip. That's the answer to your question: 'why not relax?' We have lived all our lives on a campaign or between campaigns. All Europeans of our age have and – Sorry, Julian.

JULIAN: Meanwhile we farm our land, my dear.

MARIE: Yes – but 'meanwhile' … No, I'm sorry. Take no notice of me. Go and meet them, Philip.

PHILIP: Take it easy, Marie. *(Begins to go off U/R.)*

JULIAN: *(Steadying her.)* 'For, if thou rest not, busy maggots eat thy brain, and all is dedicate to chaos.'

PHILIP: *(Turning.)* Who wrote that?

JULIAN: That? Oh, it applies to all of us, not to Marie only: to the hopeful idealists as well. 'O proud, impatient Man –' You know it?

'O proud, impatient Man, allow to Earth
Her seasons. Growth and change require their winter
As a tired child his sleep. Thou art that child;
Lie down. This is the night. Day follows soon.
Wake then refreshed, wiser for having slept.

This is old nurses' counsel, and the gods',

For, if thou rest not, busy maggots eat

Thy brain, and all is dedicate to chaos.'

MARIE: That, I suppose, is what Heron meant by 'a creative pause'.

PHILIP: I thought you were a naval officer. How do you memorize these things? That ought to be my job.

JULIAN: Oh, we got leave you know… Besides, memory is my vice. In my job, one doesn't carry things in writing. *(PHILIP goes. They are silent until he is gone.)*

JULIAN: Was he talking of Heron?

MARIE: I let him… It's you I love, Julian.

JULIAN: Yes, my darling, I know. *(A distant knock is heard.)*

MARIE: *(Rising.)* They are at the front door.

JULIAN: Yes. Stay here peacefully until they come. Philip will bring them through. *(The knock is repeated.)*

MARIE: I hate the sound of knocking at the door. *(She links her arm in his and holds it closely.)*

Curtain.

SCENE 2

The same, after dinner. On the wall U/R is an unlighted lamp. As it is summer-time, there is plenty of daylight left, but the producer can do what he likes with the sunset as time passes. When the Curtain rises the stage is empty and the windows are dark. Movement is visible inside and the women's voices are heard. Enter from the drawing room MARIE, followed by MRS. MURIVEN and VALERIE.

MARIE: I don't think we should be cold out here. But you decide, Mrs. Muriven, please.

MRS. MURIVEN: I wouldn't dream of sitting anywhere else. It is an enchanting evening. I have arranged with the sun not to set at present. To sit out after dinner in England is an extremely rare luxury. Let us indulge in it until it is taken from us.

VALERIE: It isn't one that any Government is likely to take away.

MRS. MURIVEN: I am not sure, Valerie. Nature is by no means egalitarian; the sun often shines on the Riviera when there is a fog in Merthyr Tydfil. That cannot be described as social justice.

MARIE: If you are comfortable and will forgive me I will go and fetch coffee.

VALERIE: Let me help.

MARIE: No, please. It is a secret ritual.

MRS. MURIVEN: *(Cheerfully grumpy.)* Why do you and Julian do so much of your servant's work?

MARIE: We do it so much better. *(Exit.)*

VALERIE: Godmother, how could you ask that?

MRS. MURIVEN: I? Oh, I can ask anything. I knew Julian's mother before he was born. I must be allowed to poke fun at his wife. But how she can cook!… I like your American, my dear.

VALERIE: Mine?

MRS. MURIVEN: That was the word I used.

VALERIE: I thought he talked well at dinner.

MRS. MURIVEN: I found that he listened well. A gift I appreciate more… Still, I should like to have drawn him about the River Line.

VALERIE: Some of that I *have* heard.

MRS. MURIVEN: I got only bits and pieces.

VALERIE: He puts them together like a jig-saw puzzle – as if he weren't sure of the answer himself.

MRS. MURIVEN: Julian and Marie don't give him much chance on that subject.

VALERIE: Oh?… Why do you say that?

MRS. MURIVEN: Twice at dinner, they – in effect – stopped him. The first time, Julian switched the conversation away; the second time, Marie rose from table and swept out, taking poor Mr. Sturgess's audience with her. It seemed odd to me. I was enjoying my pear.

VALERIE: Why should it be 'odd'? Isn't it only that they don't want to talk of war?

MRS. MURIVEN: I may be wrong, though that, in the nature of things, is improbable. But the two of them always refuse at the same fence. Has Mr. Sturgess talked to you of the man they called Heron?

VALERIE: A little. He often begins to talk about him. He seems to want to. Then he stops.

MRS. MURIVEN: Why does he stop – even to you?

VALERIE: I believe he's not sure of his own story.

MRS. MURIVEN: But he was there!

VALERIE: Oh yes, he was there.

MRS. MURIVEN: Julian and Marie are sure enough. But I repeat: they always refuse at the same fence.

VALERIE: How you love a mystery!

MRS. MURIVEN: On the contrary, a mystery is precisely what I don't love. If I am suddenly whisked away from the dinner-table before I have finished my desert, I like to know, quite clearly, why.

VALERIE: *(After a pause and a movement, during which MARIE appears with the coffee tray.)* You never will, dear Godmother, until you have solved the mystery of sudden death. *(MARIE stands quite still. VALERIE sees her.)* I'm sorry. I suppose that doesn't make sense. I had jumped off down a side-track from something Godmother was saying. I mean: one supposes that certain things won't happen to oneself. We have an idea that *we* are exempt. Even from death. It's against reason that we should be, but I believe that in our heart of hearts we are all incredulous.

MARIE: *(Very low but very distinctly and meditatively.)* Incredulous?

VALERIE: – of death, seen in the distance.

MARIE: Why only 'in the distance'?

VALERIE: Isn't it so?

MARIE: Why 'in the distance' only. Seen close. Seen close. That is the very word – incredulous! *(She is seeing the face of HERON as he died. Now, swiftly pulling herself together, she puts down the tray.)* Coffee? … *(To MRS. MURIVEN.)* Black or white?

MRS. MURIVEN: Black, please.

VALERIE: *(In answer to a glance.)* And for me. *(PHILIP arrives from U/R. While he is being given coffee –)*

MARIE: Is Julian on his way?

VALERIE: *(Who has wandered upstage and has been looking out over the countryside and is now returned.)* This must be one of the pleasantest views in England, whichever way you look. It's like being in a huge armchair looking over the two valleys. *(To MRS. MURIVEN.)* I'm glad you have told the sun not to set.

PHILIP: You said that in a very melancholy way.

VALERIE: Did I? This is one of my last evenings in England.

PHILIP: But your passage hasn't come through?

VALERIE: It may at any moment now.

PHILIP: You aren't looking forward to South Africa.

VALERIE: In a way, I am. My brother needs me there. Anyhow I look forward to the voyage. The trouble is that nowadays no voyage is long enough. What I should really like is to go round the world in a sailing-ship – no newspaper, no wireless, a little plain company – not too much – and all the books I want to read again.

PHILIP: Again? No new books?

VALERIE: Those as well, I suppose.

PHILIP: And what did you mean by *plain* company?

VALERIE: Seamen, doctors, soldiers – people getting on with their own jobs – does that seem dull?

PHILIP: Not if it includes schoolmasters.

VALERIE: By no means all!

PHILIP: One would do. Where do I find a sailing-ship?

MARIE: Dear Philip, what on earth are you talking about?

MRS. MURIVEN: I think he was planning to elope with my god-daughter in a seven-masted schooner.

PHILIP: I hope you approve?

MRS. MURIVEN: I approve the schooner. I must have notice of the other part of the question. *(JULIAN appears with bottles of liqueurs and cognac.)*

JULIAN: Marie, take one of these rather quickly. *(She moves to him.)*

PHILIP: *(To VALERIE.)* Anyhow, I made you forget that you were going to South Africa.

JULIAN: *(To MARIE.)* No, the one under my arm.

VALERIE: *(To PHILIP.)* Yes, you did.

PHILIP: Q.E.F. Which was to be done. *(While the others make room on the table for JULIAN's bottles, PHILIP seats himself beside VALERIE on the stone seat.)*

PHILIP: Tell me about your brother.

VALERIE: In South Africa?

PHILIP: No. The other one.

VALERIE: He was killed. I have told you.

PHILIP: Not enough.

VALERIE: He was my half-brother really. They both were. But he counted as a real brother.

(From the group at the table.)

MRS. MURIVEN: No, Julian, bless you, not cognac.

JULIAN: It's Delamain Oh Six.

MRS. MURIVEN: Even so.

JULIAN: I thought it was your favourite tipple.

MRS. MURIVEN: But it makes my heart beat.

(From the stone seat.)

VALERIE: Even Godmother is growing old. She has changed since I saw her. But that was in the weeks before Dunkirk. One always forgets how long the war went on.

PHILIP: Why didn't you meet Julian then?

VALERIE: Commander Wyburton? But I have never been *here* until now. Godmother didn't live here then. It was in Yorkshire, in the house she had shared with my Grandmamma – who was German. Does that surprise you?

PHILIP: You mean does it shock me? Why should it? You forget I'm American. We aren't all Pilgrim Fathers.

MRS. MURIVEN: My dear, your valley is becoming like a great pool in this evening light.

VALERIE: But you know, I'm really more German than one grandmother accounts for. She and Godmother used to talk German continually; so did our own mother; so did we. It's just as much my first language as English. Useful when war came.

PHILIP: In Yorkshire still?

VALERIE: In London. We rather lost touch with Godmother. But my brother and I did go to see her. When the war flared up. That was the last time I saw him. Of course he was older than me, but when I was small and even now… However, that is of no interest except to me. For everyone else, he's dead.

PHILIP: But for you – not?

VALERIE: Never, really, while I myself am alive.

PHILIP: Which means?

VALERIE: He was everything. As if we were one. And he still is. *(JULIAN has come over and is standing beside her to offer her cognac, a glass in one hand, a bottle in the other. She looks at him, then away, and is not interrupted.)* Do you know what I mean if I say that we had each other's legends?

JULIAN: I do. *(They turn to him, a little resenting his interruption at first, then with interest.)* If you watch a child playing his own secret game, you can see that he is performing his legend, and you are outside it and he is inside. It's just the same

157

later. Everyone builds a legend into his life which is – well, what is it?

VALERIE: The glow inside quite ordinary things?

JULIAN: Perhaps… Anyhow, to be inside someone else's legend is…only once in all my life have I known a *man* capable of it.

VALERIE: Who? *(But JULIAN has turned abruptly away, and she continues to PHILIP.)* My brother was in mine; I was in his. I used to feel often that he was I, and I was he. I do still.

PHILIP: How was he killed?

VALERIE: *(Shaking a puzzled head.)* He was taken prisoner. He escaped. He must have been killed escaping. Anyhow he has never come home.

PHILIP: Is that really why you are going to South Africa? Must you?

VALERIE: It's no good staying here. He and I were going to live and work together after the war. So we planned.

PHILIP: Suppose one of you had married? Wasn't that a possibility?

VALERIE: I suppose so. We should have talked the same language about that, I expect. I don't know. I wasn't eighteen. *(VALERIE gets up and crosses U/L. PHILIP, after a moment. Meanwhile, MRS. MURIVEN and JULIAN enter U/R. JULIAN carries MARIE's coat. MRS. MURIVEN, continuing a conversation we have not heard, says:)*

MRS. MURIVEN: I'm not at all sure, Julian, that you are the right person for this discussion.

JULIAN: Because I agree too much?

MRS. MURIVEN: As a naval officer, responsibility is a profession with you. *(Seeing PHILIP's approach.)* Mr. Sturgess will be more profitable to quarrel with. Come and sit down, Mr. Sturgess. Let us call in the New World to redress the indecisiveness of the Old.

PHILIP: What have I done?

MARIE: Mrs. Muriven believes that the Western democracies are dying of a sick conscience.

PHILIP: A little self-criticism may be no bad thing.

MRS. MURIVEN: Never cry over spilt decisions.

JULIAN: Certainly the Iron Duke never did!

VALERIE: It's quite useless to pull Godmother's leg about the Iron Duke. It's a nickname she adores.

MRS. MURIVEN: Do you wonder?

PHILIP: I do a little.

MRS. MURIVEN: Wasn't he a great man?

PHILIP: But he lived a long time ago – before democracy began.

MRS. MURIVEN: You forget how often, in the history of the world, democracy had failed before he was born. The epitaph is always the same: 'Here lies democracy who died of a sick conscience'. 'He wanted too much too soon; he paid too little too late'… In America you learn fast. That is your genius. Fast enough, I believe – just fast enough – to save mankind. The world moves. You with it – inevitably.

PHILIP: May I ask in what direction?

MRS. MURIVEN: I am an old Englishwoman, Mr. Sturgess, but I have American blood. I love and respect your people. May I really try to answer that? In what direction?

PHILIP: Why, please! This is off the record.

MRS. MURIVEN: Why, then, in the direction of responsibility. Which doesn't mean counting appetites and calling them progress or counting voices and calling them the voice of God. It means responsibility *within your destiny*. Like a pilot's responsibility for his ship, moving on a tide.

PHILIP: I like to believe in free will. 'Destiny' is a tough word for me.

MRS. MURIVEN: It is implied in history; it is implied in character; both tough customers if we want to please ourselves. Destiny sent your people westward across the Atlantic for three centuries and more, whether they liked it or not, and now it is drawing them back again. It drew *you* back. Do you imagine that you went bombing Germany because you wanted to?

PHILIP: Indeed I don't... But Mrs. Muriven, you are driving mankind into an intolerable dilemma. It's Hamlet's dilemma between a violent action required of him by – oh, by Destiny if you like, and the peaceful quietism that was part of his nature. It tears the conscience. The Western democracies wish to avoid that tearing.

MRS. MURIVEN: Wish? Wish to avoid?... Responsibility is a hard bread to be eaten with a rough wine, not sopped in milk. No one can eat it for us. Eat or starve.

MARIE: It is true. It is quite, quite true. Our responsibilities within our destiny select us, not we them; they select us – often quite suddenly. It is like walking into a room that you expect to be empty, and finding a man there waiting for you and looking at you and commanding you. Always you recognize him, but sometimes at first you call him by the wrong name.

JULIAN: *(To divert her, with great abruptness.)* You are shivering, my dear. Look, I brought out your coat. Put it on.

MARIE: I am not cold, thank you.

JULIAN: Shall we light the lamp?

MRS. MURIVEN: Suppose we were to stroll round the garden.

JULIAN: It will soon be dark? *(He lights it but keeps it low.)*

MRS. MURIVEN: It is the perfect time when the light is not all gone and the evening primroses are out.

PHILIP: A time to remember absent friends.

MARIE has followed, but remains detached from them at two yards' distance. From within the house comes the sound of piano music, at first scarcely audible, then clear, then disappearing – a very brief passage of the Scherzo of Chopin's Sonata in B flat minor. At the first sound of it:

VALERIE: Listen!

When the music ceases –

MARIE: What did you hear?

VALERIE: I thought…music?

MARIE: There's no one in the drawing room.

VALERIE: One imagines things, I suppose.

MARIE: Did you know it?

VALERIE: It was the Chopin Scherzo which is followed by… I have known it all my life.

MARIE: What is it followed by?

VALERIE: The Funeral March. *(MARIE turns and follows the others who have disappeared.)*

VALERIE: *(To MARIE, retreating.)* But you… *(To PHILIP.)* Why should she pretend not to hear it?

PHILIP: I think she didn't.

VALERIE: Nor you? Do you mean that I alone – ? Do you mean that –

PHILIP: I heard it.

VALERIE: Not the others? You and I?… My brother played it. It is the B Flat Minor Sonata.

PHILIP: You were thinking of your brother. His death doesn't tear you?

VALERIE: No. Do you remember that story you began to tell at dinner? About your friend – I mean Heron – how one night he wrote a poem and, because it was your rule not to carry anything written, burnt it; and how he said it made no difference whether you kept a poem or not or whether anyone ever read it or not. The thing – any spiritual thing, I suppose – was there before you had it and is still there when it seems to have gone. My brother taught me that. 'Loss without losing' was what you said.

PHILIP: It wasn't I who said it. It was Heron.

VALERIE: My brother didn't use those words, but it's what he felt and what I feel. That, you see, is why his death doesn't tear me.

PHILIP: The things I struggle after, you reach out for as if they belonged to you.

VALERIE: What things?

PHILIP: That music perhaps.

VALERIE: But you heard it too!

PHILIP: If I did, it was through you. And now I begin to doubt it. It's always like that with me… Oh I haven't the gift of… making confessions…flippantly. Perhaps with you I needn't try?

VALERIE: *(Gently.)* No, you needn't try.

PHILIP: *(Swerving to an opportunity.)* Why? Why on earth do you make special conditions for me?

VALERIE: Because I… Because you are exciting.

PHILIP: Good heavens, in what way?

VALERIE: You swerve suddenly. You…teach suddenly. *(Laughing at him.)* Are you a good schoolmaster?

PHILIP: I doubt it. I don't teach myself suddenly enough. I suppose what I'm struggling for is some kind of reasoned balance between the activities and the acceptances of life – the crusading part and the quietist part of me, if you see what I mean.

VALERIE: But why not?

PHILIP: Because, like the rest of the world, I want it both ways. It's not enough for me to hear music; I want to be quite sure I heard it and know why. But you – you did when you were speaking about Heron's poem – you speak of that balance between the two aspects of life – the active part and the accepting part – well, it's damned hard to say. You speak of it hardly at all as a *reasoned* thing. Much more as a thing to be felt, an experience within reach.

VALERIE: Not within my reach. Reachable if you like.

PHILIP: Very well. But in sight, like an apple on a high branch. Heron's attitude towards his poem seemed to me, when Frewer told me of it, anyhow to a bit of me, a kind of… indifferentism?

VALERIE: But why? To write a poem that no one will ever see and to care passionately about it – I understand that so well. It's like fighting in a part of the battlefield that no one will ever notice, or loving, not for what love takes or even for what it gives... Philip, that's not indifferentism. Why do you think it can be? It's not avoiding the fire or fearing it. It is passing through the burning, fiery furnace without the smell of fire on you. I don't know any other way to live in the modern world. I think your friend... What was he? I mean, by temperament? Did he take a hopeful view of the world?

PHILIP: He took a much blacker view of what was going to *happen* than I did, if that is what you mean, but it didn't frighten him.

VALERIE: *(To herself.)* Making himself eyes with which to see in the dark.

PHILIP: Tell me something. It's rather a naive question. Your godmother says I'm naive.

VALERIE: What is it?

PHILIP: Are you Christian?

VALERIE: Yes... I like your questions. They are sudden too.

PHILIP: I like your answers. Few people wouldn't hedge that answer... Anyhow, you see, I have to risk being thought not subtle enough. I have to take short-cuts. I haven't long to get to know you. When you answer 'yes' like that, it's a long stride between you and me.

VALERIE: Did you love him – your friend, I mean?

PHILIP: Yes.

VALERIE: That – Oh, the thing's unsayable!

PHILIP: *(Near her.)* What were you trying to say?

VALERIE: Your 'yes', too, seemed a long stride between you and me. Does that make any kind of sense about a man I never knew?

PHILIP: It makes sense to me, knowing him and knowing you. Beginning to know you both.

VALERIE: It will soon be quite dark. I must go home.

PHILIP: They will come back.

VALERIE: I think they've gone on by the lower gate... Philip, when your friend died –

PHILIP: Go on, my dear. Say it. You will say it straighter than I can.

VALERIE: I have no right to say it.

PHILIP: You have the right, if you will take it.

VALERIE: I meant that your conscience *is* torn by Heron's death. Do you know how your face changes when you speak of it or when you so terribly avoid speaking of it?... Oh, you don't know how your whole being seems to change. It's agony to watch.

PHILIP: Everything has altered since I came here. My romantic selection from the past doesn't work any more. The thing comes up and lives itself; to be with Marie and Julian is to have the stress and the ache of it; but you –

VALERIE: What have I to do with that story?

PHILIP: More than I can tell. You seem almost to be part of it, as though he really were still alive and I could stretch out my hand and take his...as I take yours. *(She makes no movement of withdrawal.)* Don't take your hand away.

VALERIE: No.

PHILIP: Never?

VALERIE: My dear, don't ask that now.

PHILIP: I do ask it.

VALERIE: Not to-night.

PHILIP: I do ask it.

VALERIE: Because to-night you are what he used to call 'out of judgement', and so, perhaps, am I. *(Their hands part.)*

PHILIP: Then you must hear the whole story first.

VALERIE: Why are you afraid of your story? Or didn't you know until now that you were?

PHILIP: I don't think I am. I don't think I am. I may not force it on Julian and Marie; they know it too well. ... But I can tell it to you. You have the right. When you have heard it, you can…take your hand away – or not. *(They are now upstage.)*

VALERIE: Tell it as we walk home… Philip, do you really want to tell me this? Better sleep on it and decide in the morning.

PHILIP: I want you to know…and judge.

VALERIE: Tell it then as you see it, but without judging yourself. How do you know that judgement lies with us?

PHILIP: We had better not leave the lamp.

VALERIE: There's no wind.

PHILIP: Safer to turn it out. *(He turns it out. She waits, then moves on as he comes up with her.)* Listen. You know already how we came to Marie's house. When we had been in her granary a week, she told us there was another Englishman coming. That night she went to bring him in and we sat up waiting… *(They are gone now. There is still light in the sky and light flows out from the drawing room windows.)*

Curtain.

ACT TWO

July 1943. Time: 11.50 p.m.. The granary at the Chassaignes', near Blaise, in the neighbourhood of Toulouse. Three-quarters of the stage-width from the actors' left is occupied by a room interior to the granary, called the Sardine Box. The remaining quarter of the stage has in the foreground a trap-door leading down to PIERRE CHASSAIGNE's room. Beyond this is dimly visible a background which suggests a huge granary piled with miscellaneous junk. This granary has been long diverted from its original purpose and has since been used as a vast boxroom and store; also as a playroom by MARIE when she was a young girl.

There will be action downstage by the trap-door and in the Sardine Box but none in the further recesses of the granary, which are suggested by a distant skylight, plainly visible as you look across the trap-door and visible also above the walls of the Sardine Box, which are wooden partition walls and do not reach to the granary's sloping roof.

The Sardine Box should be small. It has four visible walls. On the Left, the wall is part of the main outside wall of the granary. It is almost entirely occupied by a very large granary door through which, if it were ever opened (which it is not), hay, etc., could be hoisted from an outside platform. This granary door is fastened by a great bar (never used). In the granary door is a small door fastened by a wooden latch.

There are three other walls of the Sardine Box, all partitions. The first juts out above the granary door and runs parallel to the footlights to a little short of midstage – let us say from East to West, supposing the actors be looking South. The second, a short wall, runs W.S.W. far enough to contain a door. The third runs a little West of South, almost straight at the footlights, which it would reach just to the East of the trap-door if it were not conventionally cut off in order not to interrupt the audience's line of sight. At the point where this wall is cut off, a stove-pipe runs up from the room below.

This inner room or Sardine Box is the place which is ordinarily used by the officers. Except at the trap-door itself on one or two occasions, the whole action passes in the Box. The officers do, in fact, sleep and often by day sit in the other parts of the granary, but we do not see them there.

*As their whole object is so to arrange things that, if they have to make
a lightning get-away, they leave behind them nothing that could lead
Germans to believe that the granary has been inhabited, the Sardine
Box is a tangle of boxes and odd bits of furniture completely untidy and
haphazard. There are a rug and an armchair on three legs, and there is
as much else as the producer likes.*

*Over the skylight a blind has been fitted. At night this is pulled down and
all those parts of the granary which lie outside the Sardine Box are blacked
out, but the efficiency of the blackout is distrusted and lamps are used only
in the Sardine Box, not because the blind of the skylight is insufficient
but because, outside the Sardine Box, there may be wall-chinks.*

*Therefore the only artificial light outside the Sardine Box is one fixed and
sheltered lamp (which the audience does not see) throwing an inward
beam at floor-level which the audience does see, gleaming behind the
trap-door. In the Sardine Box lamps can be safely moved but the tops
of them are shaded so that they may not throw an upward light above
the partition walls.*

*Before darkness falls (that is, in Scene 2), the blind is up and daylight
penetrates from the skylight into the Sardine Box, but dimly, so that even
by day lamps are used in the Sardine Box if you want to read.*

*The scene is bleak and untidy. The producer must get his effects by lighting
and huge ominous shadows, and he is free to build up the Sardine Box,
not necessarily with partition-walls and a door, but with dressers and
other bits of furniture, and sacking on canvas.*

*When the Curtain rises, HERON, FREWER, and PHILIP are in the
Sardine Box. PHILIP is on the floor reading, propped against sacks Left.
HERON, on a packing-case Centre, has been reading but now lays down
his book. FREWER is cross-legged on the floor D/L by a bale, gouging a
piece of wood with a penknife. He is very young, a rather pathetic boy,
cheerful by act of will, but by no means a warrior by nature. HERON is
tall and dark, an efficient officer of great potential energy, but a man of
profound dignity and spiritual composure.*

HERON: *(Looking at his watch.)* Still ten minutes to midnight.

PHILIP: She couldn't be back yet – not if her rendezvous with
him is where she found us.

HERON: Still we may as well get his bed made. Your job, Dick.

FREWER: I know. I will in a second. Let me just get this bit done.

HERON: What are you doing?

FREWER: Making something... You forget that I was going to be Michael Angelo in private life.

HERON: What in fact is it? *(Taking the piece of wood.)*

FREWER: I'll show you later. *(Gets up reluctantly.)* Now I'll do the bed. Where do you want him to lie?

HERON: Next to me – anyhow at first. Make him a fling-hole too.

FREWER: I can't see anything out there with only one screened lamp. Can't I have another?

HERON: No you cannot.

FREWER: Can I move the one there is? A fixed beam at floor-level is no good to me.

HERON: It's all you can have.

FREWER: But the skylight blackout is perfectly efficient.

HERON: That may be. It's not the skylight I'm afraid of. It's wall chinks. Marie says that only this Sardine Box is dead secure with a moving light.

FREWER: I believe the outside is secure too.

HERON: Probably it is. But Marie thinks not. Anyhow it's an order.

FREWER: All right. The bed I can do. Anyone can put down straw. Making a fling-hole for him will be ticklish if I can't see.

HERON: You have the floor-beam. After eight days in this place, surely you can feel your way. If you can't, I'll come.

FREWER: Oh I can *do* it. *(FREWER goes out U/R.)*

PHILIP: Dick Frewer's a helpless child.

HERON: Not so helpless... He just doesn't like being alone.

PHILIP: He has made up his mind, poor devil, that when he gets back to England, he'll be shot down again. Of course, it's all nonsense. Still –

HERON: No, it isn't nonsense. Men often know when their number's up. Dick has to get used to it.

PHILIP: You have a pretty hard streak in you, Heron.

HERON: Have I? Ride him like a nervous colt. *(They pick up their books again.)* You'll see. When Dick comes back he'll be feeling better. *(PHILIP cannot read either and he says:)*

PHILIP: Who do you suppose this new chap is that Marie's bringing in?

HERON: She didn't tell me, and I didn't ask.

PHILIP: If he's Air Force, Dick Frewer or I may know him.

HERON: More likely a British agent being got out. That's why, as she didn't tell me, I didn't ask. Besides, this evening, she properly put me in my place. I went to hold the trap-door for her. I felt sorry for her, going out alone on this job while we sat snug in our Sardine Box; and, like a fool, I offered to go with her.

PHILIP: But that would have been against every kind of rule.

HERON: I know. I was wrong. She's safer alone. But she looked so grey. She seemed to shrunk like a young tired cat. So I said: 'I'll come with you', and though she said 'No', it wasn't a very firm 'No', and I moved to follow her. Then, my God, she didn't argue. She gave an order. She said: 'Go back to the others and wait'. I *came* back.

PHILIP: She'd have given her head to have you go with her.

HERON: You like romance, don't you, Philip? I know it's your idea she's half in love with me.

PHILIP: More than half.

HERON: She's never given a sign.

PHILIP: She can't. She's on duty.

HERON: That doesn't stop most people.

PHILIP: It stops her.

HERON: She certainly knows how to give an order – even to herself. *(HERON rises.)*

PHILIP: Where are you off to?

HERON: I was thinking of her father down there. *(He points to the floor.)* It's bad enough when she's away in the daytime, doing her school job. He always thinks she won't come back. Now the old man must be going through hell. I thought I'd go down to him. Keep him company. Divert his mind.

PHILIP: I shouldn't, Heron, if I were you.

HERON: Why not? Old Chassaigne interests me.

PHILIP: You interest him too much. He watches you like a terrier at a rat-hole.

HERON: Nonsense, Philip. He shows his teeth now and then. That's only a scholar's jealousy – very scholarly and very French. He was a professor of German, you know.

PHILIP: That isn't all. Chassiagne is obsessed. He hates Germans with a ferocity that I didn't believe could exist. *(Enter FREWER through urtains U/S Left.)* Does he talk to you of Weitbrecht?

HERON: He has. I'm not blind, Philip. I know the old man's dangerous on that subject.

FREWER: I asked Marie about Weitbrecht.

PHILIP: Did you indeed! It's not a popular subject in the Chassaigne family.

FREWER: So I gathered. That's what puzzled me. Weitbrecht has been dead for ages – before I was born. But he ticks on like a clock in the old boy's mind… Marie said they were students together in Germany forty years ago. They worshipped each other. David and Jonathan, Marie said. And Weitbrecht betrayed him.

HERON: But where do I come in? I wasn't his Jonathan. I didn't betray him or run off with his girl – which I gather Weitbrecht did. I didn't invade France.

PHILIP: Weitbrecht is Chassaigne's devil. For him all Germany *is* Weitbrecht. Somehow you link up.

FREWER: It is true, Heron.

HERON: Philip says he's dangerous.

FREWER: I don't know about that. He's near dotty, if you ask me. But somehow you do link up. Half the time I didn't know whether he was talking about you or Weitbrecht. I doubt whether he did. His terror is that he may have a German in his house without knowing it. To-day he's in a frazzle because this new chap's coming – as though Weitbrecht might crawl out of his grave… But it's you he watches.

HERON: I don't blame him. Wouldn't you watch in his place?… Is that bed made?

FREWER: Straw thrown down casual-like. Goering himself wouldn't know it was a bed.

HERON: Least of all if he slept on it.

FREWER: *(To PHILIP.)* I wish you'd have a look. Just to confirm.

PHILIP: I will if you like. *(He moves through curtain U/S.)*

FREWER: And the fling-hole. Near the dresser among the pile of empty bottles. It's full of various gubbins. Plumb in the open. No Hun would ever rummage in it. But have a look. I may have been too clever.

PHILIP: I'll make sure. *(Exit PHILIP U/R.)*

HERON: *(To FREWER, who is obviously agitated.)* Take it quietly, Dick.

FREWER: Why do you say that?

HERON: Your piece about old Chassaigne.

FREWER: It's quite true.

HERON: I don't doubt it, but it's not important. There's no need to be worked up about it.

FREWER: I am worked up.

HERON: Why?

FREWER: You know quite well… This new chap coming. Marie may bring him in at any moment now. If he's what we have been waiting for, this may be our last night here.

HERON: I don't want to go either.

FREWER: Don't you? You only say that to be kind. It doesn't rattle you. Nothing does. That's why…being with you has meant such a hell of a lot to me… I suppose, when I get back to England, the good and great may say I'm shell-shocked or that I've lost my nerve for flying. All nonsense of course. I'm just the same. It isn't even that I'm afraid of being killed. But I want to stay put long enough to grow roots.

HERON: That's what the world wants, Dick, a creative pause. When you were a child, did you have a home – I mean, a fixed, solid home?

FREWER: For a bit I did. Not long… I suppose what I really want is just that. How did *you* know? No more time-tables, no more journeys. To stay put night after night with no scheduled move next morning is pretty near my notion of heaven. This place has been that… It's damned silly, I suppose, to be frightened of moving. My nightmare is being lost in a railway station. It's only the feeling you have in – in a warm room with people you know – of not wanting to go out into the cold.

HERON: *(After a pause.)* Death isn't like that. Dying may be.

FREWER: I wasn't talking about that.

HERON: I thought you were.

FREWER: *(Facing it.)* Yes, I was… But I'm not really afraid of that any more. But I didn't want to go from here because it's here I'm not afraid. I'm not as long as I can hold on to what you said. But I shall forget that.

HERON: What *I* said?

FREWER: Two days ago. In the afternoon when it was raining, do you remember? About the thing being 'familiar'? Death, I mean.

HERON: I always used to have the idea myself that it must be one of two things – either, as you said, a going out into solitude and cold and darkness or, if it wasn't that, then at best something unknown. I don't any longer see it in that way but as a recall.

FREWER: From what? To what?

HERON: From this world with its few friends and its millions of strangers to a light and sanity which are not solitary or cold or unknown but were familiar enough in childhood and, sometimes, are, even now. In childhood it was a pretty steady light, though it grew more and more distant. Even now, there are flashes of it when a tree or a sky or even a man or a woman becomes, as you look at them, in some way timeless, just as they were in childhood, and reality – a kind of interior grace – shines through appearances. I think what is coming is a recall to that.

FREWER: But there's no proof.

HERON: No external proof.

FREWER: I wonder whether that was right – what you said about the things children feel. I don't remember much except – well, one thing I do remember. I used to sit up in bed shouting *Kubla Khan*. My mother was alive then. I was a frightfully ordinary little boy. It wasn't the meaning – pleasure-domes and caves of ice and all that. And it wasn't really the sound – I made a hideous din. It was a kind of… oh I don't know…a magic of some sort which let me go back into a world where I belonged and where there was nothing I was afraid of or didn't understand. Do you mean that death will be like that?

HERON: Don't say it so hopefully, Dick, as if my meaning it made it true.

FREWER: It almost does for me.

HERON: Only if you re-imagine it for yourself. *(Enter from curtain U/S PHILIP as the trap-door begins to open.)*

PHILIP: They have come, I think.

FREWER: Shall I go and help with the trap-door?

HERON: Stay where you are. *(The trap-door opens. A beam of light shines up vertically.)*

MARIE: *(Emerging.)* *(Père la lumière est trop forte baisse la lampe.)*

Father, move back the lamp. It's too strong. *(The vertical light dims. MARIE comes up and stands, holding the trap-door. JULIAN follows.)* Stand still while I get the trap down.

JULIAN: Let me –

MARIE: Stand still. Give me your hand. *(She lets down the trap. Darkness then.)* Follow me. This place is a store-room. I used it as a playroom once. Full of obstacles. Come. *(She leads him round and enters the Sardine Box. The three there rise. JULIAN is wearing pince-nez and a beret. He looks like a seedy and pedantic French official. He carries a walking-stick which has a straight handle and is attached to his wrist by a leather loop: it is a dagger-stick. Meanwhile the trap-door has opened again. PIERRE CHASSAIGNE comes up, and during the ensuing dialogue makes his way to the door. But time passes before his entrance. He may have been listening.)* This is Dick Frewer. This is Philip Sturgess; he's American. Both out of the air. This is Major Lang, out of Germany. We call him Heron.

JULIAN: My name is Julian Wyburton. I'll get out of fancy dress. *(He takes off his disguise.)*

FREWER: *(Ingenuously.)* Where from?

JULIAN: *(Snubbing him.)* Since you ask, last night I spent in France.

FREWER: Which Service?

JULIAN: The senior one.

FREWER: What on earth is the Navy doing in France?

JULIAN: Keeping its mouth shut. What rank are you?

FREWER: Flight-Lieutenant.

JULIAN: *(Disregarding him.)* Who is in command here?

MARIE: I am.

JULIAN: I beg your pardon. I meant under you.

MARIE: Heron is. As a naval Commander, you are senior to him. After to-night I will act through you. *(CHASSAIGNE comes in.)*

JULIAN: No, mademoiselle. He knows this outfit. I'll take my orders from him. *(To HERON.)* If you agree?

HERON: As you wish, sir.

MARIE: Thank you.

JULIAN: *(To HERON.)* What is your name again? Lang?

HERON: My name is Lang. They all call me Heron.

JULIAN: Why?

HERON: *(Smiling.)* They say I look like one. I suppose I carry myself that way.

MARIE: *(With evident tenderness.)* He holds his head back. I think it's more like a knight in chess. *(Then she returns abruptly to business.)* Father, what are you doing here?

CHASSAIGNE: I thought I would like to meet my new guest.

MARIE: You met him as we passed through your room.

CHASSAIGNE: I like to *know* my guests. My acquaintance with Monsieur Heron has been most instructive. *(He puts his hand on JULIAN's shoulder.)* You know, my friend, his German is flawless. It has even the little faults that educated Germans permit themselves. And I, as a professor, am interested in all things German.

MARIE: Father, you are leaving the room empty.

CHASSAIGNE: *(With no sign of going yet.)* That is true. I will return at once to my kennel... *(To JULIAN.)* But it is interesting, is it not? You, for example, on your journeys, play the part of a Frenchman, and these two young gentlemen also within the limits which Nature has imposed upon them, but Monsieur Heron, *tout naturellement*, is a German merchant trading for cognac in the Charente and for oak in the Limousin. He would even, I am told, make little jokes with enemy pickets. He would, as you say, pull the German leg. To do that needs great confidence.

JULIAN: I have found myself that to chatter is often the best way to avoid curiosity.

CHASSAIGNE: True... True... Admirable... And, in any case, the English have always the idea to play a comedy part upon a tragic stage. It is altogether characteristic.

MARIE: Father –

CHASSAIGNE: Yes, Marie, I will go. You will say good-night to me as you descend. I shall be awake. I am always awake. *(With little jerky bows he goes out through curtain and down through the trap-door.)*

PHILIP: You see?

MARIE: *(To JULIAN.)* I won't keep you long to-night. You will need food and drink. I will bring it. We have special rules about food and drink. It has to be possible, in case there should be an alarm while you are eating, to remove all traces of a meal in a few seconds. A meal consists of one bowl, one spoon, one jug. You eat…as certain idealists would say…communally. The others will tell you how these…implements…are disposed of. You will find in the morning that the rest of the granary is extremely large. It is full of –

FREWER: Junk.

MARIE: Junk, I always forget that word – and completely disordered. There is a zinc tub there. It is half full of broken crockery, empty tins, thick water. The addition of one bowl, one spoon, one jug would not be observed by Germans. You understand me?

JULIAN: The principle – perfectly.

MARIE: You are as safe here as anywhere in France. My old father sleeps and works below. There is no access except through his room. The passages of the house are long and tortuous. He will not be taken by surprise.

JULIAN: Does he never go out?

MARIE: Seldom… Never in my absence. There is a closet adjoining his room. You go down to empty slops.

JULIAN: Not otherwise?

MARIE: By rule not. There may be exceptions. The point is this – and this you must understand: my father receives Germans in his room.

JULIAN: I understand perfectly.

MARIE: You are quick.

JULIAN: I play your game, mademoiselle.

MARIE: As a result, the enemy regard this house as a house of collaborators. At least I hope they still do. This stove-pipe runs up from my father's stove. If he knocks on it with his pipe, that is the first alarm. You keep silence; you gather what is within reach but don't move. But if he shows signs of going up through the trap-door, you will get the second alarm. In that case you risk sound. It's not a great risk. My father's room lies there *(Pointing Left.)* beyond the stove, not directly under us. You do what Heron calls Operation Get-Away. You should be out of the granary in – how long?

HERON: We have got it down to eighty seconds up to the granary door. *(To JULIAN.)* This door. We have never opened it. *(Holding lamp.)* It's part of a huge granary door. The little one is all we need. It opens on to – go on, Marie. I've never been out.

MARIE: On to an outside platform with a ladder running down the wall into a courtyard. If the house is close surrounded and it's daylight, there's not much hope. Still there's a chance. Heron has instructions where to go. If the enemy searches this place and finds no sign that it was ever inhabited, it may not be impossible to pick you up again outside.

JULIAN: Operation Get-Away must have needed working out.

FREWER: For the last week we have done damned little else.

(JULIAN has been prowling. He has come to the granary door and his hand is on the wooden latch.)

PHILIP: *(Shouting in alarm.)* For God's sake don't open that, the light would shine out across the road.

JULIAN: I don't propose to open it. When you have exercised Operation Get-Away, have you actually raised that latch?

PHILIP: No.

JULIAN: Then I will. Wood swells.

HERON: There's no need. I tried it this morning.

JULIAN: Ah, good.

MARIE: There's one other thing, Commander.

JULIAN: Yes.

MARIE: The discipline of the River Line deprives you of all initiative. I am in charge.

JULIAN: Certainly you are.

MARIE: But in a special way. We have through our hands men without your experience. We found our rule on their stupidity.

JULIAN: Most rules are founded on the incompetence of the human race… And the rule is?

MARIE: Whoever comes through the Line obeys – without reasoning, at once – whatever order is given him. If we are in a railway-carriage and I say 'sleep', you nod and snore. If we are in a street and I say 'fall in the mud', you fall instantly. It may be necessary for reasons which I alone know; I may recognize a face which you do not. My discretion is unlimited; your obedience absolute and instantaneous. Do you take that?

JULIAN: I take it.

MARIE: I want your oath.

JULIAN: I swear it.

MARIE: Thank you… There is this point too. Apart from those papers which you have brought in, you carry out nothing written. Everything, even a bridge score, is burned as soon as made.

JULIAN: And how disposed of?

MARIE: Burn it in a saucer, break up the ashes, dispose of them in what Dick calls a 'fling-hole'. Dick will show you… Have you weapons?

JULIAN: No pistol. I have this. *(He draws the blade from his walking-stick.)*

MARIE: That is quieter… Now I will go and bring you food. What is it, Dick?

FREWER: You're tired. I don't want to delay you. Can I ask one question?

MARIE: What is it?

FREWER: The night we came, I asked – d'you remember? – I was all in myself – I asked whether we were to move on at once or whether we could come out of top-gear. You said we were waiting for something; you didn't say what. Is this – I mean the Commander – is he the something? Do we move now?

MARIE: Not yet. *(To JULIAN.)* Does that distress you?

JULIAN: Me? I can do with a few days in harbour.

FREWER: This is harbour all right.

JULIAN: What is your name?

FREWER: Frewer, sir. Dick Frewer.

JULIAN: Sorry I snapped at you... *(To MARIE.)* I beg your pardon, mademoiselle. I interrupted you. I'm in no hurry, God knows. In fact, when do we move?

MARIE: Transport on the last stage, straight though to the Spanish frontier, has been thrown out by this delay. It has to be tied up; it will take time. There are others who will have to move into your places the night after you go and others behind them. When the machine turns over again, it must turn over simultaneously all along the line to release the hold-up.

PHILIP: *(Effects cue 'tanks')* Tanks!

MARIE: It isn't easy to arrange, our communications being what they are. Once it is arranged, no revision is possible. There's no margin for a hitch. I hate that; I fear it.

HERON: You mean that, when zero hour is fixed, we must go at all costs?

MARIE: I'm afraid so.

JULIAN: However unfavourable the local conditions are? A clear night? A full moon?

MARIE: We can calculate the moon. Not the enemy. Normally one can use discretion within certain limits. This time I shall have no choice; the time-table will be inflexible. Inflexible.

PHILIP: When will it be?

MARIE: I don't know. A fortnight perhaps.

FREWER: Then we *can* come out of top-gear again.

MARIE: Poor Dick. Yes. I'll get your food, Commander.

JULIAN: Thank you, mademoiselle.

MARIE: As a matter of routine, we use Christian names. Mine is Marie.

JULIAN: Good. Then I am not 'Commander'. *(She goes out and is to be seen descending through the trap-door.)*

FREWER: She never relaxes. When we go, others come. We at least move together. She is always alone… The job of a secret agent must be blazing hell.

JULIAN: Rather colder than that… Heron, what are my orders for the night? Where do I fit into 'Get-Away'?

HERON: To-night you don't. To-morrow you will. To-night sleep fully dressed as you were when you arrived. Everything – but everything – in your pockets. If there's a second signal, walk out after me and follow me… You can't smoke. The stubs are too obvious. *(JULIAN puts away the packet of cigarettes in his hands.)*

JULIAN: As you say. *(Picks up FREWER's piece of wood. To PHILIP.)* What's this?

FREWER: It's mine, sir. Pretty ingenious, I think. It's a chair-leg. I've scooped it out. It fits on to this broken one. Like this. *(Fits it.)* The point is, it isn't a permanent mend. But it works. *(Sits in the chair.)* Then if the German shows up, off it comes. *(He pulls it off and flings it over the partition wall. The broken chair lolls over on its side.)* That chair hasn't been sat on for twenty-years – has it? *(They all laugh.)*

JULIAN: Presumably not. And if they find the chair-leg?

FREWER: Did you know it was a chair-leg?

JULIAN: No.

FREWER: Then they won't… Shall I show you your quarters?

JULIAN: Yes. Out here? *(FREWER and JULIAN go out.)*

PHILIP: Well?

HERON: Well, what?

PHILIP: The new boy?

HERON: He knows his job. The Navy often does. Well, I'm going to turn in. Whose middle-watch? Yours or Dick's? I know it's not mine.

PHILIP: It's mine.

HERON: Then you can give the senior Service its supper and tuck it up in bed. *(JULIAN comes back.)* Bed all right?

JULIAN: In so far as a bed can be in a bachelor establishment, while preserving an appearance of chaos, you seem to have dug yourselves in pretty comfortably – like a Government department. *(Turning up the rug and finding some cards.)* Ah, I see you play cards. Bridge or poker?

PHILIP: Both.

JULIAN: How do you dispose of them – the cards?

HERON: The rule is: We roll the rug back and play sitting on the floor. If there's an alarm, one man's cards go into his pocket and out with him. Dick Frewer has some in his pocket now. The rest throw in and the rug comes down. The enemy finds the incomplete remnants of a pack ten years old. No evidence of a recent game.

FREWER: Recent? Recent? You could plant potatoes on those bloody cards.

JULIAN: My God, I want to smoke like a fool. *(Noise of trap opening.)*

FREWER: I think that's your food coming. *(As light begins to show through the trap-door, the stage is blacked out.)*

SCENE 2

The same. Twelve days later. Nearly 9.30 p.m.. Still daylight. FREWER and HERON discovered. HERON (sitting on sacks D/L) writing, FREWER (sitting on packing case) reading.

FREWER: *(Laying down his book.)* Heron.

HERON: Yes.

FREWER: I'm sorry. What are you writing?

HERON: *(With a smile.)* A poem.

FREWER: Then I'll shut up… *(A hopeful afterthought.)* Is it important?

HERON: Anyhow it's done.

FREWER: I was going to say: Can I talk a bit?

HERON: As much as you like.

FREWER: Twelve days since Julian came; eight before that; less than three weeks. I thought I'd got over it, Heron, but I felt sick just the same when Marie told us our transport was fixed for to-night.

HERON: Where is she now?

FREWER: Out there with Philip and Julian. At least I think so. I didn't hear her go down.

HERON: Is she there still?

FREWER: Yes.

HERON: She's pretty… taut…poor Marie.

FREWER: To-day she is because it's the last day. Anyhow she was while she was telling us. But afterwards she was peaceful again. She's much less – oh I don't know – less tight-strung? – than she was when we came. She's peaceful inside herself. Although she loves you…or because. So am I if it comes to that. Not of course, I mean, that I'm in the same boat with you or her. She's an intellectual and I'm not.

HERON: That makes no odds once you're out of the shallows. Which am I? An intellectual or not? Don't overvalue me, Dick, I'm not in the least a leader of men.

FREWER: You are an efficient officer. I'm not even that.

HERON: Has that anything to do with it?

FREWER: I think it has. It's all part of the same thing. For most of us life is a kind of banking-account. We are always totting it up and seeing how little time there is left. And then we panic and fuss. You don't. I was learning not to, but you –

HERON: Dick, you are identifying me with this place. Don't do that. This place is quiet and included. *(MARIE comes in from U/R.)* That's what I try to be. That is all. *(Seeing her.)* Marie.

MARIE: Go on. Let me sit here and listen. It's not half-past nine yet. Nearly three hours to go. Philip says he still has scraps of paper to burn.

HERON: *(Holding up the paper on which he was writing.)* I have this.

MARIE: Time enough... It's an odd feeling to sit here peacefully talking. To-morrow there will be no one; after that, new faces. For to-night everything has arranged itself smoothly. I've seldom had such long warning. All we have to do is walk out, when the time comes and –

FREWER: Is it the old rendezvous? The same ditch where you first picked us up?

MARIE: Yes, thank heaven. I believe you have almost an affection for that ditch.

FREWER: I have. Like the beginning of the holidays. When the war's over, on a sunshiny day after a very good lunch, I shall stop my enormous Rolls-Royce beside that ditch, and I shall say – But I don't suppose I shall. Everyone says 'after the war'. What the hell will happen?

MARIE: Not too much, I hope. Quite enough has happened in the last few years.

HERON: I believe Marie has been converted to my idea of a creative pause.

MARIE: I didn't need converting. I teach history.

(From U/R enter JULIAN carrying a lamp and dirty rag.)

FREWER: It's the same with trees.

MARIE: Trees?

FREWER: Fruit-trees. My father grew them. He said: 'Don't *bother* trees or women; if you do, the sap don't rise.'

JULIAN: That's the odd thing about this place. The sap does rise. When I came, I was hellish impatient. I pestered you – didn't I, Marie? – about plans for getting on. But once I grasped that there was nothing on earth I could do about it, I found – I mean as regards my own job – that I could for once think back to the roots of policy instead of bothering my head about to-morrow's ways and means.

MARIE: Your job!

JULIAN: Why not?

MARIE: You are incorrigible, aren't you, Julian? You think of everything – even of the sap rising – in terms of your own Service…just as you everlastingly carry your dagger-stick in your hand. Why do you? You aren't going to be attacked here.

JULIAN: Habit.

MARIE: But you might put it down sometimes.

JULIAN: Why do women lose their hand-bags?

FREWER: But you needn't sleep with it!

JULIAN: Needn't I? Why do husbands lose their wives? *(He goes out U/R.)*

HERON: *(With a laugh. To MARIE.)* How you bait him about his Service. You are just as concentrated on yours.

MARIE: Perhaps that's why. I wanted to forget for half an hour. Everything that can be done has been done. Everything is set for to-night. I wanted to think of something else. Or not think.

FREWER: *(To MARIE.)* Like Heron… D'you know what he was doing just now?

MARIE: *(To HERON.)* What were you doing?

FREWER: Writing a poem.

HERON: *(Making a spill of his poem.)* Making spills.

FREWER: But Heron, do you really write poetry? Do you publish it, I mean? Ought I to have heard of you and all that?

HERON: Heard of me? Certainly not.

FREWER: What on earth do you write poetry about? Spring and love and so on?

HERON: About nothing on earth – at least I suppose not. Are you by any chance a musician?

FREWER: I like it. Why?

HERON: Music is *about* something, but not in the same way that what is written in words is about something. It's about something, inside nature and beyond the senses, which isn't even thinkable except in music – Why shouldn't poetry move towards that – away from the logic that ties words to appearances?

FREWER: I think I do see now. *(To HERON.)* About something, you mean, so far *inside* that you have to stop thinking before you can let it come through.

HERON: That's it.

'If I but had the eyes and ears

To read within what now appears,

Then should I see in every face

An innocent, interior grace,

And, as the clouds of thought unfurled,

Be native of the golden world.'

FREWER: Do you see that, Marie, you must! *(MARIE shakes head.)* Oh – but you must!

MARIE: Must I? At least I'm intellectual enough to know that I'm half-blind.

HERON: Dear Marie.

MARIE: What did you say?

HERON: Dear Marie. *(He takes her hand and almost at once releases it. It means much to her that he should have spoken those words, and, for a moment, she covers her face. FREWER, who has twisted round and has not been looking at them, goes on.)*

FREWER: I think I do see now. I suppose I shan't to-morrow morning… And even now, I don't really see. *(He turns back to HERON.)* Poetry *must* be about something. It can't just be about the music you don't hear and the things you don't touch and –

HERON: And the food you don't eat?

FREWER: Well, yes, but why do you say that?

HERON:

'For he on honey-dew hath fed
And drunk the milk of Paradise.'

Why not? Sound without hearing, truth without arguing, love without loving, loss without losing. Why not? Isn't that a subject for poetry? You can call it nonsense rhymes if you like. *(HERON strikes a light is about to burn the spill he has made.)*

MARIE: But that – in your hand – have you just written it?

HERON: Not long ago.

MARIE: Is it – the verses you just said?

HERON: No, indeed.

MARIE: Do you know it by heart – your own poem, I mean?

HERON: No.

MARIE: But you are leaving to-night. All papers have to be burned.

HERON: That's what I was doing.

FREWER: I do see what Marie means. What's the good of writing it?

HERON: To write it. *(HERON takes matches from pocket.)*

FREWER: If it was ever going to be published – or not even published; if *anyone* was going to read it, even yourself afterwards – but as things are…

HERON: Better as things are… Not better; the same. *(He lights the spill.)* I haven't the least desire to keep it or anything. It makes no difference what you keep. The thing was there before you had it, and is still there when it seems to have gone. *(The trap-door opens.)*

MARIE: Listen. What is that? *(PHILIP, holding dirty rag from the dark interior, U/R, appears at the trap-door as CHASSAIGNE emerges.)*

CHASSAIGNE: Which of them are you?

PHILIP: Sturgess. The American.

CHASSAIGNE: Marie is here?

PHILIP: You know she is.

CHASSAIGNE: I want her urgently – urgently.

PHILIP: Come then. She is in here. *(They enter through the door of the Sardine Box. JULIAN follows. The meditative atmosphere has suddenly changed.)*

MARIE: What is it, father?

CHASSAIGNE: The enemy is moving. Everything is changed. This message came. Read it. *(Hands paper to MARIE.)*

MARIE: It is in cipher.

CHASSAIGNE: I am not a fool. I have deciphered it. On the back it is *en clair*. Read it! Read it! *(MARIE turns the paper and reads silently.)*

MARIE: If they are moving, your room must not be empty. Go back, father.

CHASSAIGNE: In face of that you will not start? *(Dans ces conditions ils ne partent plus?)*

MARIE: I will decide. *(Cela me regarde.)*

CHASSAIGNE: You cannot go. Virac is too far. *(Mais c'est impossible. Virac cest trop loin.)*

MARIE: Go back, father. *(Père retourne chez toi.)*

CHASSAIGNE: Ah well, I go. *(Bon bon je m'en vais.)* *(CHASSAIGNE goes. MARIE waits until the trap-door is closing.)*

MARIE: I'm sorry. This is difficult. Plans have changed. This is a message from farther up the Line. The road which passes our ditch outside Blaise has become unsafe. You can't be picked up there.

JULIAN: In what way unsafe?

MARIE: The enemy will be moving over it to-night. Your transport has been diverted through Virac St. Just. We are to be at Rendezvous 46 – it is a grocer's shop in Virac – not earlier than one-five, not later than one-fifteen, in the morning. The car will have two others on board, by-passing Blaise. At one-fifteen it goes forward.

JULIAN: *(Looking at watch.)* It is now – nine-thirty-seven. Three hours and three quarters. How far is Virac?

MARIE: Forty-three kilometres.

JULIAN: Twenty…seven miles?

MARIE: You still think in miles…

PHILIP: In English, French, or American, it is impossible on foot.

MARIE: That is the point. Secondary transport from Blaise to Virac has to be found.

FREWER: If a car could be stolen –

MARIE: It must not be stolen.

FREWER: Borrowed then. You could take us to Virac and drive the car back.

MARIE: I cannot drive. In any case, I must not leave Blaise.

FREWER: We could drive, and scrap it short of Virac.

MARIE: No, Dick. A car stolen from Blaise and scrapped at Virac. That would stir up the hornet's nest. No.

FREWER: Then the thing's not possible…

JULIAN: Is there secondary transport?

MARIE: At present none. I have to find it. There are two possibilities – Dessaix and Félix, both loyal men.

HERON: Part of the River Line?

MARIE: No. But part of the Resistance. They know me. They will help if they can. It depends on how they are placed to-night. It may be impossible for either of them.

JULIAN: You mean you are going to ask them?

MARIE: I must. I must.

JULIAN: The risk to you is enormous.

MARIE: They will not, I think… I must have transport for you.

JULIAN: Listen. What would happen if we didn't start?

MARIE: If you stayed her, the whole Line would pile up. Within twenty-four hours I should have eight men on my hands. The block at this end would be disastrous.

JULIAN: Well, I think that, in going to Félix and Dessaix, you are running an intolerable risk. You put yourself in their hands.

MARIE: I personally?

JULIAN: Marie, I – all of us here – when we are gone and you are left behind –

MARIE: Thank you. I know. You are kind. But it isn't your job to protect me. It is my job to post my parcels.

PHILIP: The whole question is –

HERON: There is no question. Marie knows the ropes, we do not. We don't argue, and we don't suggest. We leave her in peace; we give her time to think and we take her orders. Is that understood? *(To MARIE.)* Now.

MARIE: If I can get Félix or Dessaix, you will start. The approach must be made with the utmost caution… It will take time.

JULIAN: There's time enough. Three and three-quarter hours?

MARIE: Work it back. Virac at latest one-fifteen. Allow a minimum of forty-five minutes on the road. Eight minutes from this house to the place where Dessaix's car will pick you up if it picks you up at all. Total fifty-three. We must leave this granary not an instant later than twelve-twenty-two. That leaves no margin.

HERON: Twelve-twenty-two. That gives you a little over two hours and a half to be back here.

MARIE: More than enough, if things go well. If not… Synchronize. *(She holds out her watch.)*

HERON: *(Comparing his.)* Nine-forty-one.

MARIE: Is it understood? You will be ready to start at sixty-seconds notice.

HERON: Less.

MARIE: I may, if I have luck, be back in under an hour. If not – oh well. I am sorry. It is not intelligent to operate without a margin.

HERON: We live in a world in which we have all agreed to be fooled by the clock.

MARIE: When I return, there may be no chance to say good-bye. So I say good-bye...to you all...now. *(Stage blackout.)*

SCENE 3

Three minutes to midnight. Skylight blacked out. Floor beam showing backstage. In the Sardine Box, FREWER's improvised chair-leg is fitted to the armchair. Behind a low bale Right-Centre, HERON kneels above bale, facing the audience. To the Left of the bale, close to it, is miscellaneous debris, which, together with the Left edge of the packing-case, is in the black shadow of the dark lantern. PHILIP is sitting in an armchair R of and close to bale, tin bath at his feet. JULIAN is L of packing case.

JULIAN: *(Finishing dressing – putting on his boots and coat.)* Even this room looks different now that we've broken it up for the move!

PHILIP: *(To JULIAN.)* I thought you said you were through. *(HERON hands papers to PHILIP to burn. PHILIP is burning own papers with those of HERON's.)*

JULIAN: I am, all but my make-up.

PHILIP: Make-up? *(He lights paper in tin bowl. It flares up and smokes.)*

JULIAN: Pince-nez, beret – and I have on these damned pointed boots. All dressed up and – no means of going. Marie has been away too long. I don't like it.

HERON: Two hours and more. Obviously the first man wouldn't play. It's getting late even for the second.

JULIAN: She may just not come back at all. In which case... *(But that sentence won't complete itself and he swerves from it violently.)* The debris in this room might be more evenly distributed. Too many books. I'll take some out... *(And he swerves again.)* What are you chaps doing?

PHILIP: Emptying our pockets.

JULIAN: Looks like a sacrificial altar... One thing about the River Line: it teaches you to burn your love-letters. *(Goes out U/R.)*

PHILIP: I have very little outside the wallet I'm entitled to carry. This caricature that Dick gave me. I let that go reluctantly. But go it must. It has English balloons coming out of its mouth. *(While PHILIP is speaking and burning, HERON is searching his own pockets, making a little pile on the ledge of the packing-case behind the lamp. From the pile, he takes a sheet and hands it to PHILIP.)*

HERON: Burn them one by one. We don't want the ash to fly… *(He takes up and hands over another sheet.)* And that. *(And now he comes to some blue sheets of note-paper, taken from his pocket by mistake. These he rapidly secretes. As he does so, an envelope is flicked off the bale onto the floor D/S of bale. Neither sees this. Nor does half the audience. But they will learn.)* That is all. *(He hands over one more sheet.)*

PHILIP: It's odd how one clings to paper. Strictly we oughtn't to have had even these. They ought to have been burned 'as soon as made'… Are you sure that's all?

HERON: Quite sure.

PHILIP: Let's go through our pockets once more. *(They do so, but HERON does not produce the sheets we have just seen him put away.)*

PHILIP: All clear.

HERON: I have nothing.

PHILIP: *(Taking up the bowl.)* I'll get rid of these ashes.

He carries them out, through curtain and off U/R. HERON waits a little, thinks, hesitates, then takes out the blue letter and kneels by the lamp. PHILIP has appeared R of dresser. Looks through open shelves and starts back from what he sees. The clock in the village begins to strike midnight.

With a pencil, HERON swiftly adds some amendment using bale as table. Then he claps his hands to his pockets, obviously searching for something he cannot find. Then, putting away the folded leaves, rises hastily and sees PHILIP.

PHILIP: What are you looking for?

HERON: A – a piece I wrote which I don't remember having burned. I may have done or it may still be out here. *(He goes out. PHILIP follows him with his eyes. He has seen too much. Suspicion is flowing in upon him. He wavers in hesitation, then sees the envelope lying in the dark of the lantern, darts for it, reads it. Meanwhile, CHASSAIGNE has been coming up through the trap-door. He now enters between dresser and pipe.)*

CHASSAIGNE: *(Who is in a state of distressed agitation.)* When is she coming back? She gave me no time!

PHILIP: *(Startled by the voice.)* You!

CHASSAIGNE: What is that in your hand? Are you not leaving to-night. Do you carry papers?

PHILIP: We have been burning them.

CHASSAIGNE: Good... When do you expect her?

PHILIP: Twelve-twenty-two.

CHASSAIGNE: It is close.

PHILIP: *(Struggling for decision.)* Go back, for God's sake! What are you doing here? *(CHASSAIGNE turns to go off. PHILIP is in an agony of choice.)*

PHILIP: Wait *(CHASSAIGNE turns.)* I have no choice. None. ... Read that.

CHASSAIGNE: *(Snatching the envelope, falling on one knee above bale to read it.)* Frau Gustav Keller, Leipzig, Lotzestrasse 73! ... Leipzig! Leipzig! This is not your handwriting. It is his! *(On his feet, throwing out an arm, trembling and pointing.)* It is his! Heron! Where is the letter?

PHILIP: Sh! There is no letter... On him, I think... He dropped the envelope. He was looking for it.

CHASSAIGNE: The envelope is enough. Leipzig!

PHILIP: Quiet. We have only an instant. All the evidence runs together now. Heron... My God! It is unbelievable.

CHASSAIGNE: My young friend, a man need not be base to be your enemy.

PHILIP: The right course is to tell him, to tell the others, to give him a chance to –

CHASSAIGNE: You cannot. This is not a court of law. The road is not thirty yards away. If he is warned, if there is a struggle, an outcry, he will call attention to this house.

PHILIP: But we daren't let him cross the frontier into Spain.

CHASSAIGNE: That is for Marie to decide.

PHILIP: How can I tell her? When she returns, there will be no time. If I try to tell her then –

CHASSAIGNE: I will tell her before she comes to you.

PHILIP: Somehow she must find a way to keep him here while inquiries are made. Can you make her understand that?

CHASSAIGNE: Inquiries? She will know what to do my young friend. *Il ne passera pas.* Lotzestrasse. Leipzig. Give me that envelope. It is enough. *(He tucks it away as HERON enters from U/R and between dresser and packing case.)*

HERON: Monsieur what are you doing here?

CHASSIAGNE: I came for a little company.

HERON: To-night? Your room is unguarded.

CHASSAIGNE: That is true. I am a thoughtless old man. I go at once. *(He goes out and down through the trap-door.)*

JULIAN: Are we all set? *(All except PHILIP have their equipment or disguise for travel. The difference is very slight – a raincoat, a hat, JULIAN's pince-nez.)* These things, I believe, are the best of all disguises if you have my kind of face and you put them on wide – so that they draw up the flesh under the eyes. They narrow the whole face. Stick out your teeth, stick out your neck, stoop a bit and you are transformed into a bureaucratic rabbit.

PHILIP: I still have to get my raincoat. *(Enter FREWER between desk and stove pipe.)*

HERON: Well get it. … Get out the cards, Dick.

FREWER: Cards? Now?

HERON: It's twelve-ten. Twelve minutes to zero. We may as well play a hand. Better than doing nothing and waiting for the kettle to boil. *(FREWER brings out cards from his pocket. JULIAN turns the rug back and gathers other cards from under it.*

Together, he and FREWER make up the pack. HERON meanwhile is wandering about, looking for his vanished envelope.)

JULIAN: What are you looking for so diligently?

HERON: Making sure nothing's left behind. *(He sits down ready to play. He is facing the audience. JULIAN drops down on his right. FREWER is on HERON's left, and is seen in left-quarter-face. When PHILIP comes in, he sits on JULIAN's right.)*

JULIAN: Partners as we sit? *(Enter PHILIP who crosses to sit on floor D/L corner of bale.)*

FREWER: I shan't be much good to you at nine minutes to zero hour.

JULIAN: She's running it fine.

FREWER: She may not have got either car. We may not start. I remember once, just as I was starting back from leave, I got an extension –

PHILIP: Why are we playing bridge? I can't play bridge now...

HERON: Poker if you like.

JULIAN: We are only four.

HERON: Never mind. Deal.

FREWER: We haven't any kind of chips.

PHILIP: Deal, for God's sake, chips or no chips. *(JULIAN deals.)*

HERON: Assume my ante. I'm shy.

FREWER: Assume my straddle.

JULIAN: Cards?

HERON: Four to the joker.

JULIAN: Wake up, Dick. Cards?

FREWER: Two.

PHILIP: Three.

JULIAN: Dealer Three. Who bets?... Philip? *(The trap-door rises. MARIE begins to come in.)*

PHILIP: One shilling.

JULIAN: I'll see that.

HERON: I make it – oh what does it matter – five shillings. Five bob shy. *(MARIE enters U/C unseen by players – stands by dresser.)*

FREWER: I'm in – and shy. We're all shy. This is ghost-poker.

PHILIP: I make it ten. What? What did you say?

FREWER: It's three minutes to zero.

JULIAN: I'm away. *(Throws in his cards.)*

HERON: Fifteen.

FREWER: I'm away.

PHILIP: *(To HERON.)* We two… Twenty. Your bet. *(They stir, half-rise.)*

HERON: Now?

MARIE: No. Not now. There's been a hitch.

JULIAN: What has happened? *(Leaps to her side.)* You look half-dead. My dear, what has happened?

MARIE: Sit down. Go on with your game. *(They obey.)*

PHILIP: Only you and I are left in, Heron. Your bet.
  (MARIE nerving herself to act. She is shaking violently.)

JULIAN: Marie, what have they done to you?

MARIE: *(Throwing back her head.)* No. No. No. For one moment leave me alone.

HERON: Twenty-five.

PHILIP: Thirty.

HERON: Forty.

PHILIP: Fifty. *(And now MARIE has nerved herself to speak.)*

MARIE: Commander. *(JULIAN stiffens to extreme alertness. She looks steadily into HERON's face and he at her without flinching. She raises her arm at HERON.)* Kill that man. *(JULIAN, with a violent indrawing of breath, draws his dagger and kills HERON. MARIE watches and watches. They are all upright – JULIAN last. HERON raises himself in a final agony. His face is, for a moment, visible. Then he falls forward on face.)*

JULIAN: Why?

MARIE: Now go. Leave everything. My father will deal with the lamp and… Go. *(They go out of the room, FREWER last. At the door, he turns back alone, wrenches his chair-leg off and disposes of it. Then he catches up the others. After a moment's pause, the trap-door opens again. CHASSAIGNE comes up. The envelope is in his hand. He stoops over the body.)*

CHASSAIGNE: Leipzig.

He rifles the pockets and brings out the letter on blue paper. With great avidity, crouched by the lamp, he unfolds the letter. Rises. He pauses in his reading to stare at the body and jabs at it with his foot.

Curtain.

ACT THREE

The terrace of Act I. The next morning – Saturday. PHILIP STURGESS, finishing breakfast in the garden, is sitting R of table, pouring out his last cup of coffee. JULIAN comes in, wearing old country clothes, U/R carrying large ledger.)

JULIAN: Still breakfasting. You are a man of leisure.

PHILIP: My last cup. I gather from the looks of it, you and Marie finished long ago.

JULIAN: Have you seen her?

PHILIP: For a moment.

JULIAN: I have housekeeping news to report. News for you too. I had to go down early into Tarryford. On the bridge, I met the Iron Duke. Your young woman has her sailing orders.

PHILIP: My God, since when?

JULIAN: An hour ago. Her passage was confirmed by telephone from London. She's packing now. America will have to intervene swiftly.

PHILIP: She can't pack! She was coming out with me this morning. She was to pick me up here *(Looks at watch.)* about now and we were to – When does she go?

JULIAN: Sunday.

PHILIP: To-morrow!

JULIAN: Leaves here to-morrow. One full day in London. Sails Tuesday. From your air of…controlled panic…do I gather that yesterday evening wasn't satisfactory? You followed us at so discreet a distance that I thought you were making progress?

PHILIP: I was. But not enough. I felt…you'll think me wrong… that first she must know more about me. … Or, if you like, that I must know more about myself.

JULIAN: Beware of a sick conscience. Never cry over spilt blood – anyhow not aloud… So you told her the whole tale?

PHILIP: Do you mind?

JULIAN: N-no. Not if you are going to marry her. Are you?

PHILIP: I shall find out this morning.

JULIAN: What did you call Heron?

PHILIP: Heron. The other name, Lang, was false. It never enters my mind. Anyhow what odds would it make?

JULIAN: To her none, I grant you. But names travel. Is there anything *(He hesitates and continues with a certain reluctance because he is now, in effect, lying.)* to be gained by letting the enemy know what became of their agents? *(From D/R enter MARIE carrying tray for clearing.)*

PHILIP: The enemy! The enemy! The enemy! You are obsessed, Julian. Who are the enemy?

MARIE: I will tell you. They are those who hate God, who despise the human person, who deny the liberty of thought. It is not a question of nationality. Still, dear Philip, the Rhine is not as broad as the Atlantic. Nor are the Oder and the Neisse. There are always enemies of France in the world, and of England – and of America, too. O thou of too much faith! The herd peoples are still moving westward. Twice the flood has been thrown back. There is a third to come. Be silent, be silent, be silent until Armageddon is *over*. It is by no means over yet.

JULIAN: Marie believes in keeping her powder dry.

MARIE: *Eh bien, je suis francaise. (She begins to pile the breakfast things on the tray.)*

JULIAN: Mrs. Muriven and Miss Barton are coming this evening.

MARIE: *(In consternation.)* This evening? To dinner?

JULIAN: You are indeed French. *(C'est une vrais Francaise.)*

MARIE: But there will be nothing worth eating… Nevertheless, I will arrange.

JULIAN: I said you were adorably and competently French. *(Rises.)* I must get on with my job… In fact, my dear, you may rest in peace. Mrs. Muriven is considerately English. She refused dinner. They will come up afterwards. The girl is leaving to-morrow. *(He goes out D/L carrying ledger.)*

MARIE: Valerie is leaving to-morrow?

PHILIP: Not if I can prevent it. Passages can be cancelled. *(He helps her with the breakfast things.)*

MARIE: Ah, Philip, don't press too hard for that. If she has given her word to go to South Africa, she will wish to go, at least until her brother has had time to make other plans.

PHILIP: But an engagement to marry cancels all engagements.

MARIE: That is extremely untrue. *(She is carrying the tray towards the drawing room.)* Besides, she is English.

PHILIP: English?

MARIE: *(With a smile, over her shoulder.)* They like to keep their word in strict order of priority. *(She carries out the tray through the drawing room. PHILIP follows with coffee-pot. VALERIE enters Left. She sits tranquilly on the stone seat. PHILIP returns.)*

PHILIP: Your passage has come through?

VALERIE: Commander Wyburton told you?

PHILIP: Nevertheless we go for our walk? … Or stay here? … You are tired after last night?

VALERIE: No. I was happy last night. Why were you afraid? You were, you know. I told you so then.

PHILIP: I answered you then. *(Wanting an excuse to laugh.)* You always say 'you know'. I begin to think I know very little.

VALERIE: You are a queer creature.

PHILIP: I? I'm the most ordinary creature on – After all, who does know the whole of any story? Particularly of a story in which they themselves have taken part. Ought I to loathe and despise Heron?

VALERIE: Why should you?

PHILIP: He was, in effect, a spy.

VALERIE: Commander Wyburton was a spy. One cannot despise brave men.

PHILIP: It is…interesting…to hear you say that. Marie and Julian would say it, but they are professionals, they are hard.

VALERIE: Hard? Have you watched their eyes – even their hands? His way of reaching out and just not touching her. They give me the feeling of two people with a wall of glass between them which…isn't there. And yet something is.

PHILIP: *(Quoting.)* 'Silences.' Marie's word. I don't pretend to understand it.

VALERIE: There's a part of the story I don't understand. Did Heron in fact send home an earlier letter? You saw him buy stamps. But did he send a letter?

PHILIP: In fact we know he did.

VALERIE: Did you see him?

PHILIP: No one saw him, but Frewer knew of it. Frewer told us in our ship on the way home from Barcelona. Heron had told him quite openly what he was doing. One of his fellow-prisoners, an English Major, had been dying in camp. He had a sister in Leipzig, married to a German. Heron, when he escaped, was to carry messages in his head, and write to Leipzig from France. No censorship that way. Frewer didn't doubt the story at the time. He had no possible reason to suspect Heron.

VALERIE: And the second letter? Marie must have seen and read that.

PHILIP: Her old father took it off Heron's body. It was stuck with his blood. I can't discuss it with Marie. All I know about it is through Julian. It appeared to be harmless. Outwardly, at any rate, it was written to a woman about her brother. Marie says, too, that, when she had it tested for cipher by the River Line cryptographers, the early results were negative. Beyond that she hasn't gone; maybe she can't; she herself was arrested soon afterwards.

VALERIE: And the woman? The sister in Leipzig?

PHILIP: No trace, I gather. But that goes for nothing. Leipzig is in the Russian zone.

VALERIE: Oh, Philip, all the things that used to be wild melodrama have become commonplaces. It's a kind of madness. You and Julian Wyburton and Heron himself all doing right and inevitable things –

PHILIP: But were they? That's the whole point.

VALERIE: They were right and inevitable on that plane of insane violence.

PHILIP: And dead against every intuition of our personal lives.

VALERIE: That is why I said: 'madness'.

PHILIP: But the world has gone through its periods of violence before.

VALERIE: But now violence is a condition of thought. That is new.

PHILIP: If so, it may produce new remedies.

VALERIE: Must there be a 'remedy'? Everyone assumes that there must be a Utopia round the corner.

PHILIP: Isn't there? Not even a Christian Utopia?

VALERIE: Not even a Christian Utopia. Not in political terms.

PHILIP: Then what does it mean to say: 'Thy Kingdom come. Thy will be done, *in earth*'?

VALERIE: What does it mean to say: 'The Kingdom of God is within you'?

PHILIP: We are asking questions, not answering them.

VALERIE: I think that is all we can do. Making ourselves eyes to see in the dark; not asserting beforehand what we shall see.

PHILIP: 'Preferring –'

VALERIE: Preferring?

PHILIP: I was trying to remember the phrase. It was on one of the scraps of paper we burned that night. 'Preferring knowledge before power, and wisdom before knowledge and love before wisdom; but preferring also the faculty of wonder before the faculty of sight.'

VALERIE: *(Listening to an echo but not yet recognizing it as such.)* Did he write that? *(And the actress, with a puzzled gaze from PHILIP to help her, leaves us to wonder who VALERIE meant by 'he' – her brother or HERON or, almost, both? PHILIP leaves the question as needing no answer and kneels beside her. Suddenly she turns to him and lays her hand on his hand with a movement so simple and spontaneous that he is astonished by it. She says:)* There is nothing to fear.

PHILIP: You put your hand on mine!

VALERIE: To tell you there is nothing to fear. *(She takes back her hand naturally.)*

PHILIP: Since we have been together this morning and have been, in a way, so near, so much nearer even than we were last night, I am not afraid of anything except…of myself. Perhaps I am just one of those people who make drastic decisions because they are themselves indecisive and have a kind of false naiveté because they aren't genuinely simple. If so, I'm not of much use to you. Still, I might grow. I did in that granary. I have since I knew you… Suddenly one meets someone who isn't muddy or cloudy, someone who – you said once that your brother had… serenity. You loved him for that. I'm not calm, I'm not unruffled.

VALERIE: But serene doesn't mean only 'calm'. It means also 'clear, translucent, with light shining through'.

PHILIP: Like you. Valerie, listen… What have you there?

VALERIE: *(Hands him the case she has taken from her bag.)* This is my brother's photograph. *(The photograph is enclosed in a case fastened by a strap. He fumbles with it, but, his thought being elsewhere, does not instantly open it.)* No. Turn it over. It snaps open.

PHILIP: *(Taking her hand as she stretches it out towards the case.)* Sit quite still. I'm not looking at you. You know better what I am than I know myself. You must decide…peacefully… whether, being so different… Last night, before I told

you that story, I asked you not to take your hand away
and now – *(He drops her hand, and draws away from her. The
photograph-case has fallen open. Silence.)*

VALERIE: Philip!

PHILIP: *(With a violent effort he stands up, holding the open case. He
has gone suddenly into reverse.)* What was his name?

VALERIE: John – John Lang.

PHILIP: Not your name?

VALERIE: I told you: he was my half-brother.

PHILIP: How old was he?

VALERIE: He would have been now – thirty-three.

PHILIP: And that uniform. What regiment is it?

VALERIE: Philip, what is the matter?

PHILIP: It's extraordinary how he carries his head. Upright.
Almost backward, you'd say. Even in the photograph you
can see – Can I keep it?

VALERIE: *(Surprised.)* Yes. Why?

PHILIP: It is…almost of you. A memento.

VALERIE: My dear, what is wrong?

PHILIP: Nothing.

VALERIE: But there is something.

PHILIP: No.

VALERIE: You look ill? Why? What has happened?

PHILIP: *(Takes her in his arms but does not kiss her.)* Once…
*(Releases her, moves abruptly away towards the drawing room.
Stops. Looks back.)*

VALERIE: *(Quietly.)* Something has happened. If you can, tell
me.

PHILIP: Is it true you leave to-morrow?

VALERIE: Yes.

PHILIP: Then this is…good-bye.

VALERIE: *(Accepting this without understanding it.)* Good-bye,
dear Philip… I mean it in the old sense.

PHILIP: The old sense? *(He does not wait for an answer but goes out.)*

VALERIE: *(Alone. She is standing near the squab D/S/R.)* God be with you, my dearest, in all your strange troubles, and me in mine. *(Exhausted by shock she sits down on squab staring before her, making herself eyes to see in the dark; and says to herself:)*

'If I but had the eyes and ears

To read within what now appears,

Then should I see in every face

An innocent, interior grace,

And, as the clouds of thought unfurled,

Be native of the golden world.'

If I but had the eyes – *(She rises now, covers her eyes, uncovers them, lifts her head, crosses to wall D/S, picks up bag. JULIAN enters D. Left in her path.)*

JULIAN: Alone?

VALERIE: Yes. *(In a light tone.)* I must go home and pack. *(They pass. VALERIE exits D/L.)*

JULIAN: See you to-night. *(He goes to the wall L and looks after VALERIE. PHILIP re-enters from U/R. To above table.)*

JULIAN: What has happened? I met her going.

PHILIP: What did you say to her?

JULIAN: Nothing, I couldn't. But I saw... Oh, I said something to pass it off. I said: 'See you to-night.'

PHILIP: She won't come to-night... Sit down, Julian. I have something to say... Sit down for God's sake. *(They sit at the table.)* Will you consider that? It's an interesting photograph. She gave it to me. It's her brother... No, turn it over. It snaps open. *(JULIAN opens it, stares, but gives no sign.)* Well, Julian?

JULIAN: How much does she know?... How much does Miss Barton know?

PHILIP: No more than she did. That her brother is gone, presumed dead.

JULIAN: But that Heron was her brother?

PHILIP: No.

JULIAN: *(Challenging what he thinks is a lie.)* Then why were you so sure she wouldn't come here to-night?

PHILIP: *(Angry.)* Why in heaven's name do you ask that? What does it matter? You look at a photograph which tells you that the man we killed was a loyal officer, and all you ask is how much Valerie knows and why she should not dine here! Isn't that a personal matter between her and me?

JULIAN: I have known for nearly four years that we were mistaken. As soon as I reached England, I sent for Lang's *dossier*. It tallied beyond question. I have seen that photograph before.

PHILIP: And you wouldn't tell me?

JULIAN: I have told no one.

PHILIP: *(Angrier.)* But when you saw what was happening between Valerie and me, surely, if you are not inhuman, your precious rule of secrecy –

JULIAN: Listen. Get this straight. That Heron was genuine I have known for nearly four years. That he was her brother I have this moment learned. The name of Barton didn't appear on the *dossier*. Only Lang. The next of kin was Lang, a younger brother – presumably the chap now in South Africa. The names Lang and Barton didn't link in my mind until three minutes ago. That was new. You have to accept that or we shall talk at cross-purposes.

PHILIP: *(More calmly.)* Very well. I accept it. I'm sorry I flared up. *(Then he flares up again.)* My God, though, you and Marie must have thought me a pretty fool! Coming here, all agog to chatter about 'our Blaise adventure', and understanding not the first thing about it! There was I, the complete sucker, rather proud of myself for having been 'professional' enough to save the River Line from an enemy agent and to kill the man who – *(He breaks off in shame and indignation.)* And there were you and Marie, smiling at me up your sleeves, letting me babble on, allowing me day by day to –

JULIAN: Steady!

PHILIP: Well, isn't it so?

JULIAN: No, it is not so.

PHILIP: Anyhow, you saw fit not to tell me – you and Marie.

JULIAN: I couldn't tell you… And Marie has nothing to do with it. *(He leans across the table, taut with anxiety.)* At any moment, Marie may come out. If she does, keep your mouth shut. And keep that photograph out of sight. *(His own hand has been covering it. He pushes it across.)* Put it away now.

PHILIP: Take it. Do what you like with it.

JULIAN: *(Drawing it back under his hand, flat on the table.)* I'm sorry to be so excitable. To see that photograph within Marie's reach shakes me.

PHILIP: Are you telling me that she still believes that Heron was false?

JULIAN: Yes.

PHILIP: And you have let her go on believing it for four years. It seems mad to me.

JULIAN: *(With tired patience.)* Does it? You forget that I love her… And it hasn't been four years. I had no contact with her from the night we left Blaise until the war ended. I found her in a Swiss hospital with the marks of Ravensbrück still on her. I had more or less taken it for granted that she'd know as much as I did, but she didn't. I didn't rush my fences. There she was, propped up in bed, great scars on her face, eyes like black holes in a skull, wrists like matches – I can tell you, the subject of Heron's death wasn't one for me to plunge into. And, anyhow *(A lightened, mocking tone.)* as you know, Philip – you have cursed me for it often enough – I have a habit of not being the first to talk. So I held my hand and left her to lead… She didn't lead – or avoid. She talked about Heron sometimes, always with admiration, as one does

speak calmly and dispassionately of the dead; she talked
of him as someone…above the battle, who had to die, but
was exempt from judgement. Not a hint of knowing that
she and I – and you – had been wrong. And gradually it
dawned on me that she really didn't know… Thank God…
I wouldn't tell. It would be wanton cruelty to tell. If I can
do nothing else, I can keep my mouth shut… Well? Do you
still blame me?

PHILIP: No. The cases are different.

JULIAN: What cases?

PHILIP: Yours and mine. Your marrying with…that silence,
and my – not asking.

JULIAN: Is that what happened this morning?

PHILIP: I – quite suddenly – didn't ask.

JULIAN: But you will?

PHILIP: No.

JULIAN: But she understands nothing. You must ask.

PHILIP: No, Julian.

JULIAN: Nor tell her?

PHILIP: Wouldn't that be towards her, too…'wanton cruelty'?

JULIAN: If you and she love each other, it is a thousand times
more cruel not to marry her. The world is what it is. We
are lonely animals.

PHILIP: Do you mean I should marry without telling her?

JULIAN: I did.

PHILIP: And have lived with – a silence between you ever
since. Isn't that true?

JULIAN: We have lived together… Oh, Philip, the world is
a desert until we build ourselves a roof… *She* has been
happy, I think… Why is it impossible that you – ?

PHILIP: For the moment, leave me out. My responsibility
is all my own. I judged Heron. I gave that envelope to
Chassaigne. Your responsibility is secondary. Such as it is,
you and Marie share it.

JULIAN: There you are wrong. If Marie knew, she would see the whole responsibility as hers. It was my knife, but it was her order.

PHILIP: You are bitterly consistent.

JULIAN: Just consistent…

PHILIP: And you mean to go on like this for ever – always afraid that some poor fool like me will blurt it out.

JULIAN: Who could? Frewer's dead.

PHILIP: Always afraid, then, to talk to her of the one subject which, because you daren't speak of it, grows bigger and bigger in your mind. Is that possible?

JULIAN: It hasn't proved impossible yet.

PHILIP: Happy?

JULIAN: Happy! Happy! Happy! You talk like the mob.

PHILIP: Who are the mob?

JULIAN: Those who wish to be happy at other men's expense! Wherever two or three are gathered together in self-pity, there is the mob.

PHILIP: I still ask: Are you happy?

JULIAN: We farm our land.

PHILIP: Even if Marie did assume the whole responsibility, isn't she strong enough?

JULIAN: *(Roused to fierce retaliation.)* Isn't that a question you had better ask yourself? It needs courage to take risks with other people's lives. It needs a courage which – Quiet! *(MARIE has come in from D/R.)*

MARIE: No post yet?

JULIAN: No, but –

MARIE: What's the matter with you, Julian? *(Looking from one to the other.)* What have you been saying, you two? I heard your voices.

JULIAN: What did you hear?

MARIE: Raised voices… Nothing.

JULIAN: Listen, Marie. *(He is turning the photograph-case over and over in his hands.)* I have this. You had better see it. *(She looks at the photograph, not with visible shock but with searching interest.)*

JULIAN: He was an English officer. He was an officer of the Hussars. You had better know.

MARIE: Oh, Julian! *(She sits, trembling. The photograph falls. She keeps her eyes on JULIAN.)* So terribly long. *(It is a cry of relief.)* Poor Julian, this is new to you.

JULIAN: No. I might have told you long ago. I thought I had the guts to keep my mouth shut. I haven't, that's all.

MARIE: My dearest, it is not new to me.

JULIAN: Not new! How did you know?

MARIE: From Brussels. Just before I was taken.

JULIAN: Tell me, then –

MARIE: Not now. I don't want to talk now. Oh, Julian!

JULIAN: But if all this time –

MARIE: Not now. Not yet. *(JULIAN puts his arms round MARIE, kisses her.)* All words are dangerous. *(They embrace again.)*

Curtain.

SCENE 2

The same. After dinner that night. MARIE sitting chair D/L/C by wall D/S and PHILIP, looking out over wall U/L, discovered.

PHILIP: She will not come.

MARIE: If not, you must go to her.

PHILIP: No, Marie.

MARIE: You are *naïf*, Philip. I am not. Both ways one can be self-deceived.

PHILIP: Naïve? My mother says: 'guileless'.

MARIE: I wonder whether you have ever asked yourself why people are fond of you – people quite different from one another and miles apart from you… Or why, if it comes to that, Valerie loves you. She does, you know.

PHILIP: I know. At least –

MARIE: Don't qualify it! One knows that it is so or that it is not. One knows by the touch of a hand, the feel of the air. I know that Heron did not love me. And you know that Valerie – but do you know why? Do you in the least know what is lovable in you? It is the fact that you don't know. You are loved because, in that respect, you are without vanity. The miracle happens because, to you, it always is a miracle. People are desired who expect to be desired, and envied who expect to be envied, but no one is ever deeply loved who is not as incredulous of love as he is of death. Julian and I have been happier to-day than ever in the past. We love each other without silences now and – yes – with all our hearts, such as they are. But our love is limited by our personalities. There are great lovers as there are great poets, and we are not among them. I shall never be greatly loved because my intellect is too quick: I am not naïve enough. I know the reason for everything; – even for love, and so I shall never be loved as you are loved, and I shall never – oh well, let it go.

PHILIP: Say what you were going to say, Marie.

MARIE: I shall never know how to die as Heron died. Do you understand that?

PHILIP: No.

MARIE: I have not wonder enough. It is the grace to receive Grace. Not granted to me. Do you understand that?

PHILIP: Perhaps, in time, I might understand if –

MARIE: Ah, don't try. Don't have the killing arrogance to try. That is my own intellectual sin.

PHILIP: I think she won't come.

MARIE: Your mind goes back! How rightly and simply!

PHILIP: And if she does, it will only be because not to come might create an…awkwardness greater than her coming. You know, Marie, she has that too in common with her brother. I can't imagine circumstances in which Heron would ever have made a scene.

MARIE: *(With a smile.)* That might have told us that he was English… Philip, don't walk about. Come and sit beside me. I have something to say… *(He moves towards her.)* Upon what happens or does not happen to-night, not your life only but her life depends.

PHILIP: Are you suggesting, as Julian did, that I should marry without telling her?

MARIE: Did Julian say that?

PHILIP: He said in effect: 'Keep your mouth shut. Marry. Do as I did.'

MARIE: That was foolish. You are incapable of doing as he did. *(Touching his hand affectionately.)* You have not…the gift of reticence… No, that is not what I suggest. But is there any reason that Valerie should not be told and allowed to judge for herself?

PHILIP: I think there is.

MARIE: What you did, you did unknowingly. Are you to blame?

PHILIP: Do you really believe that only the sins we commit knowingly are to be expiated and forgiven?

MARIE: Isn't that the accepted modern code?

PHILIP: It is the accepted modern avoidance. You don't believe it yourself. The whole of Greek tragedy denies it. *(JULIAN comes in, from D/R, and quietly listens.)* Go to Fate and say: 'Please, I didn't know! Please, I didn't mean it!' A man may let you off. Fate won't.

MARIE: If there is such a thing as Fate.

PHILIP: Very well, go to Nature and say: 'I didn't understand! I didn't intend!' Nature will flick you away like a dead fly.

MARIE: Even the Greeks sometimes allowed man to be reconciled with the gods. Tragedy doesn't always demand catastrophe finally ruinous. It isn't compassionless.

JULIAN: No. But the terms of its compassion are inexorable.

PHILIP: *(Going his own way.)* That's what I mean. You can't cry off. You have to bear responsibility for the wrong that came through you until you are...purified of it. Absolved. In my case, how else than by silence?

JULIAN: My God, you have changed.

PHILIP: Yes, I have changed. But I am not seeing myself as the hero of a Greek tragedy, believe me. I am only a little teacher trying to be honest – a little boaster whose pet melodrama has caught him in a trap.

MARIE: *(Firmly.)* It is her life as well as yours. May not she decide for herself?

PHILIP: Oh, Marie, do not torment me! You speak as if there were only she and I. It isn't a question of what she decides or I decide. Our marriage is...prohibited...by Heron's death... Prohibited, do you understand?

MARIE: No. I do not. Of course, if she were told, she might feel that it was intolerable to be the wife of the man who was responsible...who was partly responsible...for killing her brother. That you must risk. But the decision is one that she is entitled to make for herself.

PHILIP: It is not one that she can make or that I can make. The prohibition is not hers or mine. It is absolute. Its origin is not in either of us; it is in him. My responsibility is to him; my debt, not repayable. He alone might have forgiven it.

MARIE: You are binding yourself to the dead.

PHILIP: I don't feel it so. If I did, I should not be bound. He is alive for her. He is always alive for me – above all, here. From the first evening in this house – in the place that he might have had at your table; among us on this lawn – among us now. And quite unspeakably alive in *her*, as though he were looking out from the windows of her eyes.

MARIE: *(After a long pause.)* Ah, my poor Philip, if it is *in her* you see him, then I have no more to say. *(VALERIE comes out of the shadows U/R at the back of the stage. JULIAN sees her first and rises; PHILIP next. The ensuing scene opens fast and lightly. They are talking at haphazard. Anything to keep talk on a level that is of not dangerous.)*

JULIAN: You have climbed the hill alone?

VALERIE: Godmother has been helping me pack. *(PHILIP brings chair from D/L to L of table.)* She was tired and has gone to bed. *(To MARIE.)* I must stay only a little while. I have an early start. Really, I only came to say good-bye and because – Thank you Philip.

MARIE: All your packing is done?

VALERIE: Except the very last things.

MARIE: Then you can be peaceful here a little while… At any rate, your last evening in the English country will be spent among friends all of whom…love you. May I say that?

VALERIE: Thank you… Who was it, in your Revolution I think, who on the night before he was guillotined looked out of his window and said – and now I can't remember. Isn't it absurd and humiliating how the thread of what you were saying, quite suddenly, snaps? When it happens I feel always as if someone had come up behind me and taken… do you see what I mean?…and taken the telephone out of my hand.

MARIE: Listen! *(A silence.)*

PHILIP: You said that as if you were hearing music.

MARIE: I was hearing nothing. How still the night is. I used to have the idea when I was a little girl that, if ever there was *no* sound, not even the turning of a leaf, nothing, then time stopped too; no one died, no one was born, no one grew older. I used to hold my breath. *(Silence.)* Oh, but one has to breathe again and pour out coffee and light cigarettes… Give me a cigarette.

JULIAN: You never smoke.

MARIE: Never mind.

VALERIE: What I meant about the telephone was – *(They all freeze to listen as VALERIE continues.)* That often when memory snaps over something utterly unimportant as mine did just now, I feel as if someone behind me – or someone *in* me perhaps – had said: 'Do stop talking nonsense. Do get off the line. I have something real to say. Do let me talk on your line.' … And then I stop…

PHILIP: Isn't it because a person can have being in our minds without having physical existence?

VALERIE: *(Withdrawn a little now.)* If that is true of the living, it must be true of those we say are dead. You must feel it of Heron, as I do of my brother. *(JULIAN gets up, books in hand, crosses to below table.)*

JULIAN: Isn't it best to let the whole thing go?

VALERIE: I'm sorry. I meant to this evening. We did talk at first of quite casual things. *(Under stress, she moves away. MARIE lays a hand on PHILIP's arm.)*

MARIE: Philip, you must help her by telling her.

PHILIP: No!

MARIE: But she speaks of Heron and her brother as different people. She speaks quietly of her brother in the presence of us who killed him. We can't sit here and let her do that.

PHILIP: … Be patient.. There is something in *her* to-night that I have never seen before. You must not disturb it. She is possessed, but not yet fully.

MARIE: Possessed?

PHILIP: Not by an evil spirit… By an interior grace. It is – look at her now.

VALERIE: He has been in my mind all day – this evening more and more. That's what made me forget what I was trying to say. It was he who…took the receiver out of my hand. It did seem then that he was standing behind me… And now. *(She looks slowly at them all, one by one, but none speaks, and she continues:)* To-morrow it will be different. There will be a broken day in London, I know, but this is really my last night in England, one at any rate I shall remember as the last. If he had been alive I shouldn't have been going and there was a time this morning when I felt that my going was a new separation from him – a kind of desertion. Now, I don't feel that, but more as if –

PHILIP: As if he were here!

VALERIE: More, even, than that. As if. *(Wrenching herself back to normality, with change of tone and speed, to JULIAN.)* I'm sorry.

It must be tiresome of me to speak like this of someone you and Marie have never known. Philip and I have talked of him so much that – *(To JULIAN.)* How I wish that you had known him too!

JULIAN: I – *(He shifts, starts up, and while she continues, strides R along back wall to U/C in nervous agitation, returning to midstage in time for his next speech.)*

VALERIE: *(Calmly.)* Not that the appearance of anyone matters ultimately, I suppose. Anyhow, one can't communicate it. If in my ship, two or three days from now, I were speaking of this evening to some stranger and tried to describe Philip so that the stranger should have a picture of him in his mind, I should fail utterly. The eyes, the mouth, the nose, the shape of the head – yes, all that, all the separate bits, but never the whole appearance recognizably. Language simply doesn't provide.

JULIAN: *(Vehemently.)* Nor does thought. Not only will you be unable, two or three nights hence, to describe Philip's face but you will be unable to see it. Look away now! Look out there, over the other valley! *(He points. She looks straight out over the audience.)* Can you see his face distinctly, clearly, completely, as you do when your eyes are on it? Can you?

VALERIE: I can see *him*!

JULIAN: But his face, his features?

VALERIE: No, not as one sees with one's eyes. Or even in a photograph. But *him* I can see. *(She turns back to them.)* Of course Philip knows what my brother looked like. He has a photograph.

JULIAN: *(Steadily.)* Marie and I know what he looked like. We –

MARIE: *(On her feet, crosses to below table.)* Valerie –

PHILIP: Be patient. Wait. *(PHILIP and MARIE and JULIAN have spoken almost together. The secret is almost out. MARIE goes defensively to JULIAN's side. But VALERIE goes on quietly:)*

VALERIE: You have seen the photograph?

MARIE: Yes, Philip showed it to us. *(And the danger is past.)*

VALERIE: I'm glad. Not that it tells anything. I'm glad, all the same, that you have seen it... My trouble – I mean the stubborn part of it, the bit I couldn't disentangle – was: I didn't know how he died. He just vanished. I didn't even know in what country – in Germany, perhaps, or Belgium. It was a long time before I felt sure it was in France.

JULIAN: How were you sure? What proof was there of that?

VALERIE: None... Of course no proof. *(She has picked up some leaves and now, rubbing them, lets the fragments fall from her hands.)* Not in the least to know how he died was for a time a bleak gap in my knowledge of him. It prevented me from being with him imaginatively as he died. As though I had abandoned him. I couldn't help trying to see the place and trying to go to it – sometimes it was a field, or a black, muddy street, or a brick cell with a bare electric bulb – but it was all false, I knew it inside me; images of loneliness, that was all. ... And sometimes, as a corrective, I used to imagine that he died amongst friends who had learned to know and love him.

MARIE: That may have been true.

VALERIE: And that he hadn't the shudder of loneliness when he died. *(Very slowly, feeling for the last word.)* Only a moment, perhaps, of – incredulity... But that is long ago – my trying and trying to picture the scene and revisit it. That is all past... I was completely wrong. The way in which he died was not, for him, of the least importance. *(And now she begins to speak with an authority not her own. She is no longer speculating or feeling her way. She is narrating facts.)* When he was dying and those who killed him watched him die... *(She breaks off, rises.)* Even when his body was dead and a foot...jabbed at his body... You see, there was no question of his forgiving or not forgiving them. They bore their responsibility in the predicament of the world. Blame and forgiveness he was leaving behind. All our debts and credits were emptied out. He let them go – *(She falters.)* He let them – *(She falters.)* I let them go. They went quite naturally, as sleep goes when one wakes or waking goes when one sleeps, easily and simply. Just for a moment, between waking and sleeping, I was…incredulous that they should go so easily, afterwards not. Without wrench, without struggle – 'loss without losing'… Who said that?

PHILIP: *(Close to her, on terrace step above VALERIE.)* 'Loss without losing' – who said that?

VALERIE: My brother did… Heron did. *(She turns to PHILIP as understanding flows into her and looks, puzzled at first, from face to face.)* You…and you…and you…and he! Ah! *(She sways and covers her face with her hands. PHILIP, thinking she is about to fall, holds her.)* No, I am alright… *(She sits.)*

MARIE: For me, and Julian too, the word we cling to – only Heron could have spoken it, is: 'They bore their responsibility in the predicament of the world.' That is the condition of amnesty for all our generation. The only one, I think.

VALERIE: Did *I* say that? *(MRS. MURIVEN comes in D. Left, Crosses R to below chair R of table.)*

MRS. MURIVEN: I am old but, as you see, extremely energetic.

JULIAN: We thought you were in bed.

MRS. MURIVEN: I was. But I am not. We all spend too long in bed. I thought suddenly: up there life is going on. It is quite a short hill. I will go and see. The time will come when that may not be possible.

JULIAN: The party begins again. Look. This is your own Delamain – Oh Six.

MRS. MURIVEN: Thank you. A little glass… But it is cold here.

MARIE: Then shall we carry it in?

MRS. MURIVEN: I think that would be better.

JULIAN, MARIE and MRS. MURIVEN go out, but at the entrance to the drawing room MRS. MURIVEN pauses and says to JULIAN:

MRS. MURIVEN: Do you remember that ridiculous Russian who wrote plays? I thought it was all nonsense. But it isn't. My little dog really does eat nuts. *(Exits D/R.)*

VALERIE: *(When alone with PHILIP.)* Was it that – that Heron and my brother were the same – which you would not tell me?

PHILIP: Yes, Valerie.

VALERIE: Would you never have told me? Why, Philip?

PHILIP: Some day I will tell you the reasons. Not now. I was imprisoned by the past; now I am free. I was guilty and now – oh it isn't easy to say.

VALERIE: Does it need saying? Be at peace; my dear, be at peace.

PHILIP: I think it does need saying. In a way, it is the treaty between us. The solution of tragedy, I suppose, can never come from outside, but only from a power within the tragedy itself. If this morning I had told you and asked to be forgiven, and you had forgiven me, it would have been meaningless. Our knowledge would have been like a locked room in our house. We should have tried every key, but the room would still have been locked. That is why I didn't tell.

VALERIE: One cannot shut one's eyes to things not seen with eyes… As it is…

PHILIP: As it is? *(PHILIP kneels L of VALERIE.)* For me, when you were letting little pieces of leaf and stick fall through your hands, you were Heron; it was an interior grace.

VALERIE: If you mean that, this evening, he was within me – yes, that is true. And you had the grace to receive it. Otherwise it would not have been true. That is the…the absolution we have received together.

PHILIP: From him.

VALERIE: Through him.

PHILIP: But I killed him.

VALERIE: *(VALERIE's hand on PHILIP's shoulder.)* No, my dear, you did not. You could not. There is peace Philip… between us? Between us and him. *(PHILIP lays head in VALERIE's lap as curtain descends.)*
Curtain.

THE BURNING GLASS

Characters

CHRISTOPHER TERRIFORD
(34) *head of the Terriford Research Unit*

HELEN TERRIFORD
(59) *his mother*

MARY TERRIFORD
(24) *his wife*

TONY LACK
(perhaps 40s) *his second at the Unit*

TAMAS DOMOKOS ('GERRY') HARDLIP
(perhaps 38)

LORD HENRY STRAIT
(35-45) *on the Prime Minister's personal staff*

MONTAGU WINTHROP
(62 or more) *Prime Minister*

INSPECTOR WIGG
a police officer

The Burning Glass was first performed at Apollo Theatre, London, on 18 February 1954 with the following cast (in order of speaking):

CHRISTOPHER TERRIFORD	Michael Goodliffe
HELEN TERRIFORD	Dorothy Green
MARY TERRIFORD	Faith Brook
TONY LACK	Michael Gough
TAMAS DOMOKOS	
('GERRY') HARDLIP	Robert Speaight
LORD HENRY STRAIT	Basil Dignam
MONTAGU WINTHROP	Laurence Naismith
INSPECTOR WIGG	Gerald Welch

Directed by Michael Macowan
Décor by Alan Tagg

The action of the play takes place in the South Room at Terriford House, near Lamberton, near the Channel, sixty miles from London.

Time: Soon

Act I.
A Monday evening before dinner in early September

Act II.
The same night; 1.30 a.m.

Act III.
Scene 1. The following Sunday, near nightfall
Scene 2. Eight days later; tea-time

ACT ONE

*A room at Mitton, a large country-house sixty miles from London and near
the Channel coast. The house was built in the middle of the eighteenth
century and is to be thought of as being long and low. Half of it, known
as the Private House, is still the home of CHRISTOPHER TERRIFORD,
his young wife MARY and his mother LADY TERRIFORD; the other half
was converted in the nineteen-twenties by his father, Sir George Terriford,
into a Meteorological Research Unit, particularly devoted to problems
of Weather Control. Since his father's death, CHRISTOPHER, who was
his father's partner in research, has directed the Unit.*

*This room in the Private House is large and beautiful, but friendly and
very much lived-in. In the centre, upstage, is a wide bay shaped as the
segment of a circle. A double door, partly of glass, occupies the middle
of the bay's curving wall, and on each side of it is a window with a
window-seat. The prospect is West of South so that, in the evening,
sun-glow will flood in from the Left (the actors' Left). To the audience,
nothing but sky is visible through the glass, for beyond the windows a
great lawn falls away to the Lower Garden; but between the windows
and the lawn is a secondary approach to Mitton through Mitton Woods,
and when a car comes by this way (from Left to Right), intending to
round the house's eastern end on its way to the front door on the north
side, the sound of its engines may be heard.*

*On the Left (always the actors' Left) of the bay, against the upper wall,
is a grand piano, carrying a lamp and flowers, and littered with music.
This piano is set back into the up-left corner of the room. A player faces
D/S, the wall on his left hand as he sits contains a window.*

*In the Left Wall, below the piano, is a door which leads to other rooms
in the Private House and ultimately to the staircase by which one goes to
bed. It leads also to the Pass Door, at the foot of the staircase, by means
of which the Private House communicates with the Unit. None of this
is visible. The point is that whoever comes from the Unit, comes in Left.*

*Upstage in the Right Wall is another door which leads through an ante-
room and hall to the front door. Again, none of this is visible. The point*

is that anyone who comes in from outside the house enters either through the bay (from the garden) or through the door up right.

Below the door right is a fireplace with a fire-stool before it, and a large gilt-framed Regency looking-glass standing on the mantelpiece. Immediately above the fireplace and at right angles to it, a sofa runs out into the room. Near to the sofa is a formidable writing-desk with a heavy ink-stand. There are two telephones on this desk: the white one connects with the exchange; the black one, on which two numbers only are dialed, is a house-telephone connecting with other rooms in the Private House and with the Unit. A third and green telephone will be added when the Prime Minister requires a secret line to Lamberton Manor.

The other principal pieces of furniture are: a low chess table, with an unfinished game set out on it, which stands near the fire; on the mantel right, a clock, small and elegant, which chimes and strikes unobtrusively and rather merrily; a tea-trolley (off stage) that can be moved without difficulty; at the writing-table, a high-backed writing-chair with arms, the occupant of which can turn rapidly while still seated; at the end of the piano nearest the player (that is to say within easy reach of the bay), a small table on which drinks and glasses are always standing; and, downstage and left of Centre, a chair with matching stool.

The chair and stool are placed at an angle of about forty-five degrees to the footlights, the stool close to the chair so that the occupant must put his feet up, if he does not wish to move the stool.

It is evening of early September about an hour before dinner. The curtains are back, for there is still daylight.

He and his wife, MARY, and his mother, LADY TERRIFORD, are discovered. He is a highly-strung but self-controlled man of about thirty-five, with now and then a darting humour at his own expense and a tendency to be more surprised than impressed by his own intellect. He so values his private life that he dislikes intensely having 'importance' thrust upon him, but he is by no means a crank and, confronted with a power and responsibility that he did not seek, he makes his decisions firmly and un-hysterically and stands by them. MARY is of great value to him, partly because they deeply love each other (and this, in crisis, is sure ground under their feet), and partly because he is convinced that, though nearly ten years younger, she is intuitively wiser than he – and perhaps, spiritually, she is. She is beautiful and gentle, simple and direct; so full of happiness and inward peace that nothing shakes her. The roots of her life are her love of God, which saves her from panic in the upheavals of the world; her love of her husband, which gives her vitality and balance; and her sense of proportion, which prevents her from condemning human frailty, even TONY LACK's. But because she is no respecter of persons, she has sometimes a certain ingenuous abruptness which the worldly wise have not, and when she finds herself opposed in conscience to the great and good (for example, to the Prime Minister), she says so in an unhesitating way that diplomatists would not recommend.

At the moment she is sitting, already dressed for dinner, on the fire-stool.

CHRISTOPHER, in a sweater and slacks, is seated in the armchair in front of the desk, while LADY TERRIFORD is in the one behind it. She is not dressed for dinner.

They are at the end of a long discussion. When the curtain rises there is silence for a moment while CHRISTOPHER looks first at MARY and then at his mother.

CHRISTOPHER: Well, so be it. *(He rises and moves up to the drink table.)* Now, mother, do your piece and get it over. *(His consent is given with intense unwillingness. MARY rises and looks into mirror over mantelpiece, watching CHRISTOPHER.)*

LADY TERRIFORD: You agree then?

CHRISTOPHER: *(Curbed irritation.)* Ring the Manor, for Heaven's sake. *(He moves to below piano.)* If he won't come, that will settle it for us, and we shall have our evening in peace.

MARY turns from the mirror to face into the room.

LADY TERRIFORD: That won't do, Christopher, and you know it won't. If I ask the Prime Minister to come here tonight and if you tell him…what you have to tell him, it must be by your own consent – freely given. *I* think he must be told. But the Burning Glass is yours. So is this house. It is for you to decide.

MARY: It is true, Christopher.

LADY TERRIFORD: I've no wish to force your hand.

CHRISTOPHER: Circumstances force it – not you. *(He puts his hand on the telephone.)* I'll get the number for you.

LADY TERRIFORD: *(Checking him.)* Ought not Mr. Tony Lack to be told of this?

CHRISTOPHER: Later – if the Prime Minister agrees to come. He may not, you know. Then we can play our chess.

MARY: With you all on edge and tearing your hair?

CHRISTOPHER: *(His back to the fire.)* I'm not tearing my hair.

MARY: You were – by the drink table. I saw you in the mirror. We'd better get it over, darling.

LADY TERRIFORD: *(Rising and moving to door L.)* Then I'll go to my own room and make the call from there.

CHRISTOPHER: You're very secretive with your Prime Minister, Mamma.

LADY TERRIFORD: Not at all. But he will come if I talk to him in my own way.

MARY: Why are you so sure?

LADY TERRIFORD: Because I have known Monty Winthrop for forty years and have never asked for anything yet. Men like that.

LADY TERRIFORD goes out L. MARY looks at CHRISTOPHER who is lost in thought. She rises and, moving him to kisses him lightly. He puts his arms round her and they embrace.

CHRISTOPHER: *(Still with his arms round her.)* That for the moment seems to solve all problems.

MARY: There aren't any.

CHRISTOPHER: Not even the Burning Glass?

MARY: That isn't a problem between you and me; only between us and the world. If I'm of any use to you, it's because I love you first for what you are – only afterwards for what you do.

CHRISTOPHER: *(Releasing her and moving to above desk.)* In a way, the Burning Glass does touch even that. I feel almost a different being with that monstrous power over Nature in my hands – in *my* hands. How much I tell the Prime Minister does go to the root of things. You see, Science has never yet kept back its knowledge. If it comes to that, mankind has never rejected power. We have always said: 'Ah, but this power has beneficent uses as well. Let's go for it!' We have never yet said: 'We are unfit for it.' The time may have come to say that.

MARY: It isn't a decision on the...on the Prime Minister level. That's what I meant. It isn't policy. It's one of those decisions that just can't be made when we argue; only when we listen.

CHRISTOPHER: Or pray.

MARY: To pray is to listen, not to talk.

CHRISTOPHER: I have to decide tonight.

MARY: My darling, don't force it. *(Putting out her hand and stopping him.)* You will decide naturally. When you are ready you will know what to do. *(This marks a period in their dialogue.)* Christopher, when you agreed that the Prime Minister should be invited, was that against your judgment?

CHRISTOPHER: He *had* to be. It *is* common sense. The Burning Glass had to go to that level as a matter of Defence. I saw it coming before this evening, and I have taken...certain steps provisionally. But it was against every private and personal wish I have. I'm not a man of power; I just don't deal in Prime Ministers. I have always thanked heaven I'm not an atomist *(Sits U/S R corner of desk facing MARY.)* and that this particular Terriford Unit has never been, in any military sense on the secret list, in my father's time or in mine. Just Weather Control, if we could get it. Rain on parched land and...well, sunshine on Derby day, I suppose. It sounded beneficent and harmless, and I never wanted it otherwise.

MARY: Tony doesn't see it in that way.

CHRISTOPHER: Oh, I know. More than half of him has always wished our job weren't so damned civilian. Some people are...so made. The very words Top Secret give them a thrill. Tony's like that. So is his curious friend Gerry Hardlip. From Tony's point of view, I'm a babe unborn.

MARY: *(She rises and goes to him.)* That is why I love you.

CHRISTOPHER: Because I'm a babe unborn?

MARY: Because from his point of view you are... *(She starts to move away but he stops her.)*

CHRISTOPHER: *(After a pause.)* Mary, how tiresome is he?

MARY: Tony? To me? Not at all. Why he wants to flirt with me I don't know – he who can have twenty women.

CHRISTOPHER: And does – or did... He isn't...so tiresome... that you want him to go?

MARY: From this house? From the Unit?

CHRISTOPHER: Either or both if you wish it.

MARY: There's no need. He's your friend...and mine, Christopher. As your scientific partner, he's valuable, isn't he?

CHRISTOPHER: Enormously.

MARY: *(As though that settled it.)* Well, then...

CHRISTOPHER: You said 'flirt with me'. He's going through a kind *(Rises from corner of desk and sits in armchair in front of it.)* of hell, I believe. I only thought that 'flirt' was too... gentle a word?

MARY: Not if you see the thing in my way.

CHRISTOPHER: He doesn't.

MARY: But I do.

CHRISTOPHER: *(Smiling at her calm, unshakable absolutism.)* I was only trying to rescue you, my sweetheart.

MARY: You did that once and for all, when we were married... Tony isn't what troubles me.

CHRISTOPHER: What does?

MARY: *(She sighs. They have talked about it so often during the last six weeks.)* The Burning Glass. We always come back to it.

CHRISTOPHER: You said that wasn't a problem between you and me.

MARY: That is true. But it affects us. Since you made that discovery six weeks ago, we have become – quite different in…in our relationship to other people. We didn't have any power over them; they had none over us. There was nothing we deeply valued that the world could give or take away – certainly not our peace of mind. Now…

CHRISTOPHER: My dearest, isn't that still true?

MARY: Not quite.

CHRISTOPHER: What has it taken from us?

MARY: The simplicities. The blessed fact that from – well from Tony's point of view or from the Prime Minister's if it comes to that – we were as unimportant as a bank clerk… or a poet. Our walks, our special trees, the books we shared and the music, our games of chess when your day's work was over… *(She is trying to express something intensely personal that she can't quite express, and so she is not finishing her sentences.)* Our *little* things…they were our life…and the Burning Glass has changed their proportion. *(Stops at chess table.)* Look –

CHRISTOPHER: At what?

MARY: Our chess table. We were playing that game…so long ago that it wants dusting. *(She lifts up a piece.)*

CHRISTOPHER: We'll finish it tonight.

MARY: In spite of the Prime Minister? *(She puts the piece back.)*

CHRISTOPHER: When he's gone.

MARY: *When* he's gone! *(She moves to him.)*

CHRISTOPHER: *(Taking her hand.)* My dearest, I know what you mean. This thing breaks in.

MARY: *(She kneels beside him.)* Now, when we are…lovers, even that isn't any longer just our two selves. It has become also a shutting out of 'this thing'. Our private peace was something we didn't know we had to defend. Now we have to.

CHRISTOPHER: *(Almost throwing the words away because there is nothing between them that is not instantly understood.)* From all the crafts and assaults of the devil.

MARY: Your mother would say that was medieval.

CHRISTOPHER: My dear mother? To her, knowledge is always progress. It always was among the men of science of my father's day. No devils for them... *(He rises, helping her up as he does so. They stand facing each other.)* ... Mary, before she comes, there's something I want you to do. You have a memory.

MARY: Not yours, but yes, visually very strong.

CHRISTOPHER: For example that chess board. *(MARY turns to face the chess board.)* Keep your back to it. *(She turns back to him.)* You looked at it just now.

MARY: I wasn't trying to remember it.

CHRISTOPHER: No, but you examined it. Could you now give me the positions?

MARY: Of course. White: base-line: two blanks; Rook, Queen, blank, Rook, King, blank. Second line: two blanks; Bishop, two Knights, two Pawns, blank.[1] Third line –

CHRISTOPHER: *(Laughing.)* Good. Bless you. But the day after tomorrow? Would it still be there?

MARY: Possibly not. I wasn't trying to plant the memory. It isn't planted deep.

CHRISTOPHER: If you had been trying, it would be?

MARY: What am I to remember?

CHRISTOPHER: *(Giving her a piece of paper.)* This.

MARY: What is it?

CHRISTOPHER: It is the Upper Intensity Setting on Machine Six – the one which produces the effect of the Burning Glass.

MARY: The Upper Setting? Are there two?

CHRISTOPHER: Upper and Lower. That *(the paper)* is a half – less than a half, strictly – of what I carry in my own mind.

MARY: I don't understand.

CHRISTOPHER: For a moment, don't try to. I will explain. Read it. Eleven five-figure groups and three non-active

---

1   Lasker v. Blackburne, 1899 (Tartakower and du Mont, *500 Master Games of Chess*, P.67)

zeros. Photograph it in your mind. This time, plant it deep. *(She gazes at it and, from time to time, after his mother is come, MARY will gaze at it again.)*

MARY: If it is in writing, here, on this paper, why must I memorize it?

CHRISTOPHER: Because it won't stay in writing. Not for anyone. Not for the Prime Minister. If anything should happen to me, I want a half of the setting to exist in your memory alone. It gives you an absolute veto on the use of the Burning Glass. One part is there, in your hands. The other I have sent – *(LADY TERRIFORD enters L.)*

LADY TERRIFORD: Well, it's done. *(She closes door.)*

CHRISTOPHER: *(To MARY.)* Plant it deep.

LADY TERRIFORD: Who would have believed that Monty Winthrop – who was really an exceedingly quick and intuitive young man when we danced together – could become so dense as Prime Minister… But perhaps it isn't his fault. Telephones are really a great handicap to women.

CHRISTOPHER: Few appear to think so.

LADY TERRIFORD: *(Moves above desk to CHRISTOPHER.)* Well, my dear, it's all a question of how you were brought up. A smile is a weapon or should be. So is an eyebrow. So is a letter if tactfully written – so much can be conveyed by starting a new sentence and not quite crossing out the old one. But of course if a woman is illiterate or has no eyebrows, she takes to the telephone, quack, quack, like a duck to a puddle.

MARY: You persuaded Mr. Winthrop, all the same?

LADY TERRIFORD: When I got through to the Manor, I didn't ask for his host, but for the Prime Minister himself. A young man on his staff spoke to me first. Very young, very courteous, very pink and clean; even on the telephone one almost smelt the soap. He was soothing and plummy, like the BBC announcing the death of a film star to an audience of twelve million half-wits.

CHRISTOPHER: There may not be twelve million half-wits.

LADY TERRIFORD: That is what the BBC appear so often to forget...

CHRISTOPHER: What happened then?

LADY TERRIFORD: Then Lord Henry Strait came to the abominable instrument. *(To MARY, whose eyes are on her paper.)* My dear, what are you studying so intently? The crossword?

MARY: *(Who has been planting it deep.)* No.

LADY TERRIFORD: Because I have done it. 'Conflagration, in the White House, perhaps' is, quite obviously, Casabianca. How I hate the word 'perhaps'. It always means the man is cheating. Or do you think crosswords are composed by women?

CHRISTOPHER: *(Angrily.)* What did Lord Henry say? ... Mother why are you prattling? I hate clever-clever Edwardian prattle as much as the cling-clang of a modern cocktail party. And it's not in your nature. *(He has spoken sharply – and it is a mark of the tension in him that he is impatient with the mother he respects and loves.)*

MARY: Gentle.

CHRISTOPHER: *(Not gently.)* I am gentle. But why now? *(But he bends over to his mother and, puts his hand on her shoulder, and says – gently:)* Why now, Mamma?

LADY TERRIFORD: Only because I am tired, my dearest. When a thing is too serious to be...easily borne, it is often best to talk nonsense for a little while. At least so I was taught. ... Some people, when the world looks ugly, are silent; I prattle in its ugly face. You must allow to each generation its own idiom... In any case the Prime Minister is coming.

CHRISTOPHER: At what time?

LADY TERRIFORD: Not to dinner. Late. They have a large dinner-party. He and Lord Henry were to have left by car at eleven-fifteen and to have been in Downing Street before one. I said: 'Two will do. You can spend an hour here.' But he was stubborn. He had to know why. I told him that the national interest required him to come. And I had to add – how I detest it! – that what I had to say could not be said on an open telephone.

CHRISTOPHER: I suppose that is true.

LADY TERRIFORD: It is horrible that it should be true! It isn't a pretty world in which, on a September evening within sixty miles of London, you daren't speak openly on your own telephone.

MARY: *(Who, since she last spoke has been listening intently, the paper loose and visible in her hand.)* It isn't a pretty world… outwardly. But it ought to be simple in one's own conscience. And it's not.

LADY TERRIFORD: Conscience is a great book but a difficult one. I used to think that it was an easy text-book on conduct that would tell me exactly what to do; but it isn't, you know. It is a great work of art, and we, who are children, have to learn to read it – not without tears. Forgive me if I say that I think you and Christopher are learning to read it too *(And she makes a joke of the word.)* compli-cate-edly.

MARY: *(It is not a question.)* Or too simply.

LADY TERRIFORD: Perhaps we mean the same thing. *(To her son.)* You know, Christopher, if what has happened to you had happened to your father – I mean, if his science had put into his hands this overwhelming power, it would never have entered his mind to keep that knowledge to himself and let it die with him. And, after all, your own impulse was the same. In the first place, you didn't keep it to yourself.

CHRISTOPHER: *(And he speaks less to her than to himself, with a quickening tempo of self-discovery.)* Because at that time, when the Reflex Indicators, quite suddenly, gave me that *effect*, I didn't see it as a military effect. I didn't see it even as an industrial effect – an infinite supply of pure heat, spilling out from heaven just because my puny hand turns on the tap… Or spilling out of hell. I didn't then see it in that way at all, but as a scientific result. It was much as if I had been playing the piano and a miracle had happened, and such music had come out of it as 'never was on sea or land'... I leapt up from Machine Six. I switched off the power and left the setting. I came running out –

LADY TERRIFORD: And told *me* –

CHRISTOPHER: *(And now he has come back, humorously to little things.)* Didn't I always tell you when I won a prize at school?

LADY TERRIFORD: And Mary? And Mr. Tony Lack?

CHRISTOPHER: Well, he's my partner in Weather Control. If, quite suddenly, you get the hell of a result, isn't it natural to say, 'Tony, come and look! Come and look at this!'

LADY TERRIFORD: You took him to Machine Six and he saw the setting?

CHRISTOPHER: We switched on. He saw the result in the Indicators and he saw the setting and I broke the setting up.

LADY TERRIFORD: But it is in your mind?

CHRISTOPHER: Of course.

LADY TERRIFORD: Then why not in his?

CHRISTOPHER: Because, because, because...he hasn't that freak of memory. He couldn't remember the positions of a chess-board, much less –

LADY TERRIFORD: One minute. I want to get this clear. I know and Mary knows and Mr. Tony Lack knows that the Burning Glass exists, but, except you, no one knows how... to apply it?

CHRISTOPHER: No one.

LADY TERRIFORD: Not Mr. Tony?

CHRISTOPHER: No one.

LADY TERRIFORD: Doesn't it trouble him that you haven't given him the...setting? *(CHRISTOPHER does not answer.)* He is your partner in Weather Control. This is, or was, part of it. You give him the result, but not the means. Has he asked for the setting? *(CHRISTOPHER is silent, not wishing to answer.)*

MARY: Has he, Christopher?

CHRISTOPHER: Yes.

MARY: More than once?

CHRISTOPHER: Twice, in a casual way. *(He turns to face audience.)* As you know I have experimented since… Mother, what are you getting at? I don't distrust him, but this thing is new; I want time to get the dimensions of it. Certainly, as you say, Tony is my partner in Weather Control. But the Burning Glass is as different from that as a jet bomber from a kite. It gives us power, by use of the sun's rays, to burn up the earth or any part of it. As I see it, that opens a new volume in your book of conscience. Almost a new language. And I'm trying to learn to read it; Mary knows. So meanwhile I have shut up. I haven't given Tony the know-how, or Mary, or you.

LADY TERRIFORD: You see, my dear, Mr. Tony has, in my judgment *(And she chooses the word.)*, adhesive friends. There is, for example, this Mr. Hardlip who comes now and then. Is his name Hardlip?

CHRISTOPHER: It is an adaptation of his name to make it pronounceable… You musn't be prejudiced, Mama, although I know you like to call a spade a spade.

LADY TERRIFORD: That isn't the point. I like a spade to call *itself* a spade. *(CHRISTOPHER makes a gesture of despair at her suspicions and says to MARY.)*

CHRISTOPHER: *(Turning to MARY and moving towards her.)* Where is Tony?

MARY: Dressing for a party.

CHRISTOPHER: In London?

MARY: Mr. Hardlip is calling and driving him up.

CHRISTOPHER: That is impossible now. If the Prime Minister is coming Tony must be here. *(He goes to the house telephone and dials two numbers.)* No answer from his bedroom. I take it, he has gone across to the Unit to fortify himself. *(Dials again.)* Unit?... Terriford. ... Mr. Lack there? No, I don't want him on the telephone... Ask him, from me, to come over to the Private House when he's finished his drink... Not urgent, but important – when he's finished his drink. ... Understood? *(He replaces the receiver and turns to MARY.)* You are dressed! I must at least put on a black tie. And you, too, Mamma. *(LADY TERRIFORD rises. She moves towards door L.)* Is that firm in your mind?

MARY: Yes.

CHRISTOPHER: Planted deep?

MARY: I shan't forget it.

CHRISTOPHER: Then burn it. *(While she does so, she says:)*

MARY: What am I to do with it?

CHRISTOPHER: I'll tell you later.

LADY TERRIFORD: What is it?

CHRISTOPHER: One of our memory games. When Tony comes, Mary, tell him from me he must wash out his party for tonight.

MARY: He will say no.

CHRISTOPHER: With the Prime Minister coming?

MARY: All the more. The great and good always make him shrug his rebellious shoulders.

CHRISTOPHER: Not on his job. It is his job to be here. Tell him.

MARY: If you say so.

CHRISTOPHER: *(Stops as he sees LADY T. at the door.)* Mamma, when you were talking to the Prime Minister, why did you insist that he should come tonight?

LADY TERRIFORD: Intuition... I am sorry, my dear, I am a common-sensical person and intuition, I dare say, isn't in my part... But I am not comfortable this evening. There are some days in life that one would like to be safely over. No doubt, I shall be more intelligent after a hot bath. *(She goes out.)*

CHRISTOPHER: After he's gone, we'll finish that game.

MARY: That particular game? … Or chess?

CHRISTOPHER: That particular. We began it so long ago. Continuity. Private life. Peaceful life. I don't know… But I do know I want to finish that game before we sleep.

MARY: Good. *(MARY rises and moves to him, she takes his arm.)* You are a funny one, my darling. Don't make too big a symbol of too small a thing. Suppose someone upset the table?

CHRISTOPHER: *(In real alarm.)* Why do you say that? Why do you say that? *(Then with relief.)* Even if someone did, you'd remember the positions. You would put it together again… *(He kisses her lightly.)* Now, forward into battle. *(As he crosses, TONY LACK enters through the door which LADY TERRIFORD left open.)*

TONY: *(Smiling.)* What has happened? I came in from the Unit through the pass door. There was your mother beginning to negotiate the stairs. She looked at me as if I were the ghost of Hamlet's father. I said – I oughtn't to have, of course.

MARY: What did you say?

TONY: I said: 'Angels and ministers of grace, defend us.' And she said: 'Yes, indeed.' What does one make of that?

CHRISTOPHER: Are you going to London tonight?

TONY: Yes, indeed.

CHRISTOPHER: You can't.

TONY: *Can't I?*

CHRISTOPHER: Mary will tell you why. *(He goes.)*

TONY: What is all this?

MARY: *(Soothing his evident excitement.)* Sit down peacefully.

TONY: *(Not obeying. TONY moves round desk towards drink table.)* You are quite right. I have, as you perceive, had three doubles. But I can take that.

MARY: *(Cheerfully playing with and not against his mood.)* If you will, out of consideration for us, not dine out in London tonight, and take off your white tie –

TONY: *(TONY turns to face her.)* As for the tie, that's easy. *(He rips it off.)* Always your obedient servant.

MARY: *(And she can't help smiling at that.)* Not always obedient.

TONY: *(TONY crosses to behind sofa and leans over her.)* I was born masterful where beautiful women are concerned – a Casanova of the cradle, a Bryon of the bassinet. *(From this moment onwards the scene between them is, so to speak, an exercise in counterpoint. His rash and insensate love-making (insensate because without hope) clashes with his fear that he may have already said too much to HARDLIP, and both these clash with her gentleness, her self-control, her determination to hold firmly to the theme of the PRIME MINISTER's coming. The speed is to be very high in bursts, with intervening slow passages; the volume of sound is to be marked by violent contrasts like a night-sea on a beach.)*

MARY: The Prime Minister has been staying at the Manor. He is coming here after dinner on his way back to London. Christopher wants you to stay. *(Rather late:)* So do I.

TONY: I shall do nothing of the kind. Prime Ministers as a species are not my cup of tea. Nor do I want tea. In any case, why is he coming? *(He turns to MARY.)*

MARY: Be serious, Tony.

TONY: I was trying, out of consideration for you, not to be. The only thing I want to be serious about is you, which doesn't please you, I can't think why.

MARY: Yes you can.

TONY: Oh, you are married and love your husband and so on, I know that; I don't really blame you for saying no, but why should you blame me for asking? You can regard it, if you please, as a politeness. It's so much pleasanter for a woman to say no, than never to be asked at all. Be honest, isn't it? Unless the chap bores you. And I don't… Or do I?

MARY: No.

TONY: Well, then, I revert to the previous question… Isn't it?

MARY: *(Smiling.)* Not if one's happy, Tony…and if one doesn't want to make the other chap unhappy and –

TONY: *(He rises and pours himself a drink.)* And drink three doubles? Now, whatever else you are, you aren't the guardian angel of my wine-bill. In fact, I am so made that I link women with song, not with wine. The Porter in *Macbeth*, you know, said a mouthful on the subject of wine and women. 'Lechery it provokes and unprovokes. It makes him stand to and not stand to. It droppeth as the gentle rain from heaven. 'Tis mightiest in the mightiest.' *(MARY breaks out laughing.)* Or has Scotland wandered into Venice? I *must* learn not to telescope the plays of Shakespeare! It leads one into every kind of moral entanglement... *(Rallentando.)* Very well, I revert from poetry to prose. Why do you steadfastly refuse to discuss the one subject I want to talk about?

MARY: I don't, if you would talk sense.

TONY: You want to talk about Prime Ministers. *(Allegro.)* It is, I grant you, a solemn subject, a noble subject, a pompous-historical subject, but it is not a sensual one. *(There is a silence – They have been fencing. Now the tone hardens.)*

MARY: Tony, I'm not a fool. Lately, you have seemed almost to hate Christopher – and sometimes, me. I know quite well that, though you...prattle...as if it were, this isn't a...a flirtation. *(TONY rises and crosses to the fire. Swiftly and with intent.)* And I know your value. And I know you are going through some kind of hell. And I want – for my own sake, not only for yours – *(TONY puts his glass on mantelpiece.)* I want not to be a blind, selfish fool.

TONY: And so?

MARY: How can I be of any use? What, in reason, do you want?

TONY: To go to bed with you. *(He sits on firestool.)* Well, I'm not sorry. You asked me. I thought you played chess. Princess's opening accepted. Knight's gambit declined. Why are there no princesses in that lamentable game?

MARY: Since you are direct, so will I be. Why do you want to go to bed with me?

TONY: Pleasure. You would be charming naked. And one would forget the twentieth century, and the Burning Glass would make no odds… Isn't that a good reason?

MARY: But not the whole reason? There are other women as good…naked. Why do you want *me*?

TONY: Because, when I thought I was through with all that, you have cropped up as the one…sentimentality in my life that I haven't annihilated. I want to press that grape and spit out the skin. And that would be that.

MARY: 'Sentimentality.'

TONY: Remove the quotes and call it love. You see, you believe in…you represent…you *are* all the things in which I used to believe. Including loyalty. Oh yes, I know…

MARY: And so you wish to destroy them.

TONY: Since I can't regain them. Milton knew what he was talking about. Trust a Puritan to know the Devil. *(He rises and sits beside her on the sofa.)* As it is…put a bracket round one night…or two. Wouldn't it be pleasurable? Be honest, wouldn't it? Even the young and beautiful grow old.

MARY: No.

TONY: Are you saying it wouldn't be pleasurable or are you just saying no?

MARY: I am saying No.

TONY: And then one is buried, and no one cares a damn.

MARY: What were the things, in which you once believed, that I now represent? *(At that TONY, with an outfling of his arms, walks right away from her and says:)*

TONY: Ah, if you take that ground. *(He rises and moves to below desk.)* Angels and ministers of grace defend you. That's the trouble – they do. *(He stops.)* That is why I love you. *(Then he turns back.)* All right. You win.

MARY: And now, please, will you give me a real answer about the other thing?

TONY: What do you want to know? *(TONY moves to MARY.)*

MARY: Will you, when this Mr. … Hardlip comes, send him about his business?

TONY: No. I should despise myself if I did.

MARY: Is your evening with him so important?

TONY: *(TONY sits in chair in front of desk.)* Not in the least. That is why I go. You miss the point. In any genuine view of the world – yours, the Christian, or mine, the nihilistic view – the Prime Minister isn't important either. In certain moods we pretend he is; we were brought up that way, it is our convention; but he isn't. Christopher thinks I'm interested in power, and in a sense it's true. I can't altogether resist the trappings, again because I happen to have been brought up that way. If I had a chance, no doubt I'd be with joy Her Majesty's Principal Secretary of State for Foreign Affairs, or the First Sea Lord my luckless father might have been, or, best of all, Lord Bishop of Bath and Wells; nothing so magnificently combines cleanliness with godliness as a Bishop of Bath and Wells. I should jump at any of those jobs with delight but only with the same delight I should have in being the Black Prince on a rocking-horse. Only to laugh at my silly self in fancy dress.

MARY: And so you are not what Mr. Hardlip is?

TONY: What is 'Mr. Hardlip'?

MARY: Tony, how much do you really know of him? Where was he born?

TONY: Vaguely on the Danube. A very cosmopolitan river, I grant you, not now as blue as it was.

MARY: And where brought up?

TONY: Half in Buda – Half in Pest. Since then he has taken all the scholarships.

MARY: I'm sure he has. What happened during the war?

TONY: The Economic Section of the Ministry of This and That. No fault of his. One of his hands doesn't function. He writes with his left. I suppose he's one of the very star economists at either University. I find him astringent at a party – like the vinegar in a salad dressing. Why all this interest in Gerry Hardlip?

MARY: He's so different from you.

TONY: Ah, he takes himself seriously. He hates what he calls the System.

MARY: Ours? The British?

TONY: Much more than that: Loyalty, love, faith – all the romantic superstitions.

MARY: But, Tony, you too have renounced them.

TONY: Have I? They have renounced me. My nursery is shut, that's all. He never had one. I am *déraciné*. He is *by nature* an intellectual cosh-boy.

MARY: But you spend time with him.

TONY: *(Ruefully.)* I can't help it.

MARY: Why?

TONY: *(TONY rises and moves U/C between desk and sofa.)* I can't help it.

MARY: Why?

TONY: A drug.

MARY: Against what?

TONY: Myself, you fool. *(He turns and moves towards MARY.)* You complacent, Christian fool. … Myself, my beloved, blind, wise adored one *(He kneels in front of her, his arms round her.)* whom I strip with my eyes and my cruelty, and worship on my knees and hate with all the envies of my soul. *(And now he breaks away and sits on sofa, not looking at her.)* You say nothing. Thou foster-child of silence and slow time! A great lady never makes a scene. *(A pause. He leans back and speaks on a completely different note.)* … I am glad the Prime Minister is coming.

MARY: *(Who has been left behind by this sudden change.)* What did you say?

TONY: I am glad the Prime Minister is to be told.

MARY: But you will take no part in it?

TONY: *(He rises and goes to window.)* No.

MARY: Then how does it affect you? Why are you glad?

TONY: *(He had been going to say much more but now slides away from it.)* Oh…it puts the thing on the right footing.

MARY: What is it you are trying – *not* to say?

TONY: Nothing. *(He comes to above desk.)* … Listen, Mary, what you said just now – about my seeming to hate Christopher sometimes, it isn't true. *(The nervous and passionate intensity of the denial is, perhaps, an admission of the half-truth.)* I'm not Iago, believe me. Whatever I may have said – or done *(It is the 'saying' which is tormenting his mind and the word 'done' is added hastily as an afterthought or 'cover'.)* – hasn't been said or done in hatred of him. Or even jealousy. My little madness is self-contained. I want *you*: not to take you from *him*. I don't love you in relation to your circumstances – least of all your husband – but ringed round, isolatedly, Miranda on her island. *(He crosses to MARY.)* My island of which I've lost the chart. *A la recherché de l'âme perdu! (He turns and moves to below desk.)* What am I talking about?

MARY: You were telling me why you are glad that the Prime Minister is coming tonight.

TONY: Because it will make Christopher safe *(MARY rises.)* – as safe as it is humanely possible for him to be ever again.

MARY: Why, is he in…that kind of danger? Only we know even that the power exists.

TONY: *(Airily; he is avoiding the real answer.)* One can never be sure. Believe me, the rumour of such things gets into the air. Great power smells and the smell goes round the world – not the detail, but the smell.

MARY: How can it, if no one talks?

TONY: It can. *(He sits in chair.)* Long before Hiroshima, it was known that that power existed. However you try to divide science into water-tight compartments, the compartments leak. *(He is becoming excited.)* It isn't necessary for you or me to go out and sell the Burning Glass setting to an enemy agent for a ruby necklace and a ton of caviare. Besides, we haven't got it to sell. All the same, when men all over the world, working on parallel lines, are waiting for the scientific cat to make its next jump, one word, the tone of a voice, an air of excitement, the *refusal* of an answer, is enough to make them say –

MARY: Say what?

TONY: *(He has been talking fast and loud. Now he drops his voice.)* Might be enough to make them say: 'My God, in the Terriford Unit a very big cat *has* jumped' and might lead them to… You see what I mean?

MARY: You are frightened, Tony. *(TONY rises and moves up to drink table and pours drink.)* Is that why you stood out against Christopher's going to the Vienna Congress?

TONY: Yes.

MARY: *(MARY moves up to him.)* At first you wanted him to. You suggested it. And then you were fierce against it. Why, if you weren't frightened before?

TONY: Because – *(He turns to her.)* Because while I was shaving one morning I…

MARY: You thought Christopher wouldn't come back.

TONY: I thought he might not. *(He puts his glass on drinks table.)*

MARY: If there was danger of that kind, they could take him any afternoon when he goes out walking in Mitton woods.

TONY: At the moment they prefer a cold war to a hot. Wouldn't it be more convenient to them if he voluntarily didn't come home from Vienna? Hardlip's car… Are you sure the Prime Minister is coming tonight?

MARY: Quite sure.

TONY: Then from tomorrow all is well. There'll be a cordon round this house. No more solitary walks in Mitton Woods. No more vague honeymoons for you, my dear, wandering in Italian hill-towns. You will have a guard under your window and another at your bedroom door. *(A car sweeps up outside the French windows and stops.)*

HARDLIP: *(Off.)* Are you ready? Can I come in?

MARY: Say we're locked up in here. Make him go round to the door.

TONY: *(At the window, waves the car on.)* Go on! Go round to the door. We're barred and bolted here. I'll let you in. *(To MARY.)* Wait and receive him.

MARY: No.

TONY: He must have seen you here.

MARY: Tony. *(He turns as he is going out of the door.)* Don't mention the Prime Minister.

TONY: Cut out my tongue. *(He goes. She goes out. HARDLIP, in tails, wears a leather glove on his right hand. This hand is useless.)*

TONY: *(Off.)* Where are we to dine?

HARDLIP: *(As he enters.)* The Fourteen. We may go on later to Janet Hilford's dance – hence white ties. The others meet us at dinner. We pick up this girl of Sellin's on the way.

TONY: *(TONY at door.)* Then we ought to start.

HARDLIP: Time enough. She lives on the way to London. I have left Sellin in the car. He can wait.

TONY: Bring the poor devil in. *(Crosses to the drink table.)* What do you want?

HARDLIP: Nothing… No. He can wait. He wouldn't be approved of in this house. *(He can't be still, but is perpetually fidgeting and fingering something.)* Nor, quite obviously, am I.

TONY: *(TONY moves to above desk.)* She had to dress.

HARDLIP: She was dressed.

TONY: She may have wished to change her dress.

HARDLIP: Do women dress twice for dinner?

TONY: Lord Almighty, why not if it amuses them?

HARDLIP: You needn't bother to cover her tracks. You know as well as I do that if the most boring curate had appeared at this moment, she'd have stayed and done her stuff, wouldn't she? And given him a glass of sherry, and asked after his grubby ecclesiastical spawn? At sight of me, she goes.

TONY: Do you mind?

HARDLIP: What she thinks of me? Not in the least! But you do. ... Oh, I admit that, when you're with me or drunk, you have moments of emancipation. But an Englishman, when sober, is a domestic animal. Even when he conquers an empire, he takes out his own women and their afternoon tea. He would have been cosy with Cleopatra. In bed or battle, his highest reward is to be called a good boy. What you really want of Mary Terriford is not to possess her but that she shall love you and respect you and kiss you on the forehead and tuck you up in bed... 'Please, Nannie, may I go out to a party with Gerry tonight?' ... 'Oh, Tony, do you think you ought to go out with naughty little backroom boys?' Isn't that what you were saying when I came in?

TONY: My God what do you and I get out of each other's company?

HARDLIP: *(HARDLIP sits arm of sofa.)* A masochistic pleasure. We enjoy the jab of each other's knives. Anyhow, what was the result? Was milord Byron defiant? Or did Tony yield to persuasion, little by little? In either case, the rule stands. All the English are really in love with their nurses. That is why they make love so badly... *(A meditative afterthought.)* and why, I suppose, they always win the last battle: they fight it with their backs to the nursery wall.

TONY: And why they get under your skin?

HARDLIP: On the contrary. I value them enormously. They provide a background to my intelligence. They admit me to their colleges because they need my brains, and to their clubs – some clubs – because they need my subscriptions. Their talent is to absorb; to receive external stimulus. Hence the Normans. Hence Disraeli. Hence myself. The English have always admitted foreigners, because their own company is so intolerably boring. But the accent remains on the word 'admit'.

TONY: Even among those you so innocently call 'the smart'?

HARDLIP: Ah, they are different! So are the proletariat. They have achieved the nihilism of the night-clubs and the gutter. They are the realists of the world to come. I love the proletariat because they have no mercy. I love the smart because they have no loyalties. I –

TONY: I love camellias because they have no smell! … Come off it, Gerry. I can't have you making a philosophy of your appetites.

HARDLIP: It is a habit among moral reformers. Besides, my appetites are under strict control.

TONY: Then your reputation flatters you. I gathered that the smart admit you not infrequently to their beds.

HARDLIP: Poor darlings. The British are more bored in bed than anywhere in the world. They welcome a moment of educative depravity.

TONY: Then I don't see what you have to complain of.

HARDLIP: For myself, nothing. There is no country into which it is more profitable to be naturalized. I am extremely well paid for taking everything I want, and I remain completely independent. But you don't. You have the capacity to go to the very top – and look at you: Terriford's assistant, dangling at the apron-strings of Terriford's wife, holding the wool for Terriford's mother! … Those two women! Different generations. Different ideas. But on one point absolutely united and unswerving. They loathe my guts. They keep me out and they keep you in. *(TONY starts for drink table.)* You won't need that drink if you are coming to my party.

TONY: Listen, Gerry. How much difference would it make if I didn't?

HARDLIP: Please yourself. By all means stay, if you want full marks from teacher.

TONY: The point is this –

HARDLIP: Don't trouble to make excuses. Far be it from me to come between a man and his nurse.

TONY: Mary has nothing whatever to do with it. It's a question of work.

HARDLIP: Tonight?

TONY: Yes.

HARDLIP: In full evening-dress? … Tell me, why is your white tie hanging round your neck?

TONY: *(His hands go up. He is intensely embarrassed.)* I can't imagine! *(TONY moves to mirror and ties his tie.)*

HARDLIP: It looks like apron-strings… You're a bad liar, Tony.

TONY: I tell you, this isn't personal to me or to you or to her. It is work. There is to be – well, if you want to know, some pretty important high-ups are coming in for a conference after dinner.

HARDLIP: *(Not a question.)* On the subject you told me of at Cambridge.

TONY: *(Airily.)* Among other things.

HARDLIP: I thought Christopher Terriford had some quixotic notion of keeping that discovery to himself and letting it die with him.

TONY: Did I say that?

HARDLIP: Don't you remember what you said? … More than you ought, Tony.

TONY: What did I tell you?

HARDLIP: For example, that the power exists and the nature of it.

TONY: *(Frightened, and trying to reassure himself.)* What does that matter? I never gave you the setting. Whatever I may have said that evening, I didn't give you that. I can't have, because I don't know it. I don't know it. *(Both are standing.)*

HARDLIP: Alright… Your hysteria convinces me.

TONY: Of what?

HARDLIP: That you really don't know the setting. That you *still* don't. Until this moment I wasn't quite sure of that. I couldn't believe he'd keep it from you. Isn't he your partner? Isn't he your friend? … And I couldn't believe you'd stand for it… Well, it's your pants that are being kicked, not mine. If the Burning Glass –

TONY: I never used that name!

HARDLIP: Who else? My dear Tony, you have no need to be frightened. Let us be very simple and then enjoy our dinner with a light heart. You said that evening – what was it? Five weeks ago? – much more than it was discreet to say. But fortunately you said it to me alone in the privacy of my rooms and no harm has been done. Still, won't you look rather a fool at this…high up conference, if Terriford knows the setting and you don't? What are you, for God's sake – the office boy? And in any case, you aren't quite yourself this evening. I should have supposed that I was more suitable company for you than Mary Terriford…or the Prime Minister.

TONY: My God, how do you know that?

HARDLIP: *(Laughing, as if at a practical joke.)* Ha! That caught you. Oh, Tony! You are on edge!

TONY: How *can* you know? It was arranged by telephone not half an hour ago.

HARDLIP: *(Laughing again.)* High-up conference on the Burning Glass. Prime Minister at the Manor. Conclusion obvious. *(Maliciously.)* It wasn't necessary to tap your telephone, I promise you. Now, shall we start? I think you need a break, Tony. *(He crosses to TONY who is behind the chess table. He pushes TONY's shoulder with his hand in which he is holding his coat. He then turns so that the coat trails across the chess table scattering the pieces.)* The great mind isn't functioning at Cabinet level. Mine will be the more amusing party. *(He picks up his evening coat and trails it from his arm.)* Come.

TONY: Oh, Gerry, look what you've done! You've ruined their game. *(He drops to his knees and begins to put the pieces back.)*

HARDLIP: It's quite useless to attempt that… Get up. It's time to go.

TONY: I'll put them back for her.

HARDLIP: For her! For her! I suppose you remember the positions? Come on!

TONY: Alright! *(He starts to follow HARDLIP out.)* What's this girl of Sellin's like?

HARDLIP: Some of her habits are a little bizarre but I think you'll find her amusing.

There is a pause and then the sound of a car starting and moving off. MARY comes in through French windows and goes to the piano. LADY TERRIFORD enters and moves to French windows which she closes. Neither sees the chessmen spilled on the floor.

LADY TERRIFORD: So you didn't persuade Mr. Tony to stay.

MARY: *(MARY plays a few bars.)* No. And yet I think he wanted to. *(CHRISTOPHER enters. He halts and listens.)*

LADY TERRIFORD: There was a bad fairy at his christening.

CHRISTOPHER: *(He moves up to drink table to pour sherry.)* Whose?

MARY: Tony's.

CHRISTOPHER: Not at his christening. His early home was as solid as a rock. It crumbled when he was a fighter pilot, which isn't a good moment.

MARY: *(To LADY TERRIFORD.)* He isn't *bad*!

LADY TERRIFORD: No. I think you are right. But he keeps bad company.

MARY: He is generous and gay and sometimes very kind…and brilliant – isn't he, Christopher?

CHRISTOPHER: He is also quite insanely brave.

LADY TERRIFORD: Or rash?

CHRISTOPHER: Both. You have never seen him gamble or dive a Spitfire into a squadron of bombers. His trouble is that he hasn't any longer a personal life that he in the least minds losing, which either makes a saint of a man or – oh well, let it go!

LADY TERRIFORD: What he needs is to marry a good girl.

CHRISTOPHER: He did. She was killed.

LADY TERRIFORD: Killed?

CHRISTOPHER: By one of the bombers he didn't get.

LADY TERRIFORD: Before the family rock crumbled?

CHRISTOPHER: Just after. She was to have been his rock.

MARY: Poor Tony. He talks to me sometimes. He shrugs his shoulders and says he's like the modern world. It's true in a way. He believes in nothing except the things he has lost. And so he rebels and frivols and makes love, and goes to parties with Mr. Hardlip, and talks –

LADY TERRIFORD: And talks?

MARY: Oh, look!

CHRISTOPHER: What?

MARY: Half the chessmen on the floor. *(She drops on her knees and begins to pick them up.)*

LADY TERRIFORD: Someone upset the table.

MARY: Quiet. I can remember. *(While she is putting the pieces back into their places, CHRISTOPHER stands beside her.)*

CHRISTOPHER: All the King's horses and all the King's men – couldn't put –

MARY: But I can! I can!

Act Drop.

ACT TWO

Later the same night. The lamps are on, the curtains closed. A fire has been lighted. LADY TERRIFORD is knitting, with a book on her lap. MARY is at the piano. The clock chimes against her music and she ceases to play.

MARY: What was it struck?

LADY TERRIFORD: Half past.

MARY: Past what?

LADY TERRIFORD: One. They came nearly an hour late.

MARY: They have been ages in the Unit. *(MARY rises.)*

LADY TERRIFORD: Monty Winthrop has always liked playing with scientific toys.

MARY: If I had been Prime Minister, I should have wanted to do it the other way round. First what the thing *was*; then the effect.

LADY TERRIFORD: What concerns him is always effect. That is why he is Prime Minister. Great men don't walk patiently from A to Z. Like fleas, they jump. They have to.

MARY: *(Moving into the bay.)* Shall I let in some air?

LADY TERRIFORD: By all means. It's a lovely night. But I'll put on a log. He likes a blaze. *(While LADY TERRIFORD makes up the fire, MARY draws back the curtains, opens window and leans out.)*

MARY: *(Turning back into the room.)* There are men outside. *(LORD HENRY STRAIT comes in, carrying under his arm a despatch-case of soft black leather.)* Lord Henry, who are those men? *(LORD HENRY is about forty, smooth, distinguished and efficient. Though he is not a member of that establishment, he is very 'foreign office' in manner. His air is that of one who belongs to a separated and infallible caste, but he is too well-bred and too clever to exhibit the arrogance of power, except later on, to TONY, when TONY is 'down'.)*

LORD HENRY: Friends, Mrs. Terriford.

MARY: You mean guards? Did you bring them all?

LORD HENRY: And others, I'm afraid.

MARY: In your car? But there isn't room!

LORD HENRY: There are more cars than one.

MARY: How do you bear it?

LORD HENRY: I? Oh, it doesn't apply to me…to the same extent…when I'm off the leash.

MARY: But he?

LORD HENRY: He doesn't give it a thought. One gets used to it, you know, as one does to wearing a pair of boots. *(CHRISTOPHER (off) opens door and the PRIME MINISTER enters. CHRISTOPHER follows shutting door and going to curve of piano.)*

LADY TERRIFORD: Mary is thinking that in the Garden of Eden there were no boots. *(As the PRIME MINISTER enters with CHRISTOPHER, he overhears the last phrase. CHRISTOPHER has a foolscap folder.)*

PRIME MINISTER: 'In the Garden of Eden there were no boots.' How pregnant an isolated phrase can be on condition that you don't understand it! In my grave, I shall still be searching for the impossible context of that remark.

LADY TERRIFORD: If you applied your mind, Monty, you would see –

PRIME MINISTER: No, my dear Helen, do not tell me. I shall enjoy having something to search for in my grave. Particularly if it embraces a memory of you. *(The P.M. turns to face into the room.)* And, if I may say so, of this historic evening. For historic it is – am I right? Now *(To CHRISTOPHER.)* shall we proceed with our task? *(To MARY who has offered him a chair.)* No, I'll sit upright. At this desk. Then I can walk about. I always come alive in the small hours. *(He sits in chair behind desk.)* Tiresome for my young hostess, I'm afraid. Now, let us get on. *(LORD HENRY sits. CHRISTOPHER is standing.)* Machine Six. Why Six?

CHRISTOPHER: Because it is the sixth distinct type of Weather Control machine since my father began. You see, sir, at the beginning –

PRIME MINISTER: No. That is all the answer I want. I take it there were intermediate stages – amendments, so to speak – Four A, Four B, Four C and so on?

CHRISTOPHER: Many.

PRIME MINISTER: Up to what point communicated – I mean to other men of science – abroad?

CHRISTOPHER: Up to my father's death. He always communicated his results. Men of science did. My father died in 1940.

PRIME MINISTER: I remember well. An old friend. A great loss. *(This is only formal. He has no time now for any personal feeling.)* What was the last machine communicated?

CHRISTOPHER: One of series Five.

PRIME MINISTER: Not Six?

CHRISTOPHER: No, sir. I have given Six to the Dennistoun Foundation in California. No one else. They endow Weather Control. They finance this place.

PRIME MINISTER: The enemy could have stolen it from them.

CHRISTOPHER: There hasn't been time. Anyhow why should the enemy bother? Machine Six isn't a weapon. It's completely innocuous without the Burning Glass setting.

PRIME MINISTER: Machine Six, I confess, means nothing to me. I saw the flare in the Reflex Indicators. You say that on Istik Island in the Pacific the lizards roasted and the rocks split. How do I know?

CHRISTOPHER: You don't, sir, from what you have seen. I said you wouldn't. But you have seen the reports of previous experiments. *(He pulls out a map and spreads it.)* Not only from Istik but from three other Observation Posts spread around the world. *(LORD HENRY rises to see map.)* There…and there…and there. And that's Istik. I'll leave copies with Lord Henry. *(He hands a file to LORD HENRY.)*

LORD HENRY: How did these reach you?

CHRISTOPHER: Air-mail. These Observation Posts themselves are uninhabited islands. Nothing there but our recording instruments. But our observers in those parts visit them regularly and report what they find – chiefly rainfall, temperatures, hours of sunshine. That gave us all we wanted on Weather Control in the ordinary way. When I got the Burning Glass settings, I cabled for special reports. They are decisive and not pleasant.

LORD HENRY: They came home by open air-mail?

PRIME MINISTER: Why not in cipher?

CHRISTOPHER: Because this isn't a Government show. *(LORD H. shrugs and resumes his seat.)* The Terriford Trust was my father's private pidgin to start with. Then the Dennistoun Foundation produced a Research Endowment. This has never been a secret organization.

PRIME MINISTER: From today onwards it is… Henry, when we reach London, you will…shut all the stable doors. *(To CHRISTOPHER.)* Give Lord Henry details of your staff here and your observers outside.

CHRISTOPHER: They are included there. *(The file is already in LORD HENRY's hands.)*

PRIME MINISTER: Good. *(He rises from desk.)* Stop all communications inward or outward until new arrangements have been made. *(To LORD HENRY.)* Tell Gareth to draft what is necessary. I will see the draft myself. *(He takes off his overcoat and throws it on piano stool.)* Well, so far, so good. *(In fact, he is only opening a new chapter in his mind, but his eyes are on MARY and she rises.)*

MARY: I think we are in the way. *(CHRISTOPHER rises.)*

PRIME MINISTER: No. Pray sit down. You already know as much as I do – that under the Burning Glass lizards roast. All life disintegrates – am I right?

CHRISTOPHER: Yes, sir.

PRIME MINISTER: It is formidable. By night as well as by day?

CHRISTOPHER: This is the night, sir.

PRIME MINISTER: So I observe.

LADY TERRIFORD: If the sun has set, I don't see how –

PRIME MINISTER: No, no, Helen, not now. Never ask a man of science questions of that kind, He wallows in them – and it makes no difference to the lizard. *(To CHRISTOPHER.)* No doubt the Terriford waves bend or something of the kind. Everything bends nowadays. Am I right?

CHRISTOPHER: No, sir. Completely wrong. You see –

PRIME MINISTER: My cabinet never say that. It might be better if they did.

LADY TERRIFORD: Not for them.

CHRISTOPHER: *(Bursting to explain what is so interesting to him.)* I'm sorry, sir. But *bend* isn't the right word. What really happens is –

PRIME MINISTER: Never mind. For the moment I take it as read. Now let us return to our lizards.

MARY: Prime Minister, what Christopher is trying to say is really important and interesting. Wouldn't it be intelligent to know what the Burning Glass is as well as what it does? *(The PRIME MINISTER is at first vexed by this interruption.)*

PRIME MINISTER: Intelligent?

MARY: I didn't mean that you –

PRIME MINISTER: *(Relenting.)* You are quite right… Tell me, then, what the Burning Glass is.

MARY: Christopher must tell you.

PRIME MINISTER: *(To MARY.)* You shall tell me. I shall understand you better. Tell me, as you would a child. *But* first, let me clear the air. I know something of Radio. Am I to think of the Terriford waves in the same terms?

CHRISTOPHER: Both are electro-magnetic. There the likeness ends. Radio waves are reflected back by – call it the upper atmosphere. Terriford waves are not. They –

PRIME MINISTER: Words of one syllable.

CHRISTOPHER: They *do* things *to* the upper atmosphere… Go on, Mary. As to a child.

MARY: Fifty or sixty miles outside the earth is a vast layer, which isn't air and isn't space. It is called the Ionosphere or the Heaviside Layer. It contains *(She glances at CHRISTOPHER.)* ionized particles? Like all atoms they are little suns with electrons buzzing round them like planets. But ionized particles are freakish. They have one electron too few. Radio waves hit them, and are reflected back to earth, but –

PRIME MINISTER: Why?

MARY: I don't know.

LADY TERRIFORD: What a relief it is nowadays to hear someone say: 'I don't know.'

PRIME MINISTER: Does anyone know this, Christopher? *(He turns in his chair to speak to CHRISTOPHER.)*

CHRISTOPHER: The Radio boys have their results.

PRIME MINISTER: Without knowing why?

CHRISTOPHER: Without knowing *finally* why.

MARY: Please listen. The Terriford waves are different. Christopher's father found that they could –

CHRISTOPHER: Might –

MARY: That they might – they might polarize a section of the upper atmosphere – anyhow make it into a definite pattern so that it would act to the sun's rays as a lens.

PRIME MINISTER: That is the word I catch hold of. Lens. Go on. Make me understand it.

MARY: When you were a little boy, sir, did you ever take a magnifying glass and turn it in the sun until it burnt a hole in a piece of paper or set fire to a dry leaf?

PRIME MINISTER: Oh yes, I was a very destructive little boy… Is that it? Is that it? Go on.

CHRISTOPHER: May I break in? My father began by studying the connexion between ionization and light. His object and mine was always Weather Control. He did succeed in forming a kind of lens but he could never get enough power: the lens was always too far from being a perfect lens: he could obtain warmth but – it isn't easy in words of one syllable.

PRIME MINISTER: Let me try. I am a democratic politician. Always use kitchen-metaphor. Everyone understands that, even under a system of universal education… When your father switched on the sun, the bath-water remained, so to speak, tepid. Am I right?

CHRISTOPHER: Thank you, sir.

PRIME MINISTER: Or shall we say you had a garden hose shooting warm sunshine accurately and now you have…a flamethrower? *(They do not interrupt his long pause.)* A celestial flame-thrower… Apollo's Burning Glass… *(He has been meditating, feeling his way. Now he sees the whole thing, and speaks with the triumphant relief of a man who has been buried alive.)* That gives us absolute mastery.

MARY: *(In a tone of despair. MARY rises.)* Is that how you see it?

PRIME MINISTER: How else?

MARY: Mastery in war?

PRIME MINISTER: And in peace. You must not be shocked by the idea of *commanding* peace. Talk won't serve with totalitarians. *(To CHRISTOPHER.)* Now tell me. What is to prevent the enemy from arriving independently at your results?

CHRISTOPHER: Everything.

PRIME MINISTER: You refresh me. Why?

CHRISTOPHER: Because even if they got as far as Machine Six or their own version of it, they haven't the Burning Glass setting. And won't have it.

PRIME MINISTER: Might they not develop it?

CHRISTOPHER: I didn't develop it. It came. You must get this, sir. If you set an eternal monkey at an eternal typewriter and he went on typing and typing for ever, the time would come – must come mathematically by the laws of chance – at which what appeared on his paper would be – well, shall we say a complete sonnet of Shakespeare? The chances against my arriving at the Burning Glass setting were like that.

PRIME MINISTER: You are a very modest young man. What with your monkey and your typewriter, you make it sound as if I could have hit on the thing myself. Am I right?

CHRISTOPHER: Well sir, it would need a monkey who could type… Anyhow, monkeys or no monkeys, if I forgot it now, I should never reach it again. And *they* won't in a million years.

PRIME MINISTER: Who has the setting?

CHRISTOPHER: No one but myself.

PRIME MINISTER: Almost as important: who knows that it exists?

CHRISTOPHER: We in this room and my chief assistant, Tony Lack.

PRIME MINISTER: Where is he?

CHRISTOPHER: He's dining in London.

LORD HENRY: Didn't he know the Prime Minister was coming? *(CHRISTOPHER and MARY hesitate.)*

LADY TERRIFORD: He was told. He was asked to stay. He wouldn't let down his host.

(PRIME MINISTER looks at LORD HENRY.)

PRIME MINISTER: If it would need a monkey and a million years to reproduce the Burning Glass setting, I had better have a copy now. Even young men have died in the night. Where do you keep it?

CHRISTOPHER: In my memory.

PRIME MINISTER: You mean it is not written? My dear friend, *(P.M. puts his hand on CHRISTOPHER's shoulder.)* write it at once. Tomorrow Walter Crisp shall make contact. You shall have support at the highest level – scientific development (that's Crisp) and Gareth, security. At present, Henry, no one else. Repeat no one. When we reach London, order security on this house and this young man without delay.

LORD HENRY: In what degree?

PRIME MINISTER: Alpha Plus… Meanwhile, I will have the setting. Write, my friend. *(He puts a pen in CHRISTOPHER's hand. He moves a step or two away, his back to CHRISTOPHER.)*

CHRISTOPHER: *(After a pause, drops the pen with a little clatter.)* No, sir.

PRIME MINISTER: What? *(He turns to face CHRISTOPHER.)*

CHRISTOPHER: I can't write it.

PRIME MINISTER: Cannot?

CHRISTOPHER: Will not.

LORD HENRY: If what you are afraid of is security, that surely can be left to the Prime Minister.

CHRISTOPHER: I am not thinking of that… And I am talking to him.

PRIME MINISTER: My request is an order.

CHRISTOPHER: One I ask you not to give.

PRIME MINISTER: It is given.

CHRISTOPHER: It is one you cannot enforce. You can search me and this place. Not my mind.

LORD HENRY: To whom will you give the setting? To Crisp?

CHRISTOPHER: To no one – at present.

LORD HENRY: But that is an intolerable position. Is it a question of price? *(On that, CHRISTOPHER swings round at him.)*

CHRISTOPHER: My God, you can't say that. You… *(He stifles himself.)*

MARY: Lord Henry, you know it is not true. *(CHRISTOPHER motions her to be quiet.)*

PRIME MINISTER: In this country we do not force men's minds. That, with all our faults, is the distinction between ourselves and the evil we resist. The issue before the world is precisely that – the liberties of the mind, the sanctity and independence of the spirit. That is why I ask where I cannot compel. I ask this power. Your own conscience must yield it.

CHRISTOPHER: Isn't it true that many who were working on the atomic bomb prayed that some principle might emerge which should make the thing for ever and ever impossible?

PRIME MINISTER: That is true.

CHRISTOPHER: Were they right or wrong?

PRIME MINISTER: They were right in hoping that Providence would refuse them that gross power. But Providence did not refuse it to them – or to you. The problem stands.

CHRISTOPHER: I am not shirking it. I didn't bring you here, sir, on a fool's errand. *(And now he is struggling.)* My mother has one text by which she rules her life. It was my father's too. It's in my bones. I can't easily say it.

LADY TERRIFORD: 'Render therefore unto Caesar the things which are Caesar's; and unto God the things that are God's.' It's plain common sense.

MARY: *(Ingenously.)* You are Caesar. *(Turning in her chair to P.M.)*

PRIME MINISTER: *(With a smile at her prompting.)* Thank you, my dear. *(Turns to LORD HENRY.)* But what would the Opposition say to that? …

CHRISTOPHER: God knows I am with you on the Liberties of the Mind. They are threatened – cold and hot. They have to be protected. You had to know that the Burning Glass exists. Now, there is no threat you can't defy. In supreme emergency – and you shall be the judge of that – the *use* of it is yours. But not now. And never the setting itself. Except in supreme military emergency, the Burning Glass shall not be put to use at all.

PRIME MINISTER: Not even to beneficent use?

CHRISTOPHER: Not even to what you call beneficent use. The word begs the whole question. Suppose we could harness the Burning Glass, as we are trying to harness atomic energy. Suppose we could switch on the sun to drive all our engines for us, and boil the bath-water, and grow our food and can it, and play our music and can that, and incubate our babies and can them; suppose this huge power over Nature were really on tap in every suburb from

Purley to Peru – what then? There can be a blasphemy of applied science. We have reached that point. For five generations man has developed his power over Nature –

PRIME MINISTER: Is that wrong?

CHRISTOPHER: Alone it is. We haven't developed at the same time our spiritual or our political qualities. We are neither gentler nor wiser than we were. We are like a monstrous giant, one of whose arms has grown and grown –

PRIME MINISTER: Stop. I am not expressing an opinion, but I want to grasp the significance of this. Do I understand that now, for the first time, science is withholding knowledge?

CHRISTOPHER: Now, for the first time, science is withholding power.

PRIME MINISTER: Is not that reaction?

CHRISTOPHER: No, sir, it is revolution. It is revolution. It is revolution against the drug that has been…swelling us.

PRIME MINISTER: Power over Nature is a godlike drug.

CHRISTOPHER: It happens that we aren't gods.

PRIME MINISTER: You are holding back the clock.

CHRISTOPHER: I am refusing to put it forward. To do either is to lie. *(This is not without effect on the PRIME MINISTER, but the immediacies are what concern him.)*

PRIME MINISTER: So be it… For the moment, leave the civil uses; that is long-term, anyway. Come back to the urgent, the military. If I am not to have the setting, how am I to obtain the use? What action do you propose?

CHRISTOPHER: I will work with your scientific advisers on Machine Six. I will work on their lines. But it is I who will set the machine.

PRIME MINISTER: And if, when emergency does arise, you are dead or absent?

CHRISTOPHER: That has been provided for.

LORD HENRY: Then you have confided the setting to someone? To Mr. Lack, for example?

CHRISTOPHER: You are too quick. I said 'to no one' and I mean it. *(He moves and puts his hand on MARY's shoulder.)* Half the setting is deeply planted in my wife's memory. That half alone is useless in itself; anyhow she hasn't a notion of how to apply it. The other half is in a sealed and addressed envelope in the hands of a friend, a village doctor. He doesn't know what the envelope contains and would be no wiser if he did. In emergency, if I am absent, Mary will telephone him and give him a code word. He will post the letter. The two parts of the setting will come together.

LORD HENRY: In whose hands?

CHRISTOPHER: For the Prime Minister's use.
(He moves away to drink table.)

LORD HENRY: Through what intermediary?

PRIME MINISTER: Do not press, Henry. When the kingdoms of the world are offered to me, I can wait a little while to learn the name of the intermediary.

MARY: You said 'the kingdoms of the world'. Remembering the context?

PRIME MINISTER: *(With a snap.)* I know my Bible.

MARY: The reply was: 'Get thee behind me, Satan.'

PRIME MINISTER: But I am only Caesar. Did you not tell me so? It is hard for Caesar to make that reply… And who offered me the kingdoms…and the republics?

MARY: *(A cry of despair, rare in her. She rises.)* I wish we were peasants! I wish we had lived and died a thousand years ago! Even the choice between good and evil seems to have been taken from us.

PRIME MINISTER: Oh, no, it has not. That is despair. So the entanglements of the world always appear in our darkest hours. It seems then that we cannot stretch out a hand without wounding, or speak without denying, or kiss without betraying. The pieces of silver burn in our palm and the cock crows in our ears. The words of the Gospel itself seem to conflict with one another, good fighting against good, and we call it the modern dilemma and pity ourselves, but it is the dilemma of the two sisters, the one who served and the other who sat at Jesus' feet. It is the dilemma of Pilate, who also was a minister of Caesar: at least I have learned that we cannot wash our hands of it. What we call contradiction is often, without our knowing it, the perfect balance of truth itself. The contradictions in the words of Jesus are all a seeming that we shall grow out of; to underline them with our intellect is pride; to use them as an excuse for inaction is cowardice. We are to choose fearlessly. Tonight you and your husband have chosen. Your conscience was divided against itself, a part saying: 'Render unto Caesar,' and a part: 'Resist not evil.' And you have chosen; that is much. Do you now blame yourself that you seem to have sacrificed a part of your conscience? I have come to believe that this is a sacrifice often required of us while we live – our acknowledgment that our conscience is not infallible. *(LORD HENRY, anticipating a MOT has his notebook and pencil out.)* Let no man call himself an idealist who has never sacrificed an ideal. *(He has been so carried away by his own thought that he has not noticed that LORD HENRY is writing. Now he does.)* What are you writing?

LORD HENRY: Your last sentence. 'Let no man call himself an idealist who has never sacrificed an ideal.' I thought that might be politically useful.

PRIME MINISTER: *(Sharply.)* You are too clever. *(Then with a laugh he pats LORD HENRY on the shoulder.)* Either you are too old, or I am too young for this wicked world. *(He turns to face MARY.)* Before I return to London I want to say this, particularly to you if I may. *(MARY rises.)* If it should become known that this power exists, your Christopher may be in some danger.

MARY: I understand that.

PRIME MINISTER: Government can only help those who help themselves. You will find at first that to be protected is irksome, but it is really no more than a return to one's nursery days. One gets used to it and forgets it. In effect, I myself never go out except in a pram. Fortunately, a tolerably invisible pram. But you two *(He turns his head to include CHRISTOPHER.)* must not think it clever or amusing to give your nursemaids the slip.

MARY: We shall not do that.

PRIME MINISTER: Very well. From tomorrow –

MARY: I want to ask you something. Will you stay here tonight?

LORD HENRY: That is impossible.

MARY: I suppose it is.

PRIME MINISTER: But I am interested.

LORD HENRY: I'm sorry, sir. It is completely out of the question.

PRIME MINISTER: I am aware of that. Permit me, nevertheless, to be interested. *(To MARY.)* What is it you fear?

MARY: I don't know. If I did, I should not fear it.

CHRISTOPHER: My darling, there is nothing to fear. How can there be tonight? Tell me.

MARY: Very well. Say no more. There is nothing to fear.

PRIME MINISTER: When I am gone, what shall you do?

MARY: Play chess with Christopher. It's our bedtime peace and quiet. More than ever now.

PRIME MINISTER: And you, Helen?

LADY TERRIFORD: I? Sit here and read or knit.

CHRISTOPHER: It's long after your bedtime.

LADY TERRIFORD: There are nights on which one prefers company.

PRIME MINISTER: *(To MARY.)* My dear, I feel no present alarm. If they knew of this thing, they could have struck before now; you lay wide open. It's the future we have to worry about, and protection will be adequate as soon as it can be laid on. Nevertheless, I want you and Christopher to know that, at all times, as if I *were* here, you can have at once counsel and help at the highest level. *(To LORD HENRY.)* Give them access.

LORD HENRY: May I say, sir *(LORD HENRY moves to below chair behind desk.)* that I think that goes beyond the needs of the case. Gareth's line should be enough.

PRIME MINISTER: Give them personal access.

LORD HENRY: Very well. In extreme need you telephone the Treasury, Whitehall 1234. When they answer, you will say: Seventeen Eighty Five. They will repeat: Seventeen Eighty Five and you will correct them: One Seven Eight Nine. When they reply, you will say one word. *(He gives the P.M.'s back a quick look.)* Flashlight.

PRIME MINISTER: I said *personal* access.

LORD HENRY: So be it. When One Seven Eight Nine replies, you will say one-word: Curtain-Raiser. It gives you instant access by day and night to the Prime Minister himself if he is reachable; if he is not, then still to over-riding authority… Curtain-Raiser is not to be used unless the heavens fall.

CHRISTOPHER: It shall not be.

PRIME MINISTER: Then I will say goodnight. I think I shed an overcoat in here. *(CHRISTOPHER picks it up from piano stool.)*

LORD HENRY: I'll go ahead.

PRIME MINISTER: *(Fussing – to CHRISTOPHER.)* No! No! There's a scarf first.

LORD HENRY: *(To CHRISTOPHER.)* Comforter in the left-hand pocket. Cigar case in the right.

CHRISTOPHER: Thanks. I'd never make a nurse.

LADY TERRIFORD: *(As LORD HENRY approaches her.)* Goodnight Lord Henry.

LORD HENRY: You have been very patient with us. I'm grateful. *(He releases her hand and goes to MARY.)* Mrs. Terriford – I am a sheep-dog, you know. Not a glamorous role. That's why – sometimes – I snap. Am I forgiven?

MARY: If you don't bite… Tell me: I've never met a Prime Minister before. Why do you have to go *ahead?*

LORD HENRY: I have to mobilise the pram… *(At door.)* I'm leaving your husband with the baby! *(He goes out.)*

PRIME MINISTER: *(By now he is comfortably wrapped. To CHRISTOPHER.)* We understand each other, I think? No man has wielded so great a power with so little ambition. I live and learn. *(To MARY.)* Goodnight. Sleep well. Sleep safe. God keep you all. *(To LADY TERRIFORD.)* Goodnight, dear Helen. *(He puts out both hands to her. She takes them and rises.)* Goodnight. *(He kisses her on the forehead. They move to door.)* Some day, you and I will go up the Cher again in a punt and attend the Commem. Ball at – where was it? – New College or Worcester?

LADY TERRIFORD: Both, Monty, I'm afraid. And now will you let me tell you why in the Garden of Eden there were no boots?

PRIME MINISTER: Certainly not. I like puzzles and shall hereafter. It's a long time I shall have to spend in Westminster Abbey. *(He goes out. CHRISTOPHER follows to see them off.)*

MARY: What happened at New College?

LADY TERRIFORD: We danced, my dear.

MARY: And at Worcester?

LADY TERRIFORD: At Worcester we more frequently sat out. There are no pleasanter gardens in Oxford.

MARY: I believe, if I had been proposed to by a Prime Minister, I should say so forty years on.

LADY TERRIFORD: For that two things would be necessary; first, to break the rules; secondly, to be proposed to by a Prime Minister. I hope neither will happen to you.

MARY: *(Embracing her.)* What a pity that so charming a woman should have been so well brought up! *(CHRISTOPHER returns. Sound of departing motor-cars.)*

CHRISTOPHER: There they go. Listen. Really, it's like a circus. Do you think that from now onwards when I go down to the sea to bathe or into the village for a packet of cigarettes

I shall have to go in *three* motor-cars? Now, Mary, shall we play our game?

LADY TERRIFORD: Chess? Now?

CHRISTOPHER: Why not?

LADY TERRIFORD: Because it's tomorrow morning.

CHRISTOPHER: You show no sign of going.

LADY TERRIFORD: But I am old. Like the Prime Minister, I come alive in the small hours. Mary must be tired.

MARY: How soon will they lay on this...'security'? How long have we?

CHRISTOPHER: What do you mean?

MARY: How long before the – before the key turns in the lock? When it does, we shall never be just ourselves again. There will be guards everywhere.

CHRISTOPHER: But you yourself asked the Prime Minister to stay!

MARY: I know.

CHRISTOPHER: With his guard?

MARY: I know. *(The sound of a helicopter is heard. LADY TERRIFORD registers it but CHRISTOPHER and MARY ignore it.)* That was one thing. But he didn't. And so that's another, isn't it? – a kind of...reprieve? So let's not waste it. I never wanted to *sleep* at the end of the holidays.

CHRISTOPHER: *(Tenderly and playfully because she is on edge.)* My darling, what did you want to do? Shall we...shall we take the car and drive to the sea and swim? It may be September but the water is still warm. Shall we? *(LADY TERRIFORD shuts window and helicopter is no longer heard. She draws curtains shut.) (And he adds, out of consideration for her:)* Better than my dull chess.

MARY: Nothing is better than *our* dull chess. *(MARY rises to chess table. CHRISTOPHER follows and together they lift chess table and return to their seats, the table between them.)* I never wanted – I mean at the end of the holidays – people used to invent 'special treats'. They made it worse. I wanted everything to go on quite naturally – I do now – as if it weren't the end.

CHRISTOPHER: Then we'll play. Whose move?

MARY: Yours. I had moved my pawn – that one.

CHRISTOPHER: Venomous. I remember. *(Pause. He hands her her book and knitting bag from the sofa.)* Mother, your job is to knit or read, not to walk about. *(She is standing near him. With his eyes still on the chess-board, he reaches up an affectionate hand which she takes and holds.)* Why did you say what you did to the High Command – about preferring company tonight?

LADY TERRIFORD: There are nights, aren't there – there were in Scotland when I was a girl – on which one expects the door to open?

CHRISTOPHER: What does one do then?

LADY TERRIFORD: One knits – facing the door. *(MARY does not notice that CHRISTOPHER has moved a chessman. He recalls her by tapping with it on the board.)*

CHRISTOPHER: Mary, I have moved. Where have you gone to? *(MARY looks over her shoulder at the door. Then turns back.)*

MARY: Give me the doctor's number and the code-word.

CHRISTOPHER: Tomorrow.

MARY: Tonight.

CHRISTOPHER: When we have finished our game.

MARY: Please: now.

CHRISTOPHER: My dearest, why on earth?

MARY: Please: now.

CHRISTOPHER: Of course. *(He writes and gives it.)*

MARY: Bless you… Now we will keep our minds on the game. *(She moves a piece quickly and decisively. He moves at once. She raises her hand, then draws it back.)*

MARY: *(To herself.)* Steady! *(She pauses to think; then moves a piece.)* I mustn't be rattled. I…must *not*…be rattled.

CHRISTOPHER: You talked as if –

MARY: What?

CHRISTOPHER: As if a wolf had his paw under the door.

MARY: *(Reaching for his hand across the table.)* Go away, wolf.

CHRISTOPHER: *(Not turning.)* Has he gone, Mamma?

LADY TERRIFORD: No. *(She rises. A car is heard. No one speaks. The car sweeps past the open window. The sound dies and stops as the car rounds the end of the house.)*

CHRISTOPHER: Tony. I'll go and let him in.

MARY: He has his own key.

LADY TERRIFORD: In any case he may prefer to zigzag quietly to bed.

CHRISTOPHER: You are unjust, Mamma. It lights up his brain and his hands – never his legs. It makes him more alive, not less. *(HARDLIP comes in, supporting TONY by the arm. TONY is very pale and almost spent, but he is not drunk and bitterly resents HARDLIP's repeated suggestions that he is. He has been doped but does not know it. The effect upon him is that he is swept by waves of almost irresistible sleepiness, and he fights against them, talking in the intervals with keyed-up speed and lucidity.)*

TONY: I don't need your arm. I am not in the least drunk. Why do you pretend that I am?

HARDLIP: *(With the exasperating patronage of a nursemaid.)* Of course you're not. Only a little tired. *(To the others:)* I'm sorry to butt in at this time of night, but I thought it best to bring him in and make sure he got his head down safely.

MARY: Thank you. We will look after him if he needs looking after. *(TONY is seated on the sofa and, in spite of his efforts, his head continually falls forward.)*

CHRISTOPHER: *(Going to him.)* What's wrong, Tony?

HARDLIP: Poor chap… Coming out into the fresh air and then the drive down. He wouldn't let himself pass out. Better if he had. Anyhow, what matters is to get him to bed. Shall we do it together?

TONY: I wish you wouldn't stand over me and talk as if you were visiting my grave in a churchyard. We stopped at the roadside –

HARDLIP: Carburettor –

TONY: I know. I didn't pass out. And then cars swept past. Car after car after car. Dozens. Like a circus. And then we came on. I know. I am alive. Very, very, sleepy, but alive, all right. So are you all, sitting here. Oh, I'm glad. I'm glad. Mary at the chess table. *(To CHRISTOPHER.)* Why aren't you?

CHRISTOPHER: I was. It's my move.

TONY: Peaceful, silent game. I ought to play it. Used to once… *(His hands to his head.)* You know it is extremely odd. I'm perfectly alive and bright, but about once in five minutes sleep hits me on the head like a revolving sledge-hammer. And…now…if I let…let go, I shall…just…fall on the ground and sleep…on the carpet. So I won't. *(He rises with an effort and staggers to below chair in front of desk.)* Good night, Lady T. Give me credit: at least I go to bed under my own steam. Up those stairs. Up and up. *(He moves to door and goes out, leaving door open.)* Angels and ministers of grace defend us. *(TONY goes out.)*

LADY TERRIFORD: He has what we would call 'guts'. He deserves to sleep well.

CHRISTOPHER: *(To HARDLIP.)* Will you have a drink for the road?

HARDLIP: Thank you, nothing. I must apologise for interrupting your game.

LADY TERRIFORD: I want to lock up. I will see Mr. Hardlip out. *(She continues her move, in front of him, towards door.)*

HARDLIP: *(Disconcerted by this.)* Really, Lady Terriford, I don't think –

LADY TERRIFORD: Not at all. A pleasure. *(As she goes, he has to follow her.)*

MARY: You know, Christopher, Tony is *not* drunk.

CHRISTOPHER: Then what?

MARY: He showed me once a little glass tube that he always carried – since the last war, I believe. Small tablets, five of them. He said that, if you were in a room, it was as well to be sure that the window opened.

CHRISTOPHER: I know his 'window-opener'. Enough to kill him twice – and to spare. *(LADY TERRIFORD comes in door and sits chair in front of desk. Resumes knitting.)* Whatever he has had tonight, it isn't his own little glass tube. That has a delayed action, but minutes, not hours.

MARY: Still, go and see if he's all right.

CHRISTOPHER: I will. I'll make this move first.

MARY: But you haven't thought about it.

CHRISTOPHER: Oh yes, indeed I have. If you allow yourself to be interrupted by the Hardlips of this world, you become *(He moves a piece.)* as mad as they are.

MARY: *(Moving a piece at once.)* Now what do you do?

CHRISTOPHER: *(He rises.)* Have a look at Tony. Then I'll come back.

MARY: Would you rather stop?

CHRISTOPHER: *(He stops and turns.)* No. We finish that game before we sleep. It's a *thing. (He turns towards door. As he starts to move the knock is heard. He moves to window, opens curtains and bottom sash. HARDLIP puts his head in.)*

HARDLIP: It seems to be my fate to interrupt you tonight. My infernal self-starter has packed up. Would you give me a turn on the handle? I'm no good with this arm of mine.

CHRISTOPHER: I'll come. *(Moves towards door, then turns back.)* Easier through the garden if the front door is bolted and chained. *(He opens the long window.)*

HARDLIP: Good night again. *(Vanishes.)*

CHRISTOPHER: *(At the long window.)* You can play for me if you like. Knight to King's Bishop Two.

MARY: You had better take time to think about that one. *(There is a period of waiting, occupied at considerable intervals by these fragments which are not part of a continuous conversation.)*

LADY TERRIFORD: His car wasn't *at* the door. It was across the drive under the big elm.

MARY: Turned ready to start, I suppose. *(She sits at the piano, strikes two or three chords, then is silent.)*

LADY TERRIFORD: Yes, play…

MARY: Matthew, Mark, Luke and John
Bless the bed that I lie on.

LADY TERRIFORD: Did you have that in your nursery?

MARY: No. But Christopher did.

LADY TERRIFORD: Ah! You were saying it for *him*.

MARY: He is taking a long time.

LADY TERRIFORD: They had to go round the end of the
house… Have you ever known a machine that worked?

MARY: A piano is a machine.

LADY TERRIFORD: Yes, play.

MARY: At New College or in Worcester Gardens, what did you
hear in the very small hours of the morning? *(She begins the*
Songe d'Automne, *then stops in mid-bar and rises, listening.*
The car sweeps past the window. The sound dies away.)

LADY TERRIFORD: Go back to your chess table, my dear. He
will come. *(MARY remains quite still, listening.)*

MARY: He doesn't come.

LADY TERRIFORD: He will now.

MARY: I was foolish tonight, asking the Prime Minister to stay.
I suddenly saw myself standing here like this and saying:
'He doesn't come,' and you said: 'He will now.' … I am
going to look. *(She goes to the long window.)* Christopher!
(She goes out.) Christopher! Where are you? Where are
you? Christopher! Christopher! *(Silence. MARY re-enters.)* He
isn't there. He is gone.

LADY TERRIFORD: There may be a simple explanation. He
may have gone into the lower garden. Or he may have
– that *is* possible – he may have gone straight up to Tony
Lack.

TONY enters. He has taken off his coat and waistcoat and shoes and
undone his collar. Apart from that, he is still in crumpled evening
dress. His hair wild, his eyes staring.

TONY: *(He comes to curve of piano and leans on it.)* What has
happened? I was – oh, deeper than sleep, on the bed of the

ocean; and something came with all its hands and dragged me up…and up…as thought I were…necessary…up here.

MARY: Has Christopher been with you?

TONY: No.

LADY TERRIFORD: Mr. Lack. Was there anyone else in that car, with you and Mr. Hardlip?

TONY: There were two…two…

LADY TERRIFORD picks up the telephone receiver and holds it out to MARY. As MARY takes it from her the Curtain falls.

Act Drop.

ACT THREE

SCENE I

Six days later. Sunday. Late dusk. LADY TERRIFORD is discovered. She is at the desk finishing a letter. On the desk there is now a green telephone in addition to the other two. The door is ajar. Curtains are open. Chandelier is alight. Stool is now under piano. LORD HENRY enters carrying a file. He comes to desk.

LORD HENRY: I understand the Prime Minister is on his way from the Manor. I'm afraid he asks once more that he may have the use of this room.

LADY TERRIFORD: He shall. *(She puts the letter in an envelope and seals it.)* Though why for six days he should have picked on this room of all the others in the house – *(She rises with letters and crosses to below desk to sofa for her handbag.)*

LORD HENRY: Blame me. *(Touching the green telephone.)* This link with his own secure line which can't be tapped had to be laid on from the Manor. Quickest from this room. *(He crosses to door, closes it and returns to chair behind desk.)*

LADY TERRIFORD: So be it… At what time is the final stroke?

LORD HENRY: Soon now. We said 'at nightfall' – today, Sunday, if your son was not in our hands by then. We have given every kind of facility for his return. New guarantees were delivered last night – not of course through diplomatic channels. In reply, not a move or a word.

LADY TERRIFORD: So now we are at the end.

LORD HENRY: *(Always with heartless efficiency.)* Everything that can be done, has been. The two preliminary strokes on Wednesday and Friday ought to have made the enemy see reason. They were precisely located in advance and timed by local time. They were carried out with perfect accuracy. That we know. There is a neat hole four miles across in the Laderek forest, and on Friday the Sumahdin Lake in effect boiled over. The enemy have been left in no doubt that we can strike where we please and when. But they have said nothing.

LADY TERRIFORD: I should have thought that made the final stroke at their capital…meaningless. The Prime Minister will go forward?

LORD HENRY: I leave you to judge his mind.

LADY TERRIFORD: War won't bring my son back if the threat and two demonstrations – the forest and the lake – have failed.

LORD HENRY: It's natural you should see it from that point of view, Lady Terriford. Believe me, our whole object has been to get him back. Now…

LADY TERRIFORD: You abandon him.

LORD HENRY: I was going to say: We can't have him there and wait. If his knowledge remains in their reach, it becomes imperative to strike first.

LADY TERRIFORD: Did the Prime Minister ask you to explain this to me?

LORD HENRY: Not in so many words.

LADY TERRIFORD: If only you had left even two men as guards that night.

LORD HENRY: Who dreamed they could act so fast? Didn't Christopher say: 'There is nothing to fear.'? Still, blame me. Everyone does. *(The green telephone rings. He picks up the receiver.)*

Henry Strait. *(Listens.)* No. I will not even tell him. *(LADY TERRIFORD goes out of the French windows.)* The story is clear. He is staying at the Manor, but will preside at tomorrow's Cabinet in London. *(The PRIME MINISTER enters.)* Meanwhile, he will take no calls except Curtain-Raiser, and, of course, the Palace.

PRIME MINISTER: Who is that?

LORD HENRY: Joan.

PRIME MINISTER: More boxes? She says I'm neglecting them, poor girl. They will have answered themselves by tomorrow morning. You know, Henry, it's clever of the enemy not to answer; the one thing I didn't expect. No denial of having taken him. Laderek and Sumahdin, two acts of war; and not a protest. Not a word in their press – or even in ours. Five days of complete silence and the diplomatic patter going on all the time. Do you know why?

LORD HENRY: No, sir, I don't.

PRIME MINISTER: Nor do I… Still no reply from Washington?

LORD HENRY: There's a stream from Washington.

PRIME MINISTER: I mean about Machine Six. I must know what likelihood there is that the enemy have Machine Six. If they pinched it from America and Christopher can be made to talk… It is vital to know. As it is… I have to guess. And I have to guess right. … I observe two things. One: the enemy doesn't answer. Two: he doesn't bomb this place.

LORD HENRY: That would mean war. Maybe he's not ready.

PRIME MINISTER: From his point of view, better a premature war with existing weapons. I should have supposed he'd risk anything to bomb Machine Six. *(The door opens and TONY comes in. Throughout the following scene LORD HENRY, being morally a little man, is vindictive towards TONY, while the PRIME MINISTER gives him room to breathe – and talk.)*

LORD HENRY: Not yet, Mr. Lack.

TONY: *(Standing his ground at door.)* I have something to say which you must know, *(Commandingly.)* and at once.

PRIME MINISTER: Come in. What I want to know is the mind of the enemy. Can you prompt me in that?

TONY: That's for you to judge. I have tried to tell you all I know – what happened *before*, and what happened that night when he drugged me. I didn't understand what was happening then. Now, I can piece it together. What puzzles me is how he had a helicopter on tap.

LORD HENRY: It needn't puzzle you.

TONY: Why not?

LORD HENRY: Because it's none of your business.

PRIME MINISTER: *(Covering LORD HENRY's ill-temper.)* In fact, as we now know, he had had it at close call for nearly five weeks. He moved it in to Lamberton Common when he decided to act. Lady Terriford tells me now she heard it. Presumably they were reluctant to use that method if they could get him to walk into their parlour. What changed their mind –

TONY: What made Hardlip act when he did was knowledge that you were coming that night and security would clamp down next morning. But he knew it on his own – not through me.

LORD HENRY: We have only your word for it.

TONY: If you will believe nothing, you will learn nothing.

LORD HENRY: You had better understand, Mr. Lack, that at the moment your innocence or guilt doesn't interest us. You are not on trial in this room now. Your excuses can keep.

PRIME MINISTER: *(Impatient of LORD HENRY.)* Go on, Mr. Lack.

TONY: What I *am* responsible for is this: I had told him that I myself didn't know the Burning Glass setting. Hardlip built on that; if I didn't know, he could be pretty sure no one else did. And out of that there's a new point which I haven't told you and which –

LORD HENRY: Really, Mr. Lack, wouldn't it have been better at the beginning to have made a clean breast of the whole thing?

TONY: I have tried to. I am trying –

LORD HENRY: And yet you come here now and say there is something that, all this time, you have been keeping back?

PRIME MINISTER: Patience, patience!

LORD HENRY: No doubt he is trying to work his passage home.

PRIME MINISTER: *(Angrily.)* If not patience, then for God's sake imagination! When a man is telling the truth with all his might and all his heart and all his soul, can't you hear it in his voice? *(To TONY.)* Go on, Mr. Lack.

TONY: The point is: what are the enemy thinking now? On that last evening, I burst out at him: 'Anyhow whatever else I have told, I haven't told you the setting because I don't know it': You see, until that moment, he had never been *quite* sure that I wasn't in the secret. But from that moment he *was* sure. … And it does show you the enemy's mind. They took their information from him. They too assumed that, if they had Christopher in the bag, they had the Burning Glass too, and that it couldn't operate without him. When it did, at Laderek and Sumahdin…you see?

PRIME MINISTER: It can't have been pretty for Mr. Hardlip. He has, presumably, by now been re-gathered to the bosom of his somewhat variegated ancestors. That is something: one economist the less.

TONY: But you see what it means, sir. It does tell why the enemy haven't bombed this place and why they won't.

PRIME MINISTER: Does it? I should have supposed the contrary. *(To LORD HENRY.)* I want Mary Terriford to come here now. *(HENRY rises and moves towards telephone.)* No, not the telephone. I saw her in the ante-room as I came through. *(LORD HENRY goes out.)* Put yourself in their place. They took the risk of abducting Christopher. Why? They believed one of two things. Either that we hadn't the guts to use this thing or that we wouldn't have the knowledge once Christopher was taken. Now I give myself credit: they don't doubt my guts. Therefore, it's more than a good guess that they thought we hadn't the knowledge. And now they find we have. Isn't that a sound reason to destroy this place at all costs – at all costs?

TONY: No, sir. I don't believe it is if you go a step further –
(But the PRIME MINISTER, like so many great men, has his limitations. He is just not listening except to his own thought and he rides TONY down.)

PRIME MINISTER: Every precaution that can be taken secretly has been taken for the protection of this place, but nothing is a hundred per cent effective against a determined concentration on a single target. I must have the American machines to fall back on.

TONY: The enemy believe you have. *(This, which is the whole point that TONY has been trying to make, doesn't sink into the PRIME MINISTER.)*

PRIME MINISTER: *(Vaguely.)* What? *(And he turns away from TONY as MARY enters followed by LORD HENRY.)*

MARY: You sent for me?

PRIME MINISTER: I am sorry. I must press for what I need.

MARY: If you still want the setting, the answer is still No.

PRIME MINISTER: Do not be hasty. You stand, as you think, by your husband's principle. I honour that. But it is possible to misinterpret a principle.

MARY: It was to me that he gave the Upper Setting. Not in writing. *Why* do you think he gave it to me in that form? Not to be handed on. Twice this week I have given you the *use.* I will again tonight if you order it. He meant me to do that. But I will not give you the setting. Why do you want it, if you have the use? Isn't that enough?

PRIME MINISTER: No, it is not. For this reason – *(INSPECTOR WIGG enters.)*

WIGG: Excuse me, my lord.

LORD HENRY: Well, Inspector?

WIGG: Despatch-rider from the Manor, my Lord.

LORD HENRY: Bring it in.

WIGG: It's a young woman, m'lord.

LORD HENRY: I didn't say bring her. Bring it. I want the despatch.

WIGG: She won't give it to me. She's as stubborn as a mob of mules. Scottish, by the sound of her. Only the Prime Minister or you, m'lord, personal.

PRIME MINISTER: *(With delight.)* Go on, Henry. It's the Curtain-Raiser I'm waiting for. *(LORD HENRY goes out. WIGG turns to follow but is stopped by P.M..)* Inspector… Give that girl some tea or better.

WIGG: Very good, sir. *(Goes out.)*

PRIME MINISTER: I like stubborn security. My mother was Scottish. Thank God for the Act of Union. *(LORD HENRY returns.) (HENRY returns with government security box which he puts on desk in front of P.M. who unlocks it with a key from his pocket. He takes out a longer envelope.)* One sheet. Washington. Take this damn thing away. *(P.M. hands box to HENRY who takes it up to window-seat. P.M opens envelope which contains another inside which is a sheet of typewritten foolscap.)* One sheet. Washington isn't wasting words. *(For a few moments he reads to himself, then:)* In the event of war, the President will give me personal backing, but 'the fullest information will be needed to win the support of Congress. The disappearance of one man cannot of itself justify war. The nature of the Burning Glass and the urgent peril to all our people of its falling into enemy hands must be felt, repeat felt, from coast to coast. Above all it must be clear that nothing known to Great Britain has been, is being, or will be withheld from the United States.' … Now, Machine Six. Listen, Mary: here is your reason. He says: 'We have in the United States four operative and three under construction. They have hitherto been regarded as Weather Control instruments and have not been given military security. For the same reason, the enemy may have been more interested in other things.' … *May have!*

LORD HENRY: That leaves us all guessing.

PRIME MINISTER: Then there's a passage I won't read. … Now, listen to this: 'As the only example of Machine Six in your country is at Terriford House which may be destroyed, it is urgent and imperative that you communicate the setting to us. Without it our machines cannot help you. It is my personal request, as ally and friend, that you communicate the setting now, repeat now. I am at a loss to understand why you have withheld it.' … Now, Mary. *(MARY rises.)* If this place is destroyed, above all if the enemy have Machine Six, it is vital that the United States should operate. I claim the setting as a right.

MARY: No one but Christopher can give it.

PRIME MINISTER: The right to use the Burning Glass in supreme emergency he gave, through me, to his country. You agree?

MARY: Yes.

PRIME MINISTER: Does not that include our allies?

MARY: You press and press. I feel like a prisoner in a foreign country with no counsel to defend me.

LORD HENRY: Answer the Prime Minister's question. Does not your husband's grant of the military use of his machine extend to our allies?

MARY: The military use – yes. But the use, the use only the *use!* He would never allow the setting itself to go out of his keeping. Didn't he say, here in this room: 'I will give you the use, but I will set the machine myself'? Now I have set it for him and you have used it. And I will set it again and you shall use it again. I would set the American machines. But I cannot be in two places at the same time, and I must not let the setting go… I know quite well that when the Burning Glass was used on Laderek and Sumahdin there was a chance that Christopher would come back, and I know that, if it is used on the enemy capital tonight, I shall never, never see him again. But if the Prime Minister orders it, I will obey. Christopher would have wished that. But I will not let the setting go.

LORD HENRY: *(A pause. LORD HENRY looks at P.M. who nods. LORD HENRY rises and moves to fireplace and stands with his back to it facing MARY.)* How many people do you think would understand you? If you said: 'I will not use this power in war,' there are millions who would understand that, and would applaud you until they were bombed in their own homes. And if you said: 'I will give this power for peaceful, industrial uses – to give everyone more luxury at the cost of less effort' – they would applaud that also. But you say precisely the opposite.

MARY: Christopher said the opposite.

LORD HENRY: He would give it in war but not in peace? Why? You stand on conscience. Is not war the greatest of evils?

MARY: *(MARY turns in her chair to P.M.)* Where is he leading me? He is leading me into a trap.

PRIME MINISTER: Let him go on. You are hearing what the world would say. He knows his world.

LORD HENRY: You will not release the setting because you fear that, once out of your hands, it would be used in peace-time for what you consider evil purposes. But is not war a great evil?

MARY: It is a great evil.

LORD HENRY: Is not war the greatest of all evils?

MARY: No.

LORD HENRY: The world would say so.

MARY: That does not make it true.

LORD HENRY: What evil is greater than war? *(Pause.)*

MARY: To corrupt life. *(Pause.)*

PRIME MINISTER: *(With a certain satisfaction.)* The trap has not closed, Henry. On that line you will never shake her.

LORD HENRY: She does not know how old the world is. It is, in fact, corrupt.

MARY: At least, his science shall not corrupt it. That is what I stand out against, whether he is alive or dead.

LORD HENRY: Go out into the streets or the cinemas or the churches. Not one in a thousand would agree with him or thank him or understand him. They are aching for comfort and the power that buys it. Science has become a gigantic dole. Renounce it? Don't you believe a word of it! You are trying to change a world that doesn't want to be born again.

MARY: Then why is it so unhappy? Why are you, who have comfort and power, so bitter?

PRIME MINISTER: Ah, you fight well!

MARY: I have need to fight. Alone, against him, against you.

PRIME MINISTER: And yet, Mary, against what I ask, you must not stand out, whether your Christopher is alive or dead. Your loyalty is not to what he said in the past but to what he would say now.

MARY: Cannot I imagine that better than you?

PRIME MINISTER: I dare to think not... You are –

MARY: You are the Prime Minister and I am utterly alone. But I loved him. I knew him. *(In an outburst of grief:)* Oh, I said: 'I *loved*... I *knew*!'

PRIME MINISTER: Because you have been thinking of him as if he were dead, you are holding too close to the letter of your love and loyalty.

MARY: I trust you. You would not trap me?

PRIME MINISTER: *(Moved and weighed down by this confidence.)* I will not trap you. I will tell you what I believe, from my experiences of men, would be the truth of his mind and will – as if he were here.

MARY: Perhaps he is listening to us.

PRIME MINISTER: I will speak as if he were... You cannot go to the States. There is no time and you are needed here. Therefore, the Americans cannot be given the use of the Burning Glass except by giving them the setting. And is not the *use* of the American machines in this emergency a necessary part of the military use your Christopher granted to me? You cannot withhold it.

MARY: O please God, help me to do right!

PRIME MINISTER: If he were here, with nightfall close at hand and that paper before him – that peremptory demand – now, repeat now – would not he give me what I – must have?

MARY: *(After a struggle.)* I think he would.

PRIME MINISTER: *(P.M. rises.)* Give her paper and ink. *(To TONY.)* You too.

TONY: No, sir.

PRIME MINISTER: 'No'! By God, you will do what you're told.

TONY: Not yet. Neither she nor I. If you strike, then you can have it. You can have anything then; there will be nothing left to save. But you must wait an hour.

LORD HENRY: Must!

TONY: Must.

PRIME MINISTER: An hour, you say! What if they strike before our signal has gone? Are you mad?

TONY: They won't, sir, unless you do. You are reading their mind wrong. You asked me. You *did* ask me!

PRIME MINISTER: *(Who likes courage.)* Go on.

TONY: … Once they saw that Hardlip was wrong and that we could still operate without Christopher, what was their reaction?

PRIME MINISTER: To return him or attack. They haven't returned him.

TONY: They won't attack. We here are all thinking of what Christopher gave and what he withheld. The enemy knew nothing of that. They assume, quite simply, that if you have the Burning Glass, the Americans have it too. They are dead sure that the American machines are in reserve. They must climb down if you give them time.

PRIME MINISTER: They have said no word. They have him and, God knows, they may have Machine Six. The Burning Glass isn't a game at which I wait for an opponent to move. The stakes are too high, my friend.

TONY: You are wrong, sir.

PRIME MINISTER: Should I not be more wrong if they struck first? The decision is mine. You will set the machine.

TONY: In that, I take your order.

PRIME MINISTER: Mary?

MARY: We will set the machine.

PRIME MINISTER: Go, then, set it. *(TONY moves to door. HENRY steps to let him pass. At the door TONY stops and holds out his hand to MARY who, crossing below desk, takes it.)* Report when set. I shall act when nightfall is beyond doubt. Afterwards we will signal. *(TONY stands aside to let MARY go out first then follows her out.)* Inform the President. The setting will follow in…sixty minutes. Lay on cipher and transmission… I shall sleep for half an hour. *(He goes out.)*

LORD HENRY goes to desk sits in chair behind it and pulls the green telephone to him. He picks up the receiver and dials two numbers.

LORD HENRY: Joan. Henry Strait. No, don't talk; listen. In an hour from now, we shall have a Curtain-Raiser to go to Washington. It won't be long, as messages go; a pretty stiff series of figure groups in a rigid pattern. Probably the devil to cipher. Who have you at the Manor? Hold on. *(INSPECTOR WIGG has come in through the long windows. To WIGG.)* What is it?

WIGG: We have a man here, m'lord, I don't like the look of.

LORD HENRY: Where?

WIGG: On the lawn there.

LORD HENRY: Under guard?

WIGG: Yes, sir.

LORD HENRY: He will keep. I can't be interrupted.

WIGG: Very good, sir. *(Goes.)*

LORD HENRY: *(On telephone.)* Joan? For the moment, forget the figure-groups. I'll ring back on that. It's only a question of clearing transmission and we have an hour. Meanwhile here's an urgent one. Take it, and have it ciphered. Don't send until confirmed. Ready? Message begins. 'Prime Minister to President. Stop. Your Curtain-Raiser Twenty Three; two, three. Stop. We are acting now. Stop. The information for which you ask follows within' – hold on, I am being interrupted again… Well, Inspector? *(INSPECTOR WIGG has returned.)*

WIGG: I'm sorry, m'lord. I think you should see him. He's dressed queerly and he's talking very queerly.

LORD HENRY: Bring him then. *(WIGG goes up to long window and calls off.)*

WIGG: Let him come in. Odd sort of chap, m'lord. Says he owns the place. *(CHRISTOPHER enters, pauses, sways, looks around him without appearing to notice LORD HENRY. He is wearing clothes with which the enemy has supplied him.)*

CHRISTOPHER: *(Light-headed.)* Well, I do, you know, I do! *(CHRISTOPHER sits on sofa, stares, crumples and collapses. WIGG kneels beside arm of sofa, his arm round CHRISTOPHER. LORD HENRY's telephone receiver clicks back in to its bracket.)*

LORD HENRY: O my God! Terriford! *(To WIGG.)* Look after him. *(This WIGG is already very competently doing.)* Brandy. *(LORD HENRY goes to the drink table.)*

WIGG: Water, sir. *(HENRY comes behind sofa to CHRISTOPHER with water. CHRISTOPHER drinks it.)*

CHRISTOPHER: *(A sigh, then:)* Thank you. *(And he falls back on the cushions.)*

WIGG: He'll do, give him time.

CHRISTOPHER: Where is Mary?

LORD HENRY: In the Unit?

CHRISTOPHER: Where is Tony?

LORD HENRY: In the Unit. At the Machine.

CHRISTOPHER: Why? *(MARY comes in. She and CHRISTOPHER do not see each other.)*

MARY: Lord Henry, will you tell the Prime Minister that the Machine is set?

(CHRISTOPHER rouses himself and sits up, listening.)

CHRISTOPHER: I always seem to hear her voice, but she is never there. *(MARY runs round above desk. WIGG, who has risen, stops her. She moves away to behind desk chair.)*

WIGG: Not yet, ma'am. He's a bit light-headed.

CHRISTOPHER: 'The Machine is set.' Let me get up. That's right. A bit light-headed, that's all. Let me get up. *(He gets up and moves like a sleep-walker towards the telephone.)* The Machine ought not to be set. *(Picks up the house-telephone and*

287

presses a button.) Unit? This is Mr. Terriford speaking. What do you mean?... Don't you know my voice? Are you... light-headed? Tell Mr. Lack from me to come to the Private House... *(He clashes the receiver down.)* ...when he's finished his drink... I always seem to hear her voice and she is never – *(And now they are looking into each other's eyes.)* ... O Mary, you *are* there! Touch me. *(He slumps forward across the desk. MARY moves to him as the Curtain falls.)*

Scene Drop.

SCENE 2

A week later. Not yet quite tea-time, but on the tea-trolley now set behind the sofa, tea is laid, waiting for the silver kettle to be filled from a black kettle on the hob. The room is made cheerful by the afternoon sunshine of late September, and LADY TERRIFORD is looking out. CHRISTOPHER is on the sofa. He is wearing pyjamas, slippers and a very scruffy woollen dressing-gown and has a rug over his knees, a book in his hand.

CHRISTOPHER: Surely he can't be coming yet!

LADY TERRIFORD: To tell the truth, I wasn't looking for him.

CHRISTOPHER: For what, then?

LADY TERRIFORD: Nothing in particular. The sun. The house-martins. The lawn. My lower garden. It is such a comfort to think that my garden is still there.

CHRISTOPHER: Sentries still?

LADY TERRIFORD: I expect there always will be as long as you are here. But, being English sentries, they keep out of sight.

CHRISTOPHER: I wish the same could be said of English Prime Ministers. He has a very full report. Henry Strait and Gareth sat at my bedside for hours, with one of their Secret Women taking it all down. What more does the great man want?

LADY TERRIFORD: How should I know, darling? He just invited himself to tea.

CHRISTOPHER: *(Hoisting his legs off the sofa.)* Then I must change myself.

LADY TERRIFORD: I think a dressing-gown will do for a convalescent.

CHRISTOPHER: Not *this* one? *(Hopefully:)* Or will it?

LADY TERRIFORD: *(Inspecting it.)* Well, perhaps not *that* one.

CHRISTOPHER: Beside, these pyjamas... I think a pair of trousers if required for Prime Ministers. What maddens me is that the enemy kidnapped my evening clothes. They couldn't have needed anything less. *(He stands up.)* Heigh-ho! The trouble with being a convalescent for a week is that one begins to like it. You and the doctors say 'shock' and 'exhaustion'. May be. *(He crosses below desk and puts his book down.)* I was pretty well all in. When the enemy saw that the Prime Minister would act – and *could* – they decided to send me back. They told me that much. How they did it. I don't clearly remember. They didn't mean me to. I seem to remember crossing water and then I found myself on the edge of Mitton Wood – like coming round in a dentist's chair. And I walked home somehow. But I can't think back over that day from breakfast-time onward. I tried when Strait and Gareth were here. It's quite useless. Everything else is clear. The Burning Glass setting is dead clear.

LADY TERRIFORD: Mary has always prayed that you might forget it.

CHRISTOPHER: Have you noticed? No miracle is ever worked to relieve us of responsibility. I am back where I was unless –

LADY TERRIFORD: Unless?

CHRISTOPHER: Unless I am no longer the only person who has the whole setting. I wish I knew.

LADY TERRIFORD: What do you mean, Christopher? That you might have given it to the enemy under some drug or in your sleep?

CHRISTOPHER: Oh no! Oh no! I haven't even a moment's fear or doubt of that. It's far too long and complex to be given unconsciously. For the same reason they didn't even try torture. They would have had to use slower ways than that... Oh no! *They* haven't the setting.

LADY TERRIFORD: What do you fear, then?

CHRISTOPHER: Listen. Before Mary and Tony switched on to Laderek and Sumahdin they worked together. How did they work?

LADY TERRIFORD: They went to Machine Six. The Prime Minister had pledged himself they should not be interrupted. First, Mary says, Tony put on the lower setting from his paper. Then she, to avoid writing her part –

CHRISTOPHER: Why to avoid?

LADY TERRIFORD: They didn't trust Henry Strait. They thought that if ever the *whole* setting were written down together it might be...seized. But haven't you asked Tony about this?

CHRISTOPHER: Deliberately not.

LADY TERRIFORD: Or Mary?

CHRISTOPHER: As yet, I'd rather ask you.

LADY TERRIFORD: I think you are after a mare's nest, Christopher.

CHRISTOPHER: I hope so. That's why I'd rather ask you.

LADY TERRIFORD: At first, to avoid writing, Mary suggested she should stand beside Tony at the machine and dictate. He wouldn't have that. He thought the machine might be microphoned, and do you know, I really believe Lord Henry was quite capable of it. They wanted the setting so desperately to send to America. So instead she wrote each group on a separate scrap of paper and showed it to Tony silently and destroyed it as soon as set. When both settings were on, he made –

CHRISTOPHER: I understand. He made the normal adjustments for target – the forest or the lake – go on.

LADY TERRIFORD: Then they were ready to switch on. That was all.

CHRISTOPHER: Not quite all. Did they come away together?

LADY TERRIFORD: She came back to report that the machine was ready.

CHRISTOPHER: *(Reflectively.)* Meanwhile Tony was alone at Machine Six.

LADY TERRIFORD: He had to be.

CHRISTOPHER: Why didn't he report by telephone instead of sending her? … There must have been a fair time-margin before the switch-on. Mary's groups wouldn't take long to write.

LADY TERRIFORD: I can only say that Tony worked loyally *with* her from first to last. You can't think that he –

CHRISTOPHER: I don't think. *(MARY enters. She carries a silver muffin dish which she puts on the lower shelf of tea trolley.)* I wonder. *(CHRISTOPHER moves to door.)* Mother, would you come up and valet me a bit? At the moment I'm not good at stooping for things.

MARY: He said he'd be here at half past four.

LADY TERRIFORD: It must be quite a long time since I dressed you. In those days you hadn't far to stoop. *(As they move towards the door, TONY comes in. He is extremely taut.)*

TONY: Is Henry Strait coming too?

MARY: I don't know, Tony.

TONY: Is he, Lady T.?

LADY TERRIFORD: I think probably not.

MARY: Does it matter?

TONY: It does to me. He's like a walking criminal *dossier*, the smug little cad.

CHRISTOPHER: Calm down, Tony. No one will use anything against you.

TONY: *(Defiantly.)* No one can.

CHRISTOPHER: No one will even try. This isn't an episode that it suits anyone to shout about. If there's damning evidence against anyone, it's against me. You didn't leave your trousers behind. Nothing's more compromising.

(CHRISTOPHER and LADY TERRIFORD go out. MARY holds the silver kettle out to TONY.)

MARY: I won't make tea until he comes. But you might fill that.

TONY: Where, in heaven's name?

MARY: From the black one on the hob… Oh, Tony, matches? I'll light the spirit lamp.

TONY: You and your kettle and your matches! What does it feel like to have a mind at peace? Even when Christopher was gone –

MARY: Don't go back to that.

TONY: I won't ever again. I know what you went through. I watched your face all that week. But there wasn't hell in your face. Hell isn't that kind of suffering. Hell is chaos inside oneself. I'll fill the kettle.

MARY: I am using all your matches. This thing doesn't want to light.

TONY: I wonder if it's true.

MARY: If what is true?

TONY: What Christopher said. I wonder whether there have been other…little patches of time which it has been agreed to leave out of history. I suppose even secrets die in the end if no one is fool enough to keep them in writing. Here is one for you. *(He takes a piece of paper from his pocket and holds it out. She looks up.)* Take it.

MARY: It is Christopher's writing.

TONY: You know it perfectly well. It is my copy of the Lower Setting – the one I used with you at the Machine. The only copy. So I give it back. I wanted you to be sure.

MARY: Of what?

TONY: Of me. Take it.

MARY: What am I to do with it?

TONY: That would be a convenient flame. *(She holds the paper but does not light it. She is seated, he standing.)*

MARY: *(Not looking at him because she feels that something is wrong that she does not yet understand.)* Tony, you give me this as if it were of value.

TONY: Isn't it? It is half the Burning Glass.

MARY: Without the rest it is nothing.

TONY: *(With a shrug.)* It's all I have. I thought it proper to return it to store.

MARY: Why not to Christopher?

TONY: O Mary, because I'm a romantic animal, I suppose. I thought you might give a pat to the dog who brought you his bone. We worked together at the Machine. I've never been happier in my life – yes, *happier.* I know you hate me to say that. But to work with you made me happy. And I thought it might add to your…peace of mind…to be sure that that bit of paper wasn't sculling about… I happen to love you.

MARY: *(Rising to fire.)* I believe that is true… And yet you are lying! The moment you said: 'The only copy', I half knew. O Tony, you are a bad liar!

TONY: Hardlip said that; now you.

MARY: You *have* a copy.

TONY: I have not. I have not. And if I had? Alone it is valueless. You said so.

MARY: And yet you are lying in some way I don't yet understand.

TONY: About what? How can I be?

MARY: And yet you are.

TONY: *(And now his defences are down.)* What do I say now? This scene was to have gone quite differently. You were supposed to say: 'Thank you, Tony.' And then, with all the ridiculous simplicities of this mortal life between male and female, once I had had my hands under your shoulder-blades, and let you go, I should have felt like Sunday morning after church. And that bit of paper, because you burned it, would have burned up all my sins. And I should have been – I should have gone out as white as snow. *(He rises and moves quickly away between desk and piano to drink table.)* My God, don't stare at me like that as though I really were some kind of redeemable leper. I shall begin to believe you love me. I can lie to myself even about that – oh quite convincingly. That is precisely the sort of swine I am. Don't you grasp even now how far it has gone? It isn't a question of *half* the Burning Glass. It is all in my mind. Your part as well. The whole setting, the whole power, all, all! ... O Mary! *(He sits, his head in his hands, on stool.)*

MARY: What were you going to do with it? Not give it to the enemy.

TONY: Odd, isn't it? I wasn't brought up that way.

MARY: Were you going to exploit it? In what way?

TONY: How do I know? How do *I* know? I had to *have* it, that's all.

MARY: Why?

TONY: Not to be, any longer, second in my class, which I have been all my life... And I have it still, even after telling you; that's what makes me laugh. I can't hand it back, can I? If it were paper I could. But it's inside me, like my special, private, personal hell. I haven't your memory or his, but I can learn, you know. Of course I can promise not to use it, and I can believe myself and you can believe me. And I can pretend to trust myself and you can pretend... I believe you would trust me... You did this time. I believe you would unto seventy times seven. Even Christopher might, for your sake. *(Rises to her.)* But don't, Mary, never, never, never, *because* I love you, and that's true, and yet I should do it again. *(Turns away.)* Listen to me whining and confessing. I used at least to be gay, but the clockwork's fallen out. Never trust a self-pitier until –

MARY: *(Moves to him and takes his arm.)* Stop, Tony. Stop.

TONY: Until he's dead... *(It is between these two sentences that TONY resolves to kill himself.)* I might stop if I had a drink.

MARY: Then have one... Nothing is hopeless. You and I together can tell Christopher what you have told me. Then we shall know what to do. *(She burns paper, over 'slop' bowl on tea tray.)*

TONY: *(Pours himself a drink.)* You and he! It's such a damned silly trivial thing, isn't it, to have a particular woman in one's arms. There have been so many women, all dead, and there will be so many more. *(He puts his glass on the piano and takes tube of tablets from his pocket.)* And yet never to have had *her*, and be cold and the worms eat you…it seems a waste of…the ensuing spring? *(MARY moves from trolley and glances in mirror over mantelpiece. She sees what is happening and lets it happen.)*

TONY: *(He shakes two tablets from tube into his hand and drops the tube behind him.)* Do you know, you have never before approved of my having a drink. I promise you: this is the last. *(He takes into his mouth the white tablets contained in his glass tube and swills them down.)* Soon the Prime Minister will be here. Seems absurd to me. I'll…get off your carpet while the going's good. *(Puts his hands on her shoulders.)* Good-bye, my dear.

MARY: Good-bye, Tony. *(He backs up to the long windows. He speaks his curtain-line but though his face is convulsed and his mouth moves, even his curtain-line is a failure. No sound comes – or very little, but the actor had better know what the curtain line would have been.)*

TONY: Better to go out of harbour under one's own steam. *(He goes out. The sound of a motor-car which stops. A door bangs. The car goes on. The PRIME MINISTER enters from the garden R. MARY, hearing him, rises to greet him.)*

PRIME MINISTER: I sent the car on round the house. *(Taking her hand.)* How is he?

MARY: Christopher?

PRIME MINISTER: Who else?

MARY: *(Under stress, disjointedly.)* He will be here. They ought to have been, I know. She is helping him change. I will make tea. *(PRIME MINISTER stoops and picks up TONY's empty glass container.)*

PRIME MINISTER: This little tube on the carpet. It's glass. Someone may put his foot on it.

MARY: Thank you. I'll take it.

PRIME MINISTER: *(At the tea-trolley.)* Six cups?

MARY: We thought perhaps Lord Henry…

PRIME MINISTER: Oh no. He is at the Manor.

MARY: And I wanted… Tony…to make his peace.

PRIME MINISTER: I saw him going down over the lawn. *(Pause.)* I haven't come to bother you, Mary.

MARY: I know. It's just the fact that you are what you are… shakes me. I want us – Christopher and me – to be…

PRIME MINISTER: Among those happy being who have no history.

MARY: No public history.

PRIME MINISTER: Ah, my dear, don't make too rigid a distinction. Christians and Prime Ministers don't belong to different species. To renounce fame and power doesn't set you apart. Surrender is not peace. We are bound by the same rules. Peace, whether of a man or of a nation, has to be paid for minute by minute, hour by hour. Keep on putting your money in the slot or the lights go out.

MARY: Money?

PRIME MINISTER: Decision, decision, decision – the hardest of all currencies. Courage – to be blamed by cowards for being ruthless. The courage to move – and not to move. The courage to reject whatever has become valueless: our prides, our ideals – even our friends; to let them go; to bury the dead. We must do that – we Prime Ministers, we Christians. Isn't it true? Life demands it: the glorious courage to receive the unknown guest; the bitter courage to say good-bye. *(CHRISTOPHER comes in.)*

CHRISTOPHER: I'm sorry, sir. No one told me you were here.

PRIME MINISTER: No bugles were sounded. I hadn't even the consideration to come in by the front door. But where is your mother?

CHRISTOPHER: She left me some time ago. I expected to find her here. She always goes for a walk in what she calls *her* garden before tea.

PRIME MINISTER: Then let us cultivate ours. I have your report of the days you spent in enemy hands, and admirable it is – factually; but what interests me always is the enemy mind. I think I understand pretty well why at that stage it wasn't convenient for them to torture you. But there's a lot more I should like to understand. What is the *feel* of the place? Is it an efficient barracks – bang, bang, click, clack? Or a prison with peep-holes? Or is it, like Nazi Germany, a mixture between a perversion and a pantomime with a prima donna as the principal boy? Or is it like most revolutions, when there's nothing left to plunder: a long bleak railway-station where everyone sits and waits for the trains that never come. What does it feel like? Can you tell me that?

CHRISTOPHER: *(After a pause and speaking with intense but quiet passion.)* It feels like a loathsome prep. school.

PRIME MINISTER: Does it indeed! That is new. That should throw light – if I have the wit to see by it… Lead me a little. I'm on new ground.

CHRISTOPHER: I can't lead you, sir.

PRIME MINISTER: Then I must feel my way. *(Thinking aloud, doubtfully working out the puzzle.)* An old-fashioned and vile prep. school. For the moment that suggests to me cold radiators and rancid butter… What more? … *(And now he is on the scent.)* I see. Oh yes, I see now… A prevailing spirit of muscular profanity. A tough totalitarian prep. school with all the soccer eleven dressed up in leather-jackets and beating the little boys into shouting the old school songs. On the outside, hearty: on the inside, schoolboy-corrupt. Am I right? Baksheesh to the prefects; suck up to the masters; sneak to the matron, and lick the sixth form boots. And sing the old school songs… Strictly conventional. Nothing is more conventional than a prep. school, except a revolution. Whatever isn't school custom, isn't done.

Whatever isn't school jargon, isn't said. Whatever the whole school doesn't think, isn't thought, and what Master don't know isn't knowledge. Am I right? And beat the old school drum! Hurrah for the Hero of the School who shot six goals in the away match! Down with the reactionary hyena who whistled a tune of his own… An eternal prep. school from which no one goes home for the holidays.

CHRISTOPHER: There are no holidays; there is no home.

PRIME MINISTER: Then answer me three questions. If these creatures should swarm out against us, is the Burning Glass available to us?

CHRISTOPHER: Yes.

PRIME MINISTER: Will you arrange, as you did before, that it shall be available in the event of your death – or absence?

CHRISTOPHER: Yes. *(LADY TERRIFORD comes in from the garden. Only MARY is aware of her entrance. They exchange a look which confirms in MARY's mind that she (LADY TERRIFORD) knows of TONY's death.)*

PRIME MINISTER: Will you now make corresponding arrangements that if you, or this place, fails, the setting shall be available for use on Machine Six in the United States?

CHRISTOPHER: In war, yes.

PRIME MINISTER: A last question. In peace?

CHRISTOPHER: No.

PRIME MINISTER: Aren't you standing against the whole tide of modern thought?

CHRISTOPHER: Do you ask the question – or do you state it as your own belief?

PRIME MINISTER: I ask the question.

CHRISTOPHER: Against the tide of modern thought. I wonder whether that is as true as it was. Tides turn. The Wonders of Applied Science have become much less wonderful than they were. Only half-baked minds any longer worship that particular Golden Calf. Men of science themselves do not.

PRIME MINISTER: Do they not?

CHRISTOPHER: The mediocrities, sometimes. Never, the originating minds. They have great dread of their own miracles. So have the people in their hearts. For example, supersonic speed. It gets the headlines and it gets the movies. But who for a moment believes that *that*, or atomic energy, or the Burning Glass, is anything else than a monstrous gadget? No one believes any more that these things are the salvation of the world. And they did when H.G. Wells went bicycling. That is the revolution. History moves in phases. The time may come – has come, perhaps – in which science will be seen again as what it is: a source of wisdom, not of power; like music and poetry, a reading of Nature, not her slave-driver. Isn't it possible that the whole era of Power for Power's sake is near its end? I will do nothing to prolong it – as long as the decision rests with me alone. I doubt whether it does any more. *(This last sentence, thrown in by CHRISTOPHER so casually, does not at once penetrate the PRIME MINISTER's mind. When it does, it stings.)*

PRIME MINISTER: Say that again.

CHRISTOPHER: I said: I doubt whether the decision any longer rests with me alone.

PRIME MINISTER: Who else? *(LADY TERRIFORD rises.)*

CHRISTOPHER: I don't want to speak of it until I'm sure.

MARY: *(MARY rises and goes to him.)* You can, my darling.

LADY TERRIFORD: You can speak quite freely now. *(The effect is almost that the two women have spoken together. Now LADY TERRIFORD continues.)* Tony Lack is dead. His body is being carried in from the garden.

CHRISTOPHER: *(To MARY.)* You knew this?

MARY: He came to me and told me the truth. He had the whole setting in his mind. *(To the PRIME MINISTER.)* You are not to think he was a traitor – except to himself. *(To CHRISTOPHER.)* He would have given it back. But there's no way of giving back what is in the mind – except one. He took that.

LADY TERRIFORD: Here, in this room?

MARY: With his drink; behind my back.

PRIME MINISTER: Behind your back?

MARY: There is a mirror…there. I let him go.

PRIME MINISTER: You were brave.

MARY: It was he who had the courage to say good-bye.
(CHRISTOPHER, seeing the tube on the trolley picks it up.)

CHRISTOPHER: This tube? His? Poor Tony, his window-opener… Well, it's open now. *(He tosses the tube on to the tray where it chinks.)* I was wrong to distrust that man. *(The green telephone rings in the silence. For a moment no one picks it up; then LADY TERRIFORD does. She listens and hands the receiver to the PRIME MINISTER.)*

LADY TERRIFORD: For you, Monty.

PRIME MINISTER: I am speaking. *(Listens.)* No. It is of no consequence now. *(He puts the receiver down. They still wait for him to speak.)* I will go now. I shall like to think of…life in this house going on. *(He is speaking in emotional stress and LADY TERRIFORD takes his arm.)*

LADY TERRIFORD: I know, precisely, what made you say that.

PRIME MINISTER: Ah, my dear, we are both survivors, and that is a lonely thing to be. *(To CHRISTOPHER.)* What shall you do this evening when I am gone – you and she? Shall you play chess? … *(To MARY.)* I am trying to say good-night and finding it not easy. I have an extraordinary request to make. *(Now he moves to her.)* Once before, you asked me to spend the night in this house. May I accept that invitation now?

LADY TERRIFORD: Dear Monty.

MARY: I wanted to ask you. I didn't dare.

PRIME MINISTER: I should like to sit here quietly and know that I am to dine with you and sleep where I dine.

MARY: You are wise. And kind.

PRIME MINISTER: My dear, it is only my selfishness. *(To CHRISTOPHER.)* You are still thinking of your friend. We will go to his room at a convenient time. I value Mr. Lack together with you. To see an evil power not exercised – by young men – gives me, even now, a little hope for the future of the world.

Curtain.

WWW.OBERONBOOKS.COM

Follow us on www.twitter.com/@oberonbooks
& www.facebook.com/OberonBooksLondon